The Railways of New Zealand
A journey through history

The Railways of New Zealand

A journey through history

Geoffrey B. Churchman & Tony Hurst

transpress
New Zealand

First published in 1990 by HarperCollins Publishers (New Zealand)
Reprinted 1991
This second edition published in 2001 by

transpress New Zealand
P.O. Box 10-215
Wellington
transpress@paradise.net.nz
www.transpressnz.homestead.com

ISBN 0-908876-20-3

Designed by Geoffrey Churchman
Maps by Beryl Pimblott
Photos as individually credited
Printed in Hong Kong

Front End-paper: Pre-war electric locomotive ED 105 with the 8:00 a.m. Waterloo–Wellington suburban train on the Hutt Valley line approaches Ava in October 1967. R.J. McGAVIN

Rear End-paper: JA 1290 with an excursion train to Waiouru in the winter of 1965. R.J. McGAVIN

Half title: The smokey profile of WW locomotives at Greymouth's Elmer Lane depot on 17 December 1967. R.J. McGAVIN

Title page: Rails in the sunset at Auckland station in March 1982. The yard and the skyline have changed significantly in the meantime.

Above: J 1227 with a goods train from the north enters Paekakariki in the early 1960s. NZR

Contents

Above: Restored locomotives K 92 and AB 778 (left) make a pretty scene at Fairlight, the now southern terminus of the "Kingston Flyer" line on 30 September 2000. GRAHAM FOX

Left: Preserved locomotive AB 663 makes a run through early frosty landscape on the North Island Main Trunk central section.
TONY HURST

Introduction

The first edition of this book was published in 1990 to mark New Zealand's sesquicentenary—150 years since the signing of the Treaty of Waitangi. The beginning of a new century and millennium seemed an appropriate occasion for a new edition, particularly as the intervening period has seen substantial changes.

It is easy to overlook the fundamental role the railways have played in New Zealand's development and in the lives of its people. Today aircraft, cars and trucks dominate the scene and trains are used only by a small minority. A century ago, however, trains were the most important form of transport; aviation did not exist and motoring was in its infancy.

When the first settlers arrived from Britain in the middle of the nineteenth century the railway revolution there was in full swing and the significance and importance of railway transport to the development of the new country would have been foremost in their minds. The long, arduous and at times dangerous nature of transport and communications between the various settlements around the long coastline made the establishment of provincial governments appropriate which set about their own ambitious railway projects, not only to link the ports with each other but to open up and develop the hinterland. Yet very little was actually constructed by the provinces. By 1870 only 74 km of line had been opened—built, as in Australia, in three different gauges.

Fortunately, from this time onwards railway construction was taken over and co-ordinated by central government and in the next 10 years a further 1900 km of track was opened for traffic on the adopted national 1067 mm (3'6") gauge. Sir Julius Vogel's vision of a network of trunk lines throughout the country was slowly taking shape. However, limited resources, depressions and an extremely difficult topography saw to it that it was well into the twentieth century before some of the most important lines were completed.

Eventually by 1952 the railway network reached its zenith at some 5700 km. Since then the network has been steadily reduced in size as more and more traffic transferred from the railways to the roads and is now only two thirds the size it was 50 years ago. Yet despite this, more train tonne kilometres are run today than at any time in the 1950s and the railways are still the country's biggest freight mover.

Our objective with this book is to tell the story of the development of the main railways system in New Zealand since its beginnings 140 years ago. For the first 130 years it is in essence a story of state enterprise; like Australia, New Zealand differed from the rest of the world in that, with a few minor exceptions, the government has been responsible for the building and operation of its railways from the outset. Most overseas countries eventually saw the state-owned model as appropriate and nationalised their railways. However, in recent years there has been a world-wide trend of selling off state assets including the railways, and New Zealand has been part of this. The desirability of this is the subject of much debate and like other commentators we have considerable misgivings about it. Whatever forms of propulsion may be developed to replace the fossil-fuel based internal combustion engine, it is difficult that imagine that in one hundred years time, wheel on rail technology will not still be the most efficient means of moving freight and that preservation, even expansion, of the present network is of paramount importance.

This book is dedicated to the tens of thousands of people who have been part of the planning, building, operation and maintenance of railways over the past 160 years and to the thousands more who have keenly followed the action from the trackside and on board. We wish to acknowledge the valuable assistance we have had from those who have contributed photos, information and suggestions—in particular Bob Stott, Tom McGavin and Reid McNaught—that has helped to make this book what it is.

Le chemin de fer — c'est la vie.

Geoffrey Churchman and Tony Hurst

New Zealand Railways Network 1952

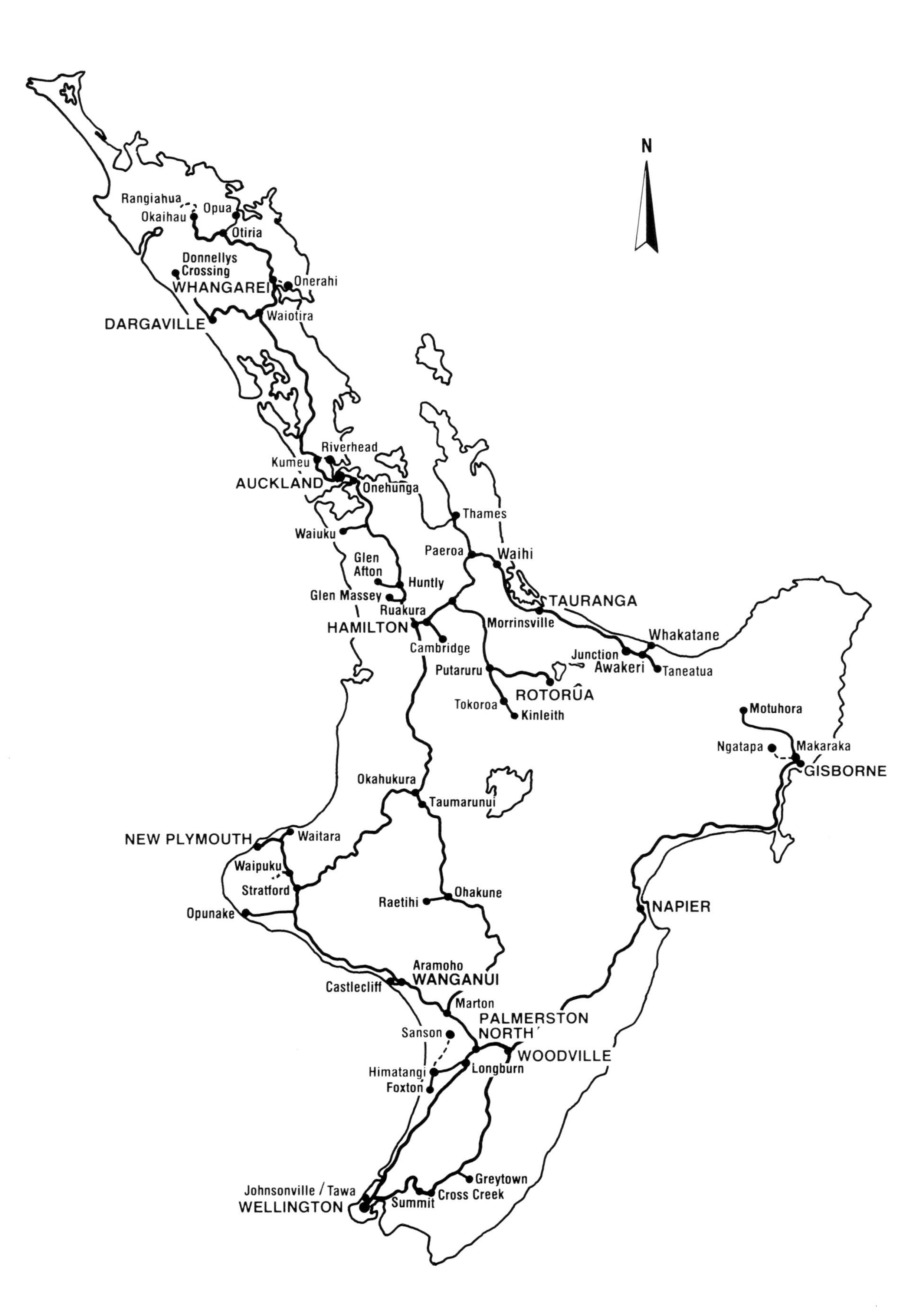

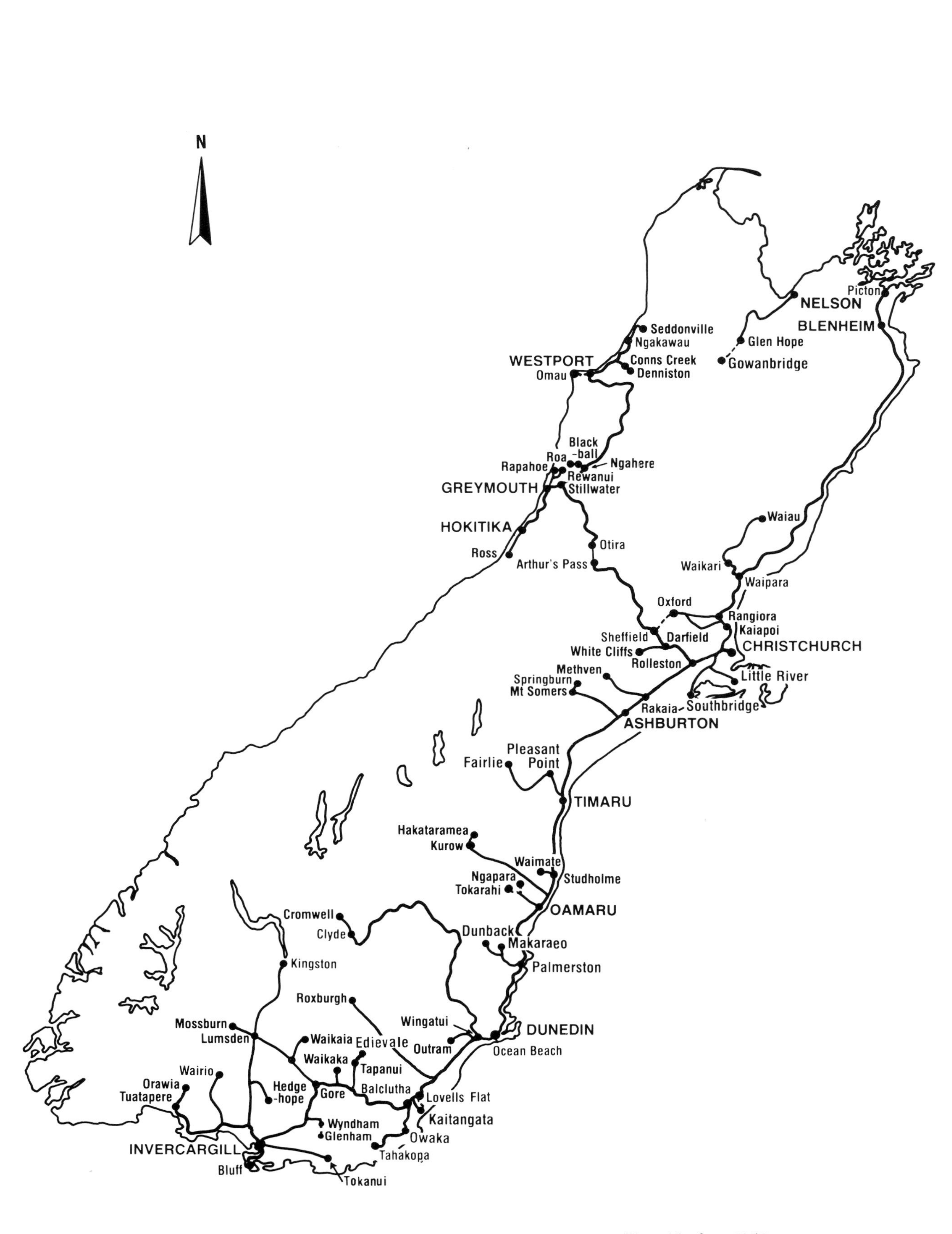
N
Picton
NELSON
BLENHEIM
Seddonville
Ngakawau
Glen Hope
Gowanbridge
WESTPORT
Conns Creek
Denniston
Omau
Black
-ball
Roa
Ngahere
Rapahoe
Rewanui
GREYMOUTH
Stillwater
HOKITIKA
Waiau
Otira
Ross
Arthur's Pass
Waikari
Waipara
Oxford
Rangiora
Kaiapoi
Sheffield
Darfield
CHRISTCHURCH
White Cliffs
Rolleston
Methven
Little River
Springburn
Mt Somers
Rakaia
Southbridge
ASHBURTON
Pleasant
Point
Fairlie
TIMARU
Hakataramea
Kurow
Waimate
Studholme
Ngapara
Tokarahi
OAMARU
Cromwell
Clyde
Dunback
Makaraeo
Palmerston
Kingston
Roxburgh
Wingatui
DUNEDIN
Mossburn
Lumsden
Waikaia
Edievale
Outram
Ocean Beach
Waikaka
Tapanui
Wairio
Orawia
Tuatapere
Hedge
-hope
Gore
Balclutha
Lovells Flat
Kaitangata
Wyndham
Glenham
Owaka
INVERCARGILL
Tahakopa
Bluff
Tokanui
--- Closed before 1952

New Zealand — land and people

New Zealand consists of three main islands—the North Island (114,489 km^2), the South Island (151,971 km^2) and Stewart Island (1746 km^2). Other small islands total 851 km^2. The total length of the North Island and South Islands is 1600 km and the widest part of the country is less than 450 km. The narrowest part of the country is the Auckland isthmus which is only a few kilometres wide. Forest, most of it native, covers nearly a quarter of the total land area, but large parts of the central North Island have been planted in Californian *Pinus Radiata* which grows much faster in New Zealand than in its native terrain.

Mountain chains are a feature of both islands, and only 26% of the country lies under 200 metres above sea level. In the North Island a hard rock mountain core extends from Cook Strait to the Bay of Plenty; the only gap across it is the gorge cut by the Manawatu River near Palmerston North. In the South Island the Southern Alps form a domineering mountain chain between east and west, extending nearly the whole length of the island. A feature of the North Island is the volcanic country of the interior with large lakes, active volcanoes, hot springs and geysers. Although high mountains occupy one tenth of the North Island land surface only four are above 1800 metres in altitude. Features of the South Island are the glaciers of Westland and the fiords of the Southwest. The longest glacier is the Tasman Glacier in the area of the 3764 metre high Mt Cook which reaches a length of 28.8 km. On the east are the alluvial plains of Canterbury. New Zealand has many long rivers, mostly swift flowing and difficult to navigate. The longest is the Waikato (425 km) in the North Island and the next longest is the Clutha (322 km) in the South Island. There are another 20 rivers in each Island over 100 km in length from mouth to source.

The country lies between 37° and 47° South and the climate is generally temperate, the north being subtropical. Average maximum and minimum temperatures in Auckland in January (summer) are 23° C and 16° C. In July (winter) the figures are 15° and 7°C. In Dunedin the respective temperatures are 18° and 11° in January and 10° and 3° in July.

The first person said to have discovered New Zealand was Kupe, about the year 950 AD. Maori migration from Polynesia followed in waves until about the year 1350. They settled mainly in the warm north. The first European to discover New Zealand was Abel Tasman, a Dutch navigator, on 16 December 1642. His initial name of Staten Land later became Nieuw Zeeland. The next European visit came on 7 October 1769 when Captain James Cook sighted land near Gisborne, landing two days later. Six months were spent circumnavigating the North and South Islands and he thus produced the first and surprisingly accurate map of New Zealand. Whaling stations sprang up along the North Island coast from 1792 onwards and a trade with New South Wales began in whale oil, seal skins, flax and timber.

On 29 January 1840 Captain William Hobson arrived at the Bay of Island to proclaim British sovereignty. The same month the first body of immigrants from England arrived in Wellington to form a settlement. On 6 February a coexistence treaty was concluded with Maori chiefs at Waitangi. By 1862 the non-Maori population of New Zealand had reached 125,000 and the Maori population was 55,000. A year later gold rush fever saw the non-Maori population jump to 200,000 with immigrants from Australia. During the 1870s Vogel's "Great Public Works Policy" saw the population double to 500,000 and over the next century it steadily climbed to reach 3.3 million by 1985. Today it stands just short of 4 million. Of the total population, some 75% are European in origin, 15% are Maori and 6% are Pacific Islanders. All other ethnic groups, Chinese being the most significant, amount to 4%.

Today New Zealand is a British Dominion, the change from colonial status having taken place in 1907. Despite large increases in manufactured exports in recent decades, the majority of national income still derives from primary products. Tourism is also significant. In most forms of transport New Zealand is well served. The country has the third highest per capita ownership of automobiles in the world which make use of some 92,000 km of roads and, on a per capita basis, internal air traffic density is the highest in the world.

Above: Canterbury high country scenery on the West Coast road. The Midland Line lies beyond the mountain ranges in the distance. G.B. CHURCHMAN

Below: Landscape of the King Country north of Taumarunui as J 1211 arrives with an excursion train from New Plymouth on 5 June 1989. G.B. CHURCHMAN

The image of New Zealand railways over a century ago. One of seven 0-6-4T class S Single Fairlie locomotives built in 1880 and 1881 is seen at Summit at the top of the Rimutaka Incline section in the 1880s. Its train consists of two bogie passenger cars and two 4-wheel wagons loaded with timber, the second possibly fenceposts. Vogel era 26 kg/m rails are in the foreground, while in the background a start has been made on clearing the native bush. As in most of the country complete hillsides were clear-felled, the hillsides which were not used for pasture eventually became covered in (introduced) gorse but in time the native bush has begun to regenerate. Today this scene, minus the houses and railway equipment, can be enjoyed by hikers on the Rimutaka Incline walkway. ALEXANDER TURNBULL LIBRARY

PART ONE

Development

CHAPTER ONE

A network takes shape

The nineteenth century

Following the arrival of the first waves of European settlers in the 1840s and 1850s, the pattern of settlement and the creation of traffic routes was strongly influenced by New Zealand's difficult geography. Most of the settlements were on the coastline separated by dense bush in the north and by mountain ranges and wide, swift flowing rivers in the south. Hence virtually all traffic between settlements in the early colonial days went by sea. Roads were very elementary and only served the immediate surrounds of each locality. The motor car and aeroplane were unheard of. Railways were seen as the fastest and best way to open up the rural hinterland by providing easy transport to and from the ports.

The first railway lines to be opened in New Zealand were both operated by horses. A very short line was laid in 1861 to serve a coal mine near Kaitangata in 1861, but a much more substantial operation was the Dun Mountain Copper Mining Company's 22.5 km long 915 mm narrow gauge track from the mines to the port at Nelson. This had been facilitated by the Dun Mountain Railway Act of 1861 and on 3 February 1862 the line was opened. However, it only ever saw horse-drawn traffic during its short life as the mines soon failed.

The first length of railway on which locomotives were used was between Christchurch and a temporary port at Ferrymead 6.8 km distant. This had been built to the broad "Irish" gauge of 1,600 mm and had been validated by the Colonial Government with the Christchurch and Lyttelton Railway Act of 1860. The first locomotive was a 2-4-0 steam tank locomotive built by Slaughter Gruning and Company (later the Avonside Engine Company) in Bristol, England, and arrived at Lyttelton from Melbourne (for which it had originally been intended) on board the schooner *Choice* on 27 April 1863 and was landed at Ferrymead wharf on 6 May 1863. It entered service as No. 1 on 1 December 1863, the opening day of the line. Three more of these locomotives numbered 2, 3 and 4 arrived from the same builders between April 1864 and May 1868.

At this time New Zealand was governed by a system of provincial governments with a central government in the capital (initially Auckland, then Wellington from 1865). Three of these provinces independently began

their own railway construction. In Southland a track with wooden rails was built from the local capital of Invercargill to Makarewa, some 12 km away, encouraged by the discovery of gold in the Lake Wakatipu region in 1861. This railway crossed swampy country where roadmaking was difficult and was an attempt to introduce railway transport with a minimum of capital expenditure. It was opened in the British standard gauge of 1435 mm on 18 October 1864. The locomotives damaged the rails, the very high maintenance costs were out of all proportion to the revenue, and the line was out of action for months at a time. The railway was for all intents and purposes abandoned in 1866. The other Southland railway project was the building of a line from Invercargill to the port of Bluff, also in 1,435 mm gauge but this time with iron rails. It was opened on 5 February 1867 and by 22 February 1871 it had extended 30 km northwards to Winton over the route of the previous Makarewa railway.

At Auckland a 35 km line to Drury was planned to assist in troop transport to the Waikato—wars with the Maori continued for several years in the North Island after the signing of the Treaty of Waitangi. Contracts were let in 1864 for construction of this 1435 mm gauge railway. Work began in 1865 but a year later, with the military need having passed, the project came to a halt.

By 1870 a total of 74 km of railway had been opened in the South Island and construction plans were well underway in various parts of the country. One of New Zealand's most far sighted statesmen, by the name of Sir Julius Vogel, could see that insular piecemeal railway construction by the provincial authorities would, through different standards of construction and operation, particularly different gauges, lead to major problems and retard the overall development of the colony. Vogel had migrated to New Zealand in 1861, the year of the first gold discoveries. He was elected to both the Otago Provincial Council and the Colonial General Assembly (Parliament). In 1869 he became Colonial Treasurer in the ministry of William Fox. On 28 June 1870, in the reading of his Financial Statement in the House of Representatives, he expounded bold revolutionary principles for "actively promoting the settlement of the country". This was to be achieved by a programme combining public works in the form of railways and roads with increased immigration.

In regards to railways he said: "We propose that the Government shall be armed with the power to conclude arrangements for the construction of certain railways within the different provinces, as desired by their respective governments. By 'certain railways', I mean that the Legislature should indicate the direction of the railways for which it is proposed to allow the Government to contract; and I think that, speaking generally, railways

The ten members of the 2-4-0T L class were built in 1877 by the Avonside Engine Company in England. Three are now preserved. L 207 is seen at Western Springs on 4 June 1984 (opposite) and L 219 at Silverstream on 31 January 1982 (right). MARK COLE

should, in each island, be designed and constructed as parts of a trunk line. According to the nature of present traffic should be the character of the respective railways....

"In America, I am told, there are what are called 'revenue railroads', that is to say, railways constructed in the manner precisely suited to the traffic, and out of the traffic returns those railways are, from time to time, improved in accordance with the traffic demands. The constructors are satisfied with a moderate speed, and, as an example of the system, they are satisfied to do without expensive stations—indeed what we should call stations .." He thus contemplated railways of low capital cost construction to enable the largest possible length of lines being laid with the funds available. This was radically different from British and European railways which were elaborately built to serve densely populated regions.

Vogel supposed that some 2,400 km to 2,600 km of railway would be built over the next ten years, at a cost of £7.5 million, together with the acquisition of 1,030,000 hectares of land, and that in addition about £1 million would be required to carry out the other proposals he was making. He had assumed that £5,000 per mile (1.6 km) would be sufficient to cover the average cost of cheap railways, including the cost of equipment and rolling stock, and he looked upon the land as a margin for contingencies or for exceptionally heavy works. The Government was so confident that a great deal of the work comprised in these proposals could be effected by guarantees or subsidies, and by land payments that they sought authority to directly borrow only £6 million.

Consequently a series of acts were passed by Parliament in September 1870. These were the Immigration and Public Works Act, the Railways Act, the Canterbury Gauge Act and the Immigration and Public Works Act. Under the Railways Act 1870, three railways were authorised to be constructed by contract with the Governor; three were to be constructed in Canterbury; and several more were authorised to be surveyed. Railways to be constructed were lines from Auckland to Tuakau with a branch line to Onehunga, at not more than £4,000 per 1.6 km; from Blenheim to Picton at not more than £5,000 per 1.6 km; Dunedin to Clutha at not more than £5,000 per 1.6 km, Addington-Rangiora, not more than £92,000; Selwyn-Rakaia Bridge, not more than £48,000 and Timaru-Temuka, not more than £67,000. The Act determined a national standard gauge of 1,067 mm (3'6"), although some exceptions were made for extensions to Canterbury's 1,600 (5'3") gauge railways.

The decision to adopt a 1,067 mm gauge was based on the recommendations of Charles Fox and Sons Ltd., a London firm of consulting engineers who outlined the advantages based on their own experiences with this

For immigrants, the New Zealand railway experience often began on disembarking. This 19th century illustration shows a train waiting on the wharf in the background to take passengers from Lyttelton to Christchurch. NZR&LS COLLECTION

One could be excused for thinking that this is a scene from a bush tramway, but in fact it shows construction work on the North Island Main Trunk in the early years of the 20th century near Ohakune, with an L class locomotive. NZR&LS COLLECTION

gauge in Canada, Norway and elsewhere. This gauge was first laid by the Public Works Department on the Dunedin to Clutha line authorised in 1871. This 82 km line to Clutha involved two tunnels and several bridges and, with construction costs working out at approximately £4,170 per 1.6 km, was regarded as a showpiece for the new order. The development of locomotive power and the carrying capacity of vehicles were, however, limited by the loading gauge and related tunnel profile. Simple, specifically designed, saddle-tank, three-axled engines were ordered for the line. This was the celebrated F class locomotive, which like the 20 kg/m iron rails for which they were tailored, were characteristic of the Vogel era. An unfortunate legacy of the Vogel era was a restricted loading gauge. Most of the surviving tunnels built in the nineteenth century had to be enlarged, sometimes more than once, to cope with larger locomotives and wagons.

In 1871 Vogel negotiated with John Brogden and Sons, contractors of London, for the construction of railways, and in August 1872 six contracts were entered into by this firm for the construction of 255 km of railway. The total value of these contracts was £558,800 to which had to be added the costs of rails, materials and rolling stock, then estimated to be about £250,000.

The Railways Act 1871, passed on 16 November 1871, authorised the construction of many more railway lines, bringing the total now authorised to 29 with an aggregate distance of about 1,230 km. The Railways Act 1872 included authorisation for the purchase of the 13 km Dunedin–Port Chalmers line which had been built by a private company by an arrangement with the Otago provincial council. The Act also required that all future contracts were to be submitted to public tender and provided that construction of any new line was not to begin before the Chief Engineer had reported that it was likely to pay working expenses from the date of completion. Lines listed as being authorised in the 1872 Act penetrated inland from coastal ports at Auckland, Waitara, Wanganui, Foxton, Napier, Wellington, Picton, Nelson, Westport, Greymouth, Lyttelton, Timaru, Oamaru, Port Chalmers and Bluff.

By June 1873, 51 km of the approved lines and the Dunedin–Port Chalmers railway were open for traffic. Construction work was actively proceeding on another 648 km, contracts were opened to be let for a further 256 km, and working surveys and plans were still to be prepared for the balance. The first Engineer in Chief of the Public Works Department, Mr John Carruthers, reported in July 1873 that public works were being pushed on as fast as the labour market would bear.

In his Financial Statement of July 1873 Vogel said the time would come when the Public Works Department would be regarded with astonishment and admiration for the rapid manner in which it was organised and the revolution completed which gave to the colony the charge of the construction of the main lines of communication. This was a reference to the central government having taken control of railway construction and the differences between "provincialists" and "colonialists" who were concerned with the development of the colony as a whole. The Provincial Governments were ultimately abolished in 1876.

In the 1873 statement Vogel outlined the Government's further proposals whereby authority would be requested to raise another £1.5 million and construct railways from the Mataura to the Clutha rivers; from Dunedin to Moeraki; and from the Waitaki River to Lyttelton. It was also proposed to extend the Auckland–Mercer railway south to the province's frontier. "And whenever opportunity offers, from the frontier south so as to join the main trunk line wherever surveys show

Left: Locomotives purchased in the 1870s and 1880s were mainly 4- and 6-wheel tank engines designed for lightweight track and severe curvature. The 0-4-0T A class was the smallest locomotive acquired by NZR. Of the 14 examples, built in 1873, three are preserved. This one, A 64, is used on the Plains Railway near Ashburton. C.E. DASH

Right: K 88, built by Rogers (USA), leads a train up the Weka Pass Railway in 1984. This loco was one of the two to head the first through Christchurch–Dunedin express. MARK COLE

that it is desirable that the junction should be effected." In the same 1873 statement, Vogel referred to the needs and desires of Marlborough, Nelson and Westland, and announced the Government's proposal to ask the House to authorise preliminary surveys with a view to deciding upon a main line which would bring Nelson and Canterbury into connection with the West Coast (and hence with each other), also if expedient into connection with Marlborough.

In 1877 the management of working railways was separated from that of lines under construction, effectively setting up a Railways Department. Administration of the lines in each of the two islands became the function of a commissioner responsible to the Government through the Minister of Public Works. In 1880 both islands became the responsibility of a single general manager, the first of whom was Mr J.P. Maxwell. The new department had to operate whatever lines the Public Works might construct but had no say in their location or possible operating conditions.

By July 1877 the Engineer in Charge of Public Works of the South Island (or Middle Island as it was called until 1907), Mr W.N. Blair, was able to report completion of the original public works scheme for that island. The final link in the 628 km trunk line between Lyttelton and Bluff had opened in January 1879; and the 140 km line from Invercargill to Kingston on Lake Wakatipu was completed in July 1878. As at 30 June 1879, a total of 1,275 km of railway lines had been completed in the South Island.

In the North Island, where a Mr John Blackett, the first engineer of the Public Works Department, was now engineer in charge, 542 km of railway had been opened for traffic, the main sections being the 150 km from Auckland south to Ohaupo, the 100 km from Napier southward to Kopua, the 138 km from Foxton to Wanganui and the 72 km from Wellington through the Hutt Valley and over the Rimutaka Ranges to Featherston. As well there were also short sections at Kawakawa, Helensville and New Plymouth, all of which were steadily being expanded as fast as available resources permitted.

Importance was being placed by the Government on the building of main lines before district branch lines and with the exception of those South Island lines that were in the course of construction by the provincial governments, works activity was confined to main lines.

However, the Government allowed any district that was able to support its own railway to build it under the District Railways Act of 1877. The first such line constructed was the Waimea Plains railway between Gore and Lumsden, which was built to open up this area and to reduce the distance between Dunedin and Lake Wakatipu. It was completed in 1880.

The first Canterbury broad gauge locomotives weighed 32 tonnes, but most of the Vogel locomotives were much lighter, the A class being only 11 tonnes, and the successful F class, of which about 60 were in stock in 1880, weighed 20 tonnes. The largest locomotives were the J class, with a separate tender for coal and water, and a total weight of 44 tonnes. Because of the severe curvature on some routes, a number of Fairlie locomotives were acquired. These used an innovative design with articulated driving bogies, and a double

The Wingatui Viaduct on the Otago Central Line was representative of the kind of engineering works facing railway builders through the difficult terrain that New Zealand's topography presented. This viaduct was actually found to require periodic shortening due to the shifting nature of the terrain. It can still be experienced on the Taieri Gorge Limited route. ALEXANDER TURNBULL LIBRARY

Fairlie was virtually two engines with one cab. Most locomotives were British built, but the American locomotive builders Baldwin of Philadelphia also contributed a growing proportion of the country's motive power stock from 1879 onwards.

By this time the 20 kg/m iron rails were proving to be inferior to steel rails in terms of the weight they could bear. The invention of the Bessemer converter had made steel much cheaper, so it was possible to relay the main routes with 26.3 kg/m steel rails.

The 1870s had been a boom period in New Zealand and in 1878 the then Minister for Public Works, James MacAndrew, announced grand plans for "filling the gaps" in the railways system. However, by 1880 the beginning of a severe world depression was being felt. This resulted in a major curtailment of Government spending programmes, and in the case of railways led to attention being focused on the amount of railway existing in proportion to its population and the cost. In the United Kingdom there were 1,250 people for every kilometre of railway—in New Zealand there were 254. This was insufficient to make the lines economic. In the previous years the deficit on the railways (equal to 2.75% in 1879-80) was less significant than the benefits seen from the settling and development of the country. In the financial crisis of 1880, however, cuts were made in staff and services and railway construction was severely reduced. One casualty was the proposed Wellington and Foxton Railway. Others were lines from Helensville to Whangarei; Te Awamutu to Taranaki; Napier to Taupo and Gisborne; Marlborough to North Canterbury; Nelson–Greymouth and Greymouth to the East Coast.

For a period of 13 years the railways had to survive on very restricted budgets: a construction cost limit of £4,000 per 1.6 km did not allow major earthworks and created extremes of gradient and curvature. Lightweight track and bridge, primitive braking and signalling, and scarcity of spare parts all imposed severe endurance tests on railway personnel.

Impetus was being given to the creation of private railway companies to construct railways in local areas. One of these was the Wellington and Manawatu Railway Company Ltd., which was formed to build the Government-shelved Wellington and Foxton railway. The company was registered the day after the passing of the Railways Construction and Land Act of 1881, which was to facilitate the building of railways by private concerns. The Wellington to Foxton line was resurveyed to connect with the Government line at Longburn rather than at Foxton, passing through Shannon to open up the land awarded by the Government to the railway. Construction began in 1882 and was fully completed in 1886. The original intention of its builders was to sell it to the Government soon after its completion. However, because of the Government's shortage of funds, the company continued to run the line until 1908, using large American-built locomotives.

Often circuitous routes or steep gradients were required. The Rewanui Incline on the West Coast featured a 1 in 26 gradient and as a result a Fell-type centre rail was employed which was grasped by brake shoes in brake vans. The centre rail was eventually removed at the end of 1966. Here WE *375, a 4-6-4 tank engine, descends from Rewanui with a miners train on 25 May 1960.* NZR

In Christchurch the East and West Coast Railway League was formed in protest at the suspension of the planned Canterbury–Westland–Nelson railway links, and following negotiations with the Government in 1884 three delegates left Christchurch for London in January 1885 to seek English capital for the formation of a railway. Consequently, The New Zealand Midland Railway Company Ltd was formed in London and accepted assignment of the contract with the Government that had been taken to London by the three delegates. Progress was slow because of shortage of capital—some five and a half years later only 61 km from Brunnerton (later Brunner) to Reefton had been built, with another 50 km from Stillwater to Jackson being added in 1894. On the grounds that the company had breached its contract and had shown excessive delay in carrying out the work, the Government took over the line in May 1895. After the failure of court action by the company and some debenture holders, the railway was finally vested in the Government in June 1900. Other railways built by private initiative were the Waimate Gorge railway, the Thames Valley and Rotorua line, and the Rakaia and Ashburton Forks Railway.

For the 20 years from 1880 to the end of the century, railway construction progressed very slowly. Between July 1879 and March 1884, 428 km of railway was built compared to 1,611 km from 1874 to 1879. In 1884 revenue was £961,304 and expenditure £655,990—representing a net return of about 2.5% on the total cost of construction to that date. The total weight of goods carried was 1,727,240 tonnes, of which 583,502 tonnes were minerals, 439,140 tonnes of grain (mainly in Canterbury), and 268,939 tonnes were timber and firewood. Ordinary passenger journeys totalled 3,272,644 and 9,026 season tickets were on issue. The advent of refrigeration for the country's meat trade around 1883 required new, more sophisticated rolling stock, the cost of which had to be met out of revenue in advance of the new traffic. This practice of charging new capital expenditure against revenue, with no contributions to a depreciation and renewals account, was standard accounting practice until 1925.

In 1887 the Government began building locomotives in local workshops. Ten D class 2-4-0 tank locomotives were built in Christchurch by Scott Brothers in 1887; production of a new W class at Addington workshops started two years later; work on reconstructing F class engines began in 1892; a U class ten-wheeled tender locomotive was created in Addington in 1894; and in 1897 the Wa class appeared out of Hillside workshops. The front line express engines of this period were the 2-6-2 U class (50 tonnes including tender), built by Baldwin in 1885, which were in turn surpassed by the 58 tonne Baldwin 4-6-0 Ub class in 1898.

Between April 1887 and March 1893 an average of 44 km of line were opened each year. This included the extension of the Napier–Woodville railway to Palmerston North in 1891, an important link as Napier,

W 192 was the first locomotive to be built by NZR and saw service on the Rimutaka Incline, for which it was suitably adapted, as well as in the Christchurch area and on the West Coast. Because of its historical importance, NZR retained it and it was returned to steam in 1979. Here it is seen with a vintage excursion train near Kaiapoi north of Christchurch in October 1988. ASHLEIGH BROWN COURTESY TOM McGAVIN

Hastings, Wellington, Wanganui and New Plymouth were all then connected by rail. As well there was the extension of the Wairarapa line northwards to Eketahuna in 1889, and the first section of the railway northwards from Helensville in 1889. In the next two years from April 1893 to 1895, construction temporarily accelerated with a total of 169 km being built, the significant sections being the 51 km from Putaruru over the Mamaku Hills to Rotorua, the 38 km from Greymouth to Hokitika, and the 26 km from Middlemarch to Hyde on the Otago Central line.

The last five years of the 19th century saw little new construction—the two completions of note being the reaching of Thames from Hamilton in 1898 and the filling in of the last gap in the all Government route from Wellington to Napier through the opening of the last link from Masterton to Woodville in 1897. At the beginning of the new century the NZ Government Railways network totalled 3,548 km, of which 1,326 km were in the North Island and 2,222 km in the South Island.

Since 1881, however, the North Island population had increased more rapidly than that of the South Island, so that the 1901 census revealed that the North Island (European) population, at 390,579, was over 8,000 more than the South Island population. This population change was reflected in the traffic density on the railways—the North Island represented 21.1% of railways revenue in 1880-81, and by 1900-01 it was 37.4%.

The profitability of the railways was improving with a return of 3% or more on the capital cost of open lines being recorded since 1896. This was accompanied by tariff reductions, among which was the introduction in 1899 of workmen's tickets at specially low rates to encourage city workers in Auckland, Wellington, Christchurch and Dunedin to live in the satellite towns. In 1900 all ordinary passenger fares were reduced to 1 1/2 pence per 1.6 km in first class and 1 penny per 1.6 km in second class.

With the decade of depression from 1880 now past, unprecedented economic expansion was making plain the deficiencies in rolling stock, track, signalling, stations and station yards at the close of the 19th century. In 1897 the annual Government appropriation for railways capital expenditure was increased to £200,000 and in 1900 it was increased again to £500,000.

The twentieth century

The new century dawned with ambitious plans for expenditure on the railways. Joseph Ward (later to become Sir Joseph Ward and Prime Minister) inherited the Railways portfolio and a five year plan involving the spending of £2 million on locomotives, rolling stock and fixed capital plant. Ward increased this figure by another £500,000 with increases in the amounts to be spent on locomotives and rolling stock, but with reductions in the amounts to be spent on bridges, signals and telegraphs. In 1901 the system of signalling known as Tyer's Train Tablet System was adopted. Signals were interlocked so that two conflicting signals could not both be lowered to "proceed" setting at the same time. The electric train tablet system employed the principle of maintaining a safe distance interval between trains rather than a safe time interval, the latter having been demonstrated as unreliable by accidents that had occurred. With the block system only one train at a time can occupy a block or section, and the legitimate user of the block carries a tablet or token. By 1903 the electric train tablet system had been deployed on several sections in the North and South Islands. In August 1905 trials were carried out between Christchurch and Rolleston with an automatic tablet exchanger and by 1907, 25 stations had been equipped with them. Along with signalling improvements came improvements in braking. Westinghouse air brakes had been first tested in Auckland and Upper Hutt in 1876, but apart from imported Baldwin locomotives already fitted with them, nothing was done to fit them as standard equipment until after a fatal collision in Rakaia in March 1899. By 1903 virtually all locomotives and rolling stock in the North Island and a large percentage in the South Island had been equipped with these automatic continuous brakes. The new century saw the appearance of the dining car on NZR and the provision of toilets as standard equipment in passenger cars, both reducing stopping times at stations. Attention was paid to improving the track with heavier rails and the closer spacing of sleepers so as to permit faster running speeds. These improvements to the track were accompanied by stronger and more robust steam locomotive power with consequently diminishing journey times.

In 1903 the first separate head office building for the Railways was ready for occupation in Wellington. The end of the first decade of the new century had seen the completion of the North Island Main Trunk and the purchase of the Wellington and Manawatu Railway Company providing a complete Auckland to Wellington link. The maximum authorised speed on the railways was now 73 km/h. Joseph Ward had become Prime Minister and his successor, William Hall-Jones, inherited a Railways Department that was now 40 years old and had an accumulated debt of £28 million. The operating ratio (working expenses to revenue) was nevertheless a quite satisfactory 75% and in some years it was as good as 66%. In recognition of the fact that much of the equipment on which the debt had been incurred was by then worn out or withdrawn, £8 million was written off this total, which still left a large £20 million, however. Under the financial policy for the railways laid down in 1897 the railways were required to return 3% on the capital cost of construction, and after this had been achieved to grant to the public, concessions in fares, rates and improved train facilities and to improve the conditions of the staff. In 1909 the policy was changed to require to give a return of 3.75% and in 1910, 4% was required.

Between 1901 and 1914 the assets of New Zealand Railways rose from £17 million to over £32 million, the increase representing an outlay of well over £1 million a year, both on railway construction and on improvements to lines. The network increased from 3,549 km to 4,597 km; busy sections around the four main centres were doubled. By 1914 all main lines had been relaid twice and most branch lines once. By 1914 the network in the North Island was 1,930 km and the network in the South Island 2,666 km. However, 8.8 million train kilometres were run in the North compared

The 0-6-0T F class saddle tank locomotives were the epitome of the Vogel era. A total of 88 of these were supplied from seven different builders between 1872 and 1888. F 163 is one of eight preserved examples, seen near Otaihanga on 6 February 1989. G.B. CHURCHMAN

to 6.1 million train kilometres in the South, reflecting the rapid increase in economic activity in the North Island over the South.

On 1 August 1914 the new general manager of the railways, Mr E. Hiley, presented a report proposing the spending of some £3.25 million on the railways over the next five years. However, a few days later came the outbreak of World War 1, resulting in a significant curtailment of expenditure on the railways which instead was devoted to the country's war effort. In fact rail traffic and the operating ratio improved, and in spite of the reduction in spending, the network was extended some 209 km between 1914 and 1919. Inflation during and after the war had pushed up operating costs from £2.9 million in the 1913 financial year to £6.2 million in the 1922 financial year accompanied by a fall in net return to little more than 1%. Thereafter, reductions in expenditure and an increase in freight traffic restored net returns from railway operations to around the 3% level.

With 1923 came another milestone—the opening of the Midland Line including the 8.6 km Otira tunnel, linking the West Coast of the South Island with the East Coast. In 1924 Gordon Coates became Minister of Railways, and in his first year in office had to cope with the country's first national railway strike, caused by the re-introduction of the 48 hour working week without an increase in pay. The week had been reduced to 44 hours in 1921 with no reduction in pay. By March 1924 the network had reached 4,915 km and in his report to Parliament, Gordon Coates presented a revised programme of railway improvements and new works. The intervention of World War 1 had made it impossible to complete the £3.2 million programme authorised by the Railways Improvement Authorisation Act 1914, although a total of £964,000 had been spent, predominantly in the Auckland area and on improvements to signalling equipment. Now an eight year programme costing some £8 million was proposed. Included in this was the Wellington to Tawa Flat deviation, the doubling of track on some Auckland sections, a major deviation at Palmerston North and a proposed tunnel through the Rimutaka Ranges estimated to cost £1 million and to begin in the fifth year of the programme. Other works proposed by Coates were electrification of sections from Auckland to Papakura and Auckland north to Helensville from Wellington to Paekakariki and Upper Hutt and extending the original Lyttelton–Christchurch scheme north to Rangiora. A deteriorating national financial position, however, ensured that much of this plan did not see realisation.

Nevertheless certain improvements occurred in the four years of Coates' office, including the electrification of passenger car and locomotive headlights, the introduction of fast overnight express goods trains and the Limited Express between Wellington and Auckland. Another milestone was the completion of the line from Waihi through Tauranga to Taneatua, some 156 km. Also in this period work started on the line to link Napier and Gisborne. The 1920s saw the first serious competition for business from the motor car and motor truck, both luring passenger and goods traffic away from the railways. Revenue from rail passenger traffic declined 20% between 1925 and 1929 while the volume of goods and livestock traffic increased, although not as fast as it would have in the absence of road transport. In 1926 Gordon Coates expressed his policy for the Railways Department as being to utilise road transport either by itself or by arrangement with others wherever economies would be effected by so doing. The outcome of this policy was the creation of the Road Services Branch of the Railways Department. The first service was between Napier and Hastings, purchased in November 1926, and a country bus service operating from Oamaru to Ngapara and Tokarahi was taken over in December of the same year. This saw the end of mixed train services on those branch lines with cost savings. In 1927 and 1928 came more bus service acquisitions in the Hutt Valley. By the end of 1930, the Railways Department owned a total of 58 petrol buses and had a road services staff of 133, with road services being provided over 127 route km. By this stage the buses were carrying close to 3 1/2 million passengers annually, 86% of them in the Hutt Valley.

The overall effect of the competition provided by the motor car and the bus was to reduce the Railways' net earnings from £2 million in the 1925-26 financial year to £921,000 in the 1929-30 financial year, with a consequent decline in the return on capital investment —by that stage totalling £57.5 million—from 4.25% to 1.61%.

Gordon Coates had gone on to succeed W. Massey as Prime Minister on the latter's death, at the same time retaining his railways portfolio until the defeat of his government in 1928. One of his moves in 1924 was to prove a twin edged sword. Sir Sam Fay and Sir Vincent Raven, renowned British railway experts, were invited to head a commission on New Zealand's railways after carrying out a similar function in Australia. While their report generally endorsed a positive development programme, some of their findings were less constructive. These included criticism of the Railways' chief mechanical engineer, E.E. Gillon, who was replaced by G.S. Lynde, a British import. Lynde gave NZR its first steel carriages, but also lumbered it in 1928 with the huge 4-6-2 + 2-6-4 Beyer Garratt "G". A combination of mechanical problems and more power than the wagon couplings could cope with, resulted in the three "G" class Garratts being eventually reconstructed into six Pacific class locomotives. Mr Lynde retired in 1930. Another recommendation of the Fay-Raven Commission was the replacement of the general manager by a board of managers, again a short-lived experiment.

The second half of the 1920s saw the completion of the new Auckland station and yard, built to a cost of £500,000, the completion of a new route from Auckland through Orakei to Westfield opened in November 1930, a new goods yard and shed at Wellington, the opening of a line from Petone to Waterloo in 1927 (eventually to extend to Taita and become part of the main line through the Hutt Valley), a new marshalling yard west of Christchurch and a new locomotive depot at Greymouth. The year 1930 saw the beginning of the Great Depression which would last for the next six years, and with it came a major slump in the Railways' operating revenue. In turn the Railways reduced staff, curtailed services and cut wages and salaries to try and keep

▲*Construction work on the Otago Central Line around the turn of the century.* ALEXANDER TURNBULL LIBRARY

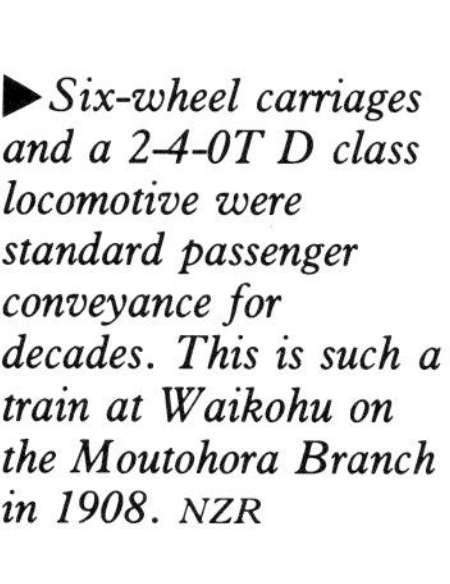

▶*Six-wheel carriages and a 2-4-0T D class locomotive were standard passenger conveyance for decades. This is such a train at Waikohu on the Moutohora Branch in 1908.* NZR

◀*Hunting rabbits by rail on the Otago Central Line about 1900.* ALEXANDER TURNBULL LIBRARY

▼*First appearing in 1908, the 18 members of the NZR (Addington) built 4-8-2 "X" class were the first of this "mountain" type class in the world. X 581 is seen with a special Wanganui–Marton goods train on 20 May 1955 near Bonny Glen.* THE LATE DEREK CROSS

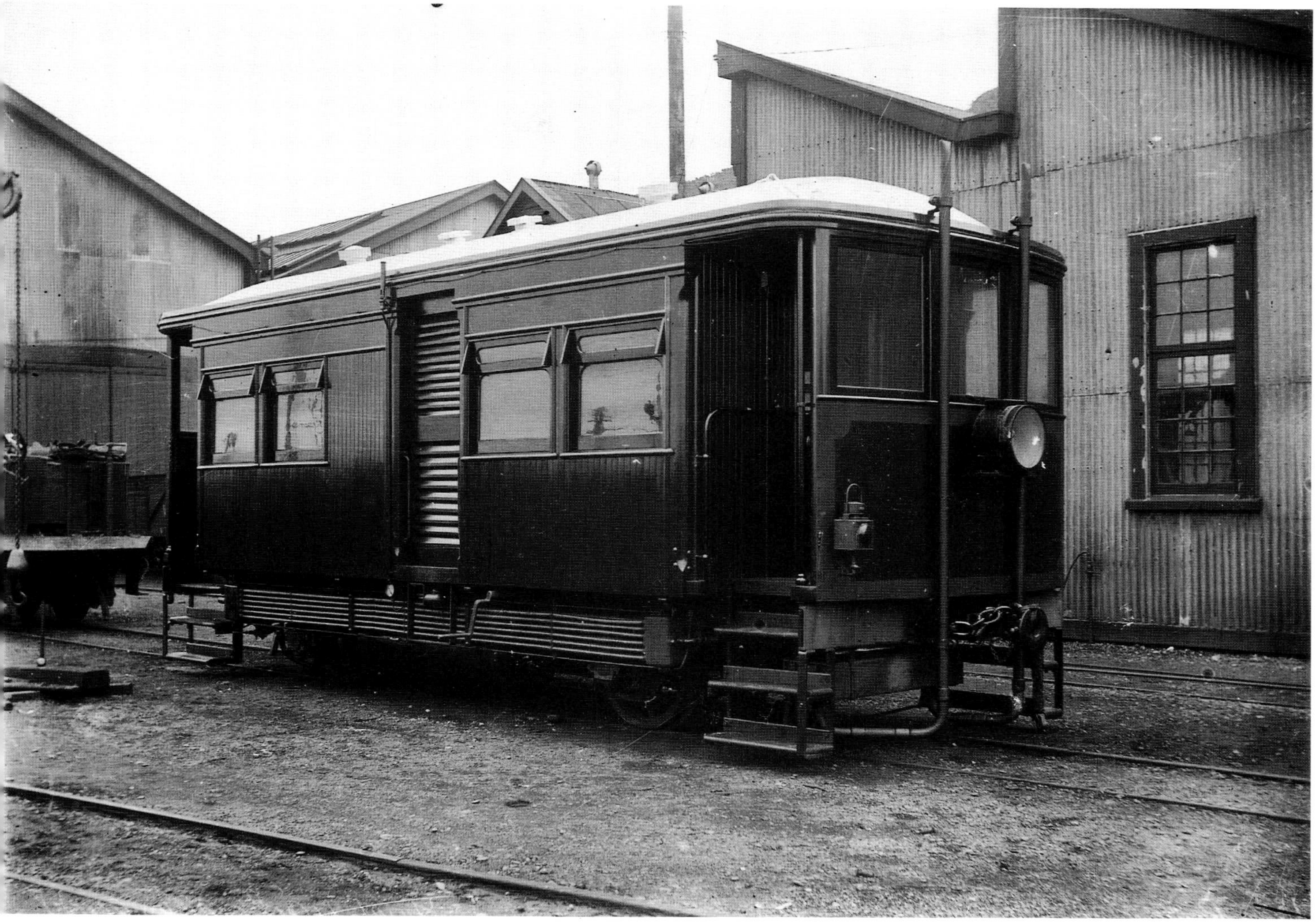

▲*This MacEwan-Pratt petrol railcar from 1912 was the first experiment with railcars on New Zealand Railways. It developed 50 km/h on a trial between Frankton and Putaruru but then broke down. It was dismantled the following year.* NZR

▶*Opening of new sections of line were usually marked by auspicious ceremonies. This is the opening of the Huiroa to Te Wera section of the Stratford–Okahukura Line on 20 June 1910. The locomotive is F 223.* ALEXANDER TURNBULL LIBRARY

Above: A scene at Palmerston North station about 1902, showing some of the occupations employed at stations a century ago.
Below: "A stop at Kaihu for refreshments." The passengers of an F-hauled train on the Donnelly's Crossing Branch. NZR&LS

The General Manager's inspection railcar from 1933 has a photo stop at Kaituna Station on the Little River Branch in the mid-1930s. It weighed 3½ tons, was powered by a 6 cylinder petrol engine, was painted red and known as the "Red Terror". In 1941 it was rebuilt for use on the Otira–Authur's Pass section as a catenary maintenance vehicle. As it seated only 7 passengers, it is to be assumed that some of the people seen here were locals meeting their VIP visitors. NZR&LS COLLECTION

their accounts in balance. In the ten years from 1923 to 1933 passenger revenue had fallen from one third of total revenue to one fifth. With the 1930s came the first closure of branch lines on any significant scale. Casualties were the 18.5 km Gisborne to Ngatapa line in the North Island, the 19.2 km Tokarahi Branch and parts of the Oxford and Wyndham Branches in the South Island. Most of the closures were of lines or parts of lines that had never seen much traffic, even in the absence of motor competition. New railway construction came to a virtual halt, the only progress being made on the Stratford to Okahukura line, which was completed in September 1933. Projects that had been completed just prior to the onset of the Depression were new workshops at Otahuhu, Lower Hutt, Addington (Christchurch) and Hillside (Dunedin), and the electrification of the 10 km Christchurch to Lyttelton line mainly to eliminate smoke nuisance in the long Lyttelton tunnel. Like the Arthur's Pass to Otira section on the Midland Line this was with 1,500 Volts DC.

The Depression saw a stop to deviations at Morningside (Auckland), Palmerston North and the Rimutaka tunnel. By 1932 the only deviation still being worked on, albeit at a snail's pace, was the Tawa Flat one. In 1933 plans for a new station and head office at Wellington were approved and preparations started for electrification of the line from Wellington to Paekakariki through the new Tawa Flat deviation and the Wellington to Hutt Valley line.

In November 1935 came the election of the first Labour Government which was committed to an expanded programme of public works and the new Minister of Public Works, Robert Semple, said in 1936, "In spite of the large mileage of highly improved main highways and the efficiency of modem motor transport, the railway still remains the predominant factor in the country's transportation system, and the completion of the present isolated systems and the linking up of the various districts by rail is, in my opinion, the proper and reasonable course to adopt." Projects given top priority were the completion of the Napier to Gisborne line, on which work restarted in May 1936, completion of the South Island Main Trunk from Picton to Parnassus, authorisation of the Westport–Inangahua line, and a deviation from Turakina to Okoia on the Marton to Wanganui line. This deviation eliminated a 22 km section of sharply curved and steeply graded line, and incorporated two long tunnels. In 1937 came the completion of the Wellington railway station, built at a cost of £350,000, full opening of the 14 km Tawa Flat deviation and the electrification of the now truncated Wellington to Johnsonville line.

In 1937 also came the decision to complete the railway to Dargaville which at that stage was the southern end of an isolated line to Donnelly's Crossing some 36 km to the north. Other works that were started or revived were the Palmerston North deviation, and a new station and yard rearrangement at Christchurch. Technically the late 1930s saw the replacement of lock-and-block signalling with automatic signalling—which first appeared between Wellington and Lower Hutt in 1922—on all double line sections of railway in the country and which was also to be found on 306 km of single line. The new Napier to Gisborne line (209 km) and the Picton to Waipara section (275 km) were also to receive automatic signalling. There was a programme

Atmosphere of a bygone age—the lines of an AB against an evening sky at Woodville with a now-removed signal cabin and semaphore signal gantry in the background.
MARK COLE

A view of how the "North Island Daylight Limited" would have appeared in the 1930s. WAB 687, built by NZR (Addington) in 1918, crosses the old Hapuawhenua viaduct with a special excursion train in 1961.
MARK COLE

for the gradual replacement of manual points with motor points at busier tablet stations and the replacement of semaphore distant signals in difficult locations with two position (yellow or green) colour light signals. Another major development in this period was the first use of Centralised Traffic Control (CTC) which was first employed on the North Island Main Trunk between Taumarunui and Okahukura (11 km) in 1938 next between Te Kuiti and Puketutu (15 km) in 1939. Centralised Traffic Control was an adaptation of three position (green, yellow or red) automatic signalling and provided for the remote control of mainline points and signals from one central location. The first major use of CTC was the 26 km between Tawa Flat and Paekakariki with control at Wellington which was commissioned in early 1940. Further major installations did not appear until the early 1950s, however. The second half of the 1930s saw the expansion of the Railways Road Services into long distance passenger traffic and in the southern part of the South Island the Railways had complete control of all passenger business on principal routes south of Timaru in 1936. This policy of expansion continued and by 1940 the total route distance of highways covered by the Railways Road Services was 4,148 km and 1,111 buses and 138 service coaches were in use. In the 1940-41 financial year they carried a total of 6.7 million passengers.

By the end of the 1930s both passenger and freight traffic on the railways had significantly recovered from the lows reached during the Depression years. Goods and livestock carried in the 1940 financial year was 7,796,733 tonnes, up from 5,578,573 tonnes in the 1933-34 financial year, although this was still lower than the 7,913,597 tonnes carried in the 1930-31 financial year—a consequence of the ever growing competition from motor transport. The issue of competition from the roads had been addressed governmentally at the beginning of the decade with the Transport Licensing Act 1931. This was a recommendation of a 1930 Royal Commission on the Railways and provided for a system of road transport licensing designed to prevent "wasteful competition" with the railways and indeed among road transport operators themselves. Despite considerable criticism from the road transport industry in later years, this system of licensing remained substantially in force for more than 50 years.

By the outbreak of World War 2 in September 1939, the network length of New Zealand railways had reached 5,430 km. The outbreak of another World War had again a profound effect on railway development in the country. Manpower had to be released to the armed forces and to essential industries, and materials in short supply had to be conserved. One new line that fell casualty to the war was an extension of the East Coast Main Trunk line from Taneatua to Opotiki and it was never revived. Work progressed, however, on the 16 km Tangowahine to Dargaville link, which was ready for traffic in May 1940, although it was not officially handed over to the Railways until March 1943. Other lines to see completion in the war years were the Napier to Gisborne line in August 1942 and the 43 km Westport to Inangahua line in December 1943. Work on completing the full Picton to Christchurch link progressed slowly during the war, and this last trunk line to be completed was officially opened in December 1945. The network length was now 5,664 km and the only isolated section remaining was the 97 km Nelson to Glenhope line. Two thirds of the population of the country was now in the North Island and the proportion of the railways network and revenue in the North Island reflected this.

As in Australia and America, the wartime years represented a tremendous boost to the railways' finances. Rationing of petrol and rubber, restricted usage of private cars and other road transport, and the movement of armed forces personnel and equipment produced

record numbers of passenger journeys and volumes of goods being transported. The net returns in the 1943-44 and 1944-45 financial years were 4.3% and 3.7% respectively. The high demand for railways services placed the whole system under considerable pressure. Fortunately much new equipment had been ordered in the late 1930s in anticipation of high traffic in 1940, the year of New Zealand's centenary. Coal consumption by the railways' steam locomotive fleet rose from a total of less than 500,000 tonnes before 1940 to 644,000 tonnes in 1943–44. Coal production could not keep pace with all reserve stocks being used up in 1944. As a result restrictions had to be placed on railway usage and the shortage of both coal and manpower lasted several years after the war. In 1946 the decision was made, due to the shortage of coal, to convert a number of North Island steam locomotives to oil-burning. The inability to provide adequate services after the War resulted in a decline in revenue and the increased cost of using imported coal added to total expenditure. The results were operating losses in the 1949 financial year amounting to £1.1 m.

During the 1940s the Government's policy of continuing the development of both rail and road transport under Railways Department ownership was maintained and by March 1951 the total number of highway route kilometres operated by the Railways Road Services peaked at 9,641 km. At that stage vehicle fleet totals were 351 buses, 398 service coaches and 301 other vehicles.

In addition to passenger traffic, most licences for goods transport along routes parallel to main railway lines were by the end of the 1940s in the hands of the Railways Department. Since 1945 the practice had been to transport, where appropriate, small consignments of goods to and from small country stations by motor truck at the same rates as if they had been transported by rail.

This was in order to achieve greater efficiency in the collection and delivery of these small lots of goods, which avoided the use of 12 to 15 tonne railway wagons for transporting good volumes of only 1 to 2 tonnes. If the destinations were distant the goods would be assembled into full wagons at the nearest large railhead. Also in 1946 the replacement of many mixed train services in country areas by buses was resumed. This again enabled greater efficiency for the railways and faster and more frequent services for passengers. The numbers of passengers transported by rail accordingly declined significantly during the second half of the 1940s, falling 45% between 1944 and 1952, with country passenger numbers falling the most. This decline in rail passenger numbers was accompanied by an increase in road service passenger numbers of 113% in the same period.

In many ways the end of the 1940s represented the end of an era and the beginning of another. Firstly road and air transport had significantly improved due to the boost given to development during the war with consequent spin-offs for civilian usage. Air travel was now in vogue for long-distance journeys and the private car was being steadily improved in terms of performance

Above: Train time at Otaki station on 5 January 1935. With at least five locomotives in steam on four different trains this was a busy place! The K and AB nearest the camera are probably heading an (extra long) NIMT express. J.D. BUCKLEY

Left: The installation of colour light signalling at Wellington in 1937 accompanied the electrification of railways out of the capital. Green over red meant "proceed", yellow over red – "proceed with caution, next signal is on red" and red over red meant "stop". ALEXANDER TURNBULL LIBRARY

Opposite above: The first length of railway to be electrified was the 14 km Arthur's Pass–Otira section in 1923. This shows a trio of the EO class with empty coal wagons about to enter the Arthur's Pass tunnel in the 1960s. R.J. McGAVIN

Opposite below: The 10 km Christchurch–Lyttelton line was electrified in 1929. Here an EC locomotive hauls a suburban train to Lyttelton over the Heathcote River near Opawa. NZR

and comfort. There was also the release of large numbers of army surplus trucks and military transport aircraft for civilian operators to set up or expand competing freight transport services to those offered by the railways. For the railways, too, changes in motive power were required. The steam locomotive, which had provided the means of railway propulsion since the beginnings 125 years previously, was now outmoded. Even before World War 2 it had become obvious that steam was on the way out—diesel and electric traction spelt the way of the future. Steam locomotive operation is physically demanding and the continual smoke, soot, coal dust, ash and oil made the job a dirty one for enginemen. Although it is these same characteristics that endear them to today's many steam locomotive enthusiasts, it nevertheless did not help to recruit enginemen for everyday operations. In addition coal and oil stocks, of which steam locomotives are avaricious consumers, were scarce and expensive, and above all else, a considerable amount of time went into preparing steam locomotives for use and then cleaning them out afterwards. In America the steam era was effec-

Right: A Thornycroft Railways Road Services bus from the 1920s. NZR

Below: A northbound electric multiple unit from Wellington to Paekakariki stops at Porirua in the early 1950s. Some of the passengers will be travelling further on the Road Services buses waiting. NZR

The handsome lines of A 428, built in New Zealand by A. & G. Price in 1909, with a nominal goods train on the Weka Pass Railway on 18 September 1995. A total of 58 of this locomotive class were built, all except one using compounding (low pressure and high pressure cylinders). REID McNAUGHT

tively over by 1948, yielding to diesel traction. In New Zealand a departmental commission started examining options for future motive power needs the same year.

In 1951 came the report of the general manager and the chief engineer in favour of electrification of the entire North Island Main Trunk, beginning with the Auckland to Frankton section, which saw particularly high density traffic. Electric traction had the advantages of using indigenous electricity rather than imported fuel, it is clean and produces no pollution (not a major consideration at that time although it was to become a concern in later years), has a favourable power to weight ratio and electric locomotives can be coupled together and operated by one crew. Another factor is that on hilly terrain as in New Zealand, when on descending sections the motors become generators and actually produce power that can be fed back into the system.

The principal disadvantage with electrification is the initial capital cost of installing catenary and substations. One can only assume that this cost was the reason why electrification of the North Island Main Trunk, while being initially decided upon, was deferred—as it turned out, for more than 30 years. In the meantime dieselisation went ahead on a large scale from about 1954 onwards. The total cost of dieselisation instead of electrification can be reckoned in retrospect. To the quantity of fuel oil consumed by the diesel fleet since 1950 can be added the higher cost of diesel locomotives over electrics and the greater maintenance and repair required. In all probability the decisions to defer electrification in the early 1950s resulted in a high net overall cost to the railways and to the country.

Work did begin on completing the electrification of the full Wellington to Upper Hutt suburban line (32.4 km) which was finished in July 1955. This was to be the last electrification work on New Zealand railways until 1984. In fact one section of electrified line—the 10 km Christchurch to Lyttelton line—was dieselised in September 1970. Reasons given were the cost of maintaining electric locomotives and substations for the section once traffic had declined as a result of the opening of the Lyttelton road tunnel.

By the beginning of the 1950s the role of the railways was starting to change. Originally the railways served to open up and develop the rural hinterland and to provide rural communities with transport facilities. This role was fulfilled by the many rural branch lines built last century but which by the 1950s no longer carried an economic volume of traffic. Some lines merely saw one up and down goods train a day, others even less than that. The average speed of trains on these lines was frequently no more than 25 km/h, hardly comparable with the speed of a motor car or truck. By the early 1950s the NZR network length had reached its zenith at some 5,700 km. Another Royal Commission in 1952 recommended the closure of certain loss-making branch lines, and several were accordingly closed, some immediately and others throughout the 1950s.

A southbound goods train with KA 946 on the North Island Main Trunk temporarily heads north as it ascends the Raurimu Spiral sometime in the 1950s. NZR

New construction, where it occurred, was primarily to serve new specific heavy industries.

The first new line to be built in the 1950s was the 28.4 km branch line from Putaruru to Kinleith where a pulp and paper mill had been established by New Zealand Forest Products Ltd and where pine forests planted in the 1930s were reaching maturity. This line was completed in October 1952 and quickly saw very heavy traffic volumes. Likewise in the Bay of Plenty a proposal to build a pulp and paper mill at Murupara in 1950 saw the authorisation of a new line to Murupara from Edgecumbe. Later it was decided to build the mill at Kawerau instead, so the route of the railway was changed to a 13.3 km branch line from a junction near Awakaponga to Kawerau and was opened in October 1953. A 57.2 km extension to Murupara was built over the next four years and was opened in January 1957, although not handed over to NZR until July of that year. These branches, like the Kinleith Branch, soon saw very heavy traffic volumes, transporting logs from Murupara to the mill at Kawerau and the pulp and paper from Kawerau to the ports for export or for distribution throughout New Zealand for local use. The Murupara Branch was thus the last branch line of any significance to be built in New Zealand. A couple of years earlier a 6.9 km branch line to serve new port facilities at Mount Maunganui had been built. One of the last major deviations to be completed in the 1950s was the 22 km relocation north of Upper Hutt through the new 8.8 km Rimutaka tunnel to the Wairarapa on which work had started in 1949. This was completed in October 1955 and the deviation was opened the following month, cutting out some 14 km of winding track over the Rimutaka ranges including the famous but expensive and time-consuming Rimutaka Incline with its Fell engines. By 1960 the total network length of NZR had declined by 305 km from that of 1950, with the 105 km of new line opened being more than offset by the closure of 410 km of lightly-used lines. One of the major closures was that of the isolated 97 km Nelson to Glenhope section, which closed in September 1955 amid much local opposition.

Perhaps the event that many people will remember most from the 1950s, however, was the Tangiwai disaster. On Christmas Eve 1953 the overnight Wellington to Auckland express carrying 285 people plunged into the Whangaehu River at Tangiwai, north of Waiouru on the North Island Main Trunk. Just before the train consisting of Ka class locomotive number 949, nine passenger cars and two vans reached the bridge, a torrent of water and mud from the Crater Lake of Mount Ruapehu came roaring down the river and swept away the concrete piles of the bridge, leaving no support when the train ran onto it. With a death toll of 151, the incident ranks as New Zealand's worst railway accident and New Zealand's fifth worst recorded disaster.

The volume of goods carried continued to increase throughout the 1950s, particularly in the Auckland region, and new yards and handling facilities were brought into use. These included a major marshalling yard at Westfield, 11 km south of Auckland, opened in January 1962. New station yards at Port Chalmers, Stratford and Hastings; new goods sheds at Frankton and elsewhere; and extra sidings for the Bluff Harbour development were all opened, and the long awaited 11 km deviation at Palmerston North incorporating a new station, goods shed and yard, and a new locomotive depot, was brought into full use at the end of 1963. Although the capital expenditure in the North Island was high, much heavier traffic enabled a net return on investment there of 2.1% in the 1962 financial year, while in the South Island, a 4.8% loss on investment was incurred. In 1962 came a major change in inter-island traffic with the introduction of the roll-on roll-off ferry *Aramoana* which provided a link between the railheads at Wellington and Picton. Since 1947 inter-island freight traffic had been carried out by the Rail–Air service mainly between Wellington (Paraparaumu) and Blenheim. By 1961 this service was carrying 54,637 tonnes annually, although the inauguration of the rail and road vehicle and passenger ferry cut this total by a quarter. With the introduction of the roll-on, roll-off rail operation it was now possible to consign goods by rail from any station in one island to any station in the other island without having to handle the load on the way. The new ferry soon attracted enough traffic to produce an operating surplus within seven months. Later in 1967 came the introduction of a second ferry, the sister ship *Aranui*. While providing a vital link, the 3 hours plus required for the 88.5 km has not been to the liking of all passengers who have to endure about half of this time through the often stormy waters of Cook Strait.

As well as improvements being made to freight handling, several new station buildings for the benefit of staff and passengers were built between the late 1950s and early 1960s. These included the grand new Christchurch station, built at a cost of £800,000 and opened in November 1960. Others were Te Awamutu, Napier, Hastings, Feilding, Porirua, Stratford, New Plymouth, Port Chalmers and Rotorua, the last being a combined road/rail terminal. The 1960s generally followed the trend that had been set in the 1950s. Further closures of branch lines that were experiencing dwindling traffic were made with the result that by 1970 the network had shrunk a further 440 km from its length in 1960, most of the closures being in the South Island. Passenger revenue as a percentage of total revenue continued to fall—in 1950 it represented 17.8% of total operating revenue, in 1960 it had fallen to 9.2% and in 1970 it was down to 6.7%. Not surprisingly very little capital was spent in this period on improving passenger facilities and on new equipment. Apart from 35 new railcars to replace passenger trains on secondary lines that were introduced between 1955 and 1958 no really new passenger stock was bought until 1971.

The main emphasis during the 1960s was on obtaining diesel locomotives to replace the remaining fleet of steam locomotives. The last steam locomotive in New Zealand to be outshopped was Ja 1274 in 1956 and

A newish English Electric Company electric multiple unit set at Paekakariki in 1949. Although only 39 km from Wellington, this was one of NZR's celebrated refreshment room stops as locomotives were changed over here (electric to steam northbound, steam to electric southbound) until 1967. NZR

▲*K 902 with a goods train climbs to Stratford from Ngaere in February 1960.* MARK COLE

▼*KA 955 on a Wellington–Auckland Sunday evening express works up speed away from McKays crossing on 26 August 1962.* MARK COLE

JA 1267 departs Christchurch with a 13 total Invercargill Express in the morning of 22 August 1966. MARK COLE

Livestock transport was the raison d'être *of many rural branchlines. This shows sheep wagons being shunted at Castle Rock on the Mossburn Branch in February 1953.* NZR

from a fleet of 473 steam locomotives and 221 diesel locomotives in 1960, by 1970 the numbers were 18 and 470 respectively. The other focus was on replacing older goods wagons with those designed for modern requirements and with higher unit capacities.

Passenger services by railcar to Whangarei, Rotorua, Tauranga and Westport were ended in 1967-68 and replaced by buses. At the same time lightly patronised services on other routes were reduced, including off-peak suburban services in the four main centres. The first moves to revamp certain passenger services came with the introduction of the "Blue Streak" railcar as a daylight service between Auckland and Wellington in 1968. These railcars featured redesigned seats, wall-to-wall carpet, catering facilities and a public address system. With an increased average speed of 63 km/h for the 680 km journey it soon attracted good patronage and a second railcar was similarly outfitted in December 1968 and a third in March 1969.

In September 1969 tenders were called for three new twin-coach air-conditioned railcars for the Auckland to Wellington daylight run. These were to be diesel-electric with an output power of 723 kW, designed for speeds up to 120 km/h and to accommodate 96 passengers inside each two coach set. These railcars were delivered from their Japanese builders in 1972 and were named "Silver Fern" on account of their external finishing of ribbed stainless steel sheathing on a corrosion resistant carbon-steel frame.

Attention was also paid to the Auckland to Wellington overnight service and tenders were called late in 1968 for twenty-four sleeping cars, three buffet cars, and four vans to house power-generating equipment and space for luggage. Again all cars were to be fully air conditioned and sound proofed. These cars were received from Japan in 1971 and the new "Silver Star" overnight trains entered commercial service in September 1971 replacing the former Night Limited Express. The new cars, which included a licensed restaurant car, represented a high standard of comfort with extensive facilities.

In the South Island plans to upgrade passenger trains on the 590 km Christchurch to Invercargill run were announced in May 1969. Twelve former first class passenger cars were completely refurbished and two other cars were refitted out as buffet cars with new modern bogies for smooth running. On 1 December 1970 diesel hauled single class "Southerner" expresses took over from the steam hauled South Island Limiteds. Like the "Blue Streak" railcars, the external livery was blue and a lighter blue waistband was chosen with gold lining. The DJ locomotives assigned to the train were at that time the newest motive power on NZR.

All three of these new trains presented significant reductions in journey times over those that they replaced. This was due to the elimination of some passenger stops, but mainly to the increased performance and lack of servicing stops of the motive power. For the Silver Stars, initially a pair of DA class diesels were used each weighing 81.3 tonnes and developing 1,060 kW gross output. Later in 1972 these were replaced with one DX class locomotive which weighed a mere 16.2 tonnes extra than a DA but developed nearly twice the power at 2,050 kW.

On 6 November 1972 a new buffet car express called the "Endeavour" entered service to replace the morning railcar on the Wellington to Napier run. Normally consisting of a Da class diesel-electric locomotive, four passenger cars, a buffet car and a guard's van, it represented another move to upgrade a prime long distance passenger service. In keeping with the trend set by the "Southerner" the external livery of the train was blue with a light blue, gold rimmed waistband and white car roofs. Internally the passenger accommodation was improved with wall to wall carpet and armchair style seats. Railcars maintained the connection from Napier to Gisborne.

Meanwhile the Cook Strait ferry service had seen some changes with the transfer of management of the ships from the Union Steamship Company to NZR in November 1971. In December 1972 came the addition to the fleet of the *Arahanga*, a freight carrying vessel with accommodation for 40 passengers, essentially the truck drivers. In April 1974 came a fourth ferry, the *Aratika*. Initially a freight-only ship like the *Arahanga*, it was converted in June 1976 in Hong Kong to carry 800 passengers and 70 automobiles. At the end of 1974, the four ships could carry 1650 standard four-wheel wagons each day every week. This was on the basis of 25 return trips a week by the *Aramoana* and *Aranui* and 18 trips by the two freight ferries.

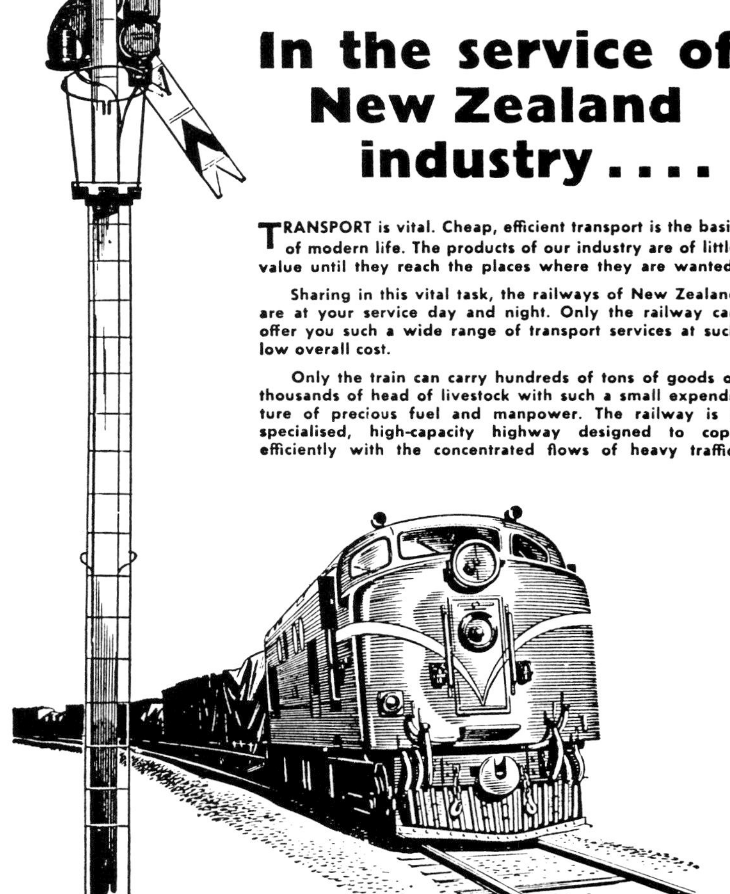

In the service of New Zealand industry . . . .
TRANSPORT is vital. Cheap, efficient transport is the basis of modern life. The products of our industry are of little value until they reach the places where they are wanted.
Sharing in this vital task, the railways of New Zealand are at your service day and night. Only the railway can offer you such a wide range of transport services at such low overall cost.
Only the train can carry hundreds of tons of goods or thousands of head of livestock with such a small expenditure of precious fuel and manpower. The railway is a specialised, high-capacity highway designed to cope efficiently with the concentrated flows of heavy traffic.
The products of the land go down to the sea . . . on rails — the high-capacity highway!
NEW ZEALAND RAILWAYS

Above: The diesel arrives. A 1950s advertisement featuring a new DF locomotive. NZR

Left: A new face in passenger travel introduced in 1955, the Fiat railcar. A Gisborne bound articulated unit crosses a southbound KA 964 at Te Horo on 26 August 1963. J.A.T. TERRY

Improvements to freight handling capability saw the building of an extensive new marshalling yard at Te Rapa, 5.5 km north of Hamilton, with 51.5 km of track and 230 turnouts covering 32 hectares. This was modelled on American practice and built to replace marshalling yards at Frankton Junction. With the merging of traffic from Thames, Kinleith, Kawerau and the Bay of Plenty with the North Island Main Trunk, very heavy traffic volumes occurred and created the need for a modern expanded and computerised yard. The Te Rapa yard opened early in 1971 and in the following years saw a rapidly expanding volume of traffic. By 1976 a total of approximately 2,600 wagons were being hump shunted in each 24 hour period during Tuesday to Friday. In later years, the number of wagons shunted decreased drastically, with moves to larger wagons and to unit trains that would not require shunting en route. As a result, the hump yard was closed in 1992, as a much smaller flat yard was sufficient.

Another major development in freight handling came with the introduction of the Traffic Monitoring System (TMS). This was initially placed into operation on the Woodville-Napier-Gisborne line on 1 February 1979 and later throughout the rest of the country. It entailed computerisation of all details on the condition and whereabouts of every one of the Railway's 30,000 goods wagons, so that such information could be obtained in seconds from a central computer file. It became possible to locate a wagon, whether in a train or in a yard, and know whether it was empty or full and what type of commodity it was carrying. This coincided with a renumbering program, so that all locomotive, carriage and wagon number had a check digit included to reduce the risk of recording numbers incorrectly. This system has been progressively improved, and amongst the functions of the current system, known as "Amicus" is the ability of customers to access it via the Internet, to locate where their consignments are on the railway system. The need for streamlined freight handling procedures was emphasised in 1977 by changes in the Transport Licensing Regulations for the cartage of goods by road transport. The general limit was increased from effective rail distances of 64 km (40 miles) to 150 km. Beyond this distance, the regulations generally prohibited road transport unless the route that included the railway was more than one third longer than the shortest road route.

The rapid growth of container traffic saw in 1978 a five-year locomotive and rolling stock programme characterised by the absence of any provision for new four-wheeled box wagons and highsider wagons, at the same time a significant provision for flat bogie type wagons designed to carry containers. By this time the growth of container traffic had seen the proportion of bogie wagons for carrying ISO containers increase from less than 2% of total bogie stock in 1970 to 26% in 1978. In 1978 came the opening of the last major new railway line—the Kaimai deviation. This was the culmination of work set in motion by the findings of a 1962 commission cumbersomely called The Commission of Inquiry into Improved Access by Land to the Port of Tauranga and Bay of Plenty. The existing rail route into the Bay of Plenty involved a slow, tortuous line via Waihi and the Karangahake Gorge. The recommendation was for a deviation and tunnel through the Kaimai range to reduce the rail distance from Kinleith to Tauranga from 226.9 km to 127.1 km. The proposal was given the green light by the Government in May 1963 and on 2 October 1965 the first sod was turned. Thirteen years later on 12 September 1978 the deviation, including the 8.85 km. Kaimai tunnel, was opened. This tunnel was now the longest in New Zealand, exceeding the Rimutaka tunnel (8.798 km) and the Otira tunnel (8.554 km). At the same time as the Kaimai

KA 945 with an excursion train seen between Mana and Plimmerton near Wellington in January 1995. REID McNAUGHT

J 1234 with an excursion train crosses the Kopuawhara viaduct on the scenic Napier–Gisborne line on 23 October 1993. REID McNAUGHT

A 50 ft wooden postal van from 1908 on the back on express 626 to Auckland, seen at Wellington in 1949. Postal sorters would work in these vans overnight, changing trains to return home at Taihape. Postal vans were withdrawn in 1971. NZR

deviation was opened, the 60 km of line between Paeroa via Waihi to Apata was closed.

Other branch line closures in the 1970s were the Catlins River branch in February 1971; the Seddonville to Mokihinui Mine section in February 1974; the Kapuni to Opunake section of the Opunake Branch in July 1976; the Methven and Tuatapere Branches in July 1976; the Balfour and Waiau Branches in January 1978; the Tapanui Branch in October 1978 and the Kingston Branch north of Mararoa in November 1979.

During the 1970s the general trend in rail passenger traffic was one of cutbacks. The last addition to the roster of passenger trains came with the "Northerner", as an alternative overnight express to the "Silver Star" between Wellington and Auckland, on 3 November 1975. Unlike the "Silver Star", which consisted of sleeping cars only, the "Northerner" comprised both sleeper and seat carriages. In June 1979, however, the "Northerner" became the only overnight express when the prestigious "Silver Star" was withdrawn. This withdrawal resulted from a decision that the train was not economic in its existing form and that it should be converted to a combined seating and sleeping car train. However, when the first car was converted it was found that the cost or removing the asbestos linings which had been identified as a health hazard made the whole exercise an uneconomic proposition. This combined with industrial relations problems led to it never being put back into operation. The carriages were eventually sold, and most were converted by A. & G. Price Ltd of Thames for metre gauge track for use on the glamour "Eastern & Oriental Express", which runs between Singapore and Bangkok.

Other rail passenger services to end in the 1970s were those between Christchurch and Lyttelton in February 1972; Greymouth and Ross in October 1972; Dunedin to Alexandra in April 1976; all remaining passenger services north of Helensville by June 1976; and the Wellington to New Plymouth "Blue Streak" railcar service in July 1977. With the decline of passenger services came the end of most railcar services. Early in 1976 it was announced that no more railcars would receive major overhauls and that all would be withdrawn from service as they wore out. The result was that from a one-time fleet of over 50 railcars, the only ones in regular operation by the end of 1978 were the three "Silver Fern" sets on the North Island Main Trunk. There had been four types of railcar in general post war use: six "Rimutaka" type used over the Rimutaka Incline from 1936 until its closure; six twin-engine (90 kW each) double bogie "Standard" type used from 1939 from Napier to Wairoa and from Wellington to New Plymouth until December 1972; nine single engine 185 kW "Vulcan" type used on various South Island services

Above: Four-wheel 25 ft long diesel railcar RM 21 at Christchurch in 1936. This was one of two built in Hutt Workshops that year for the Christchurch Press *morning newspaper run to the West Coast. It was powered by a 70 kW Leyland diesel engine, had a top speed of 80 km/h and weighed close to 8 tonnes. Seating was provided for 19 passengers but with a full load of newspapers it was reduced to 13. A popular innovation was a folding card table for those on the early morning service. In 1940 they were superseded by the Vulcan railcars and they were dismantled in 1942.* NZR

Below: Vulcan railcar RM 55 stops at Buller in the early 1960s. Railcar services between Greymouth and Westport lasted until 1967. NZR

The DA class made its appearance in 1955. It was an adaption of the General Motors (USA) G 12 class, with an extra running axle in each of the two bogies so as to spread the load more evenly on the track, as well as reduced cab measurements to take account of New Zealand's tight loading gauge. Altogether 146 of these 1,060 kW locomotives were supplied and became the standard locomotive of the 1960s in the North Island. When the Te Rapa yard was opened in 1971, the first 5 of the class were adapted for use in the yard with low speed running and radio communication with the control tower. These were denoted DAA class. The DA's were finally withdrawn in early 1989. This scene shows two on a goods train between Waimiha and Poro-o-Tarao in the early 1980s. DAVE SIMPSON

◀*The 15 of the English Electric built 490 kW, Bo-Bo class DE's when introduced in 1952–53 represented the first appearance of diesel-electric traction on NZR. DE 512 at Wellington in 1975 was the last in the original colour scheme.* NORM DANIEL

▼*The English Electric built DF arrived in 1954. The 10 members of the 1,120 kW class had a 2-Co-Co-2 wheel arrangement and were used in the North Island. Weaknesses of their V-12 motors led to their early retirement by 1975. DF 1302 photographed at Timaru after overhauling on 9 August 1970.* B.J. MCKENZIE

▼*The 17 members of the General Motors (Canada) built 705 kW, A1A-A1A Db class were introduced in 1965–66 and used on secondary lines in the North Island. The class leader is seen at Glen Afton in October 1969.* TONY HURST

▼*The five members of the 755 kW Di class arrived from English Electric's Rocklea plant in Queensland in 1966. At the time they were seen as alternatives to the DB's but in the event no more of either class were built. DI 1103 was the last in original livery, seen at Tauranga in 1978.* NORM DANIEL

▶The 42 A1A-A1A 560 kW DG class arrived from English Electric in 1955–56. All were eventually transferred to the South Island by 1976. Here DG's 787 and 756 arrive at Eastown (Wanganui) on 30 April 1961 with a train of empty Vb meat wagons. This was the first diesel hauled train in the area. MARK COLE

Rebuilds

Ten of the DG class were rebuilt between 1978 and 1980 with low nose cabs which included improved sound proofing and push-button braking. All were withdrawn by 1983. Here a rebuilt DG leads an unrebuilt DG into Timaru with Tuhawaiki Point in the background in the early 1980s. B.J. MCKENZIE

▶Eighty of the DA's were rebuilt by Clyde Engineering (Australia) between 1978 and 1980. Here one of the rebuilds, DC 4093 sporting advertising for a beer brand and a radio station is seen at Upper Hutt on 30 June 1989. MARK COLE

▲*The cab of a KA in the 1950s contrasts with the cab of a Silver Fern railcar. The attire of the personnel reflects the respective working conditions.* NZR

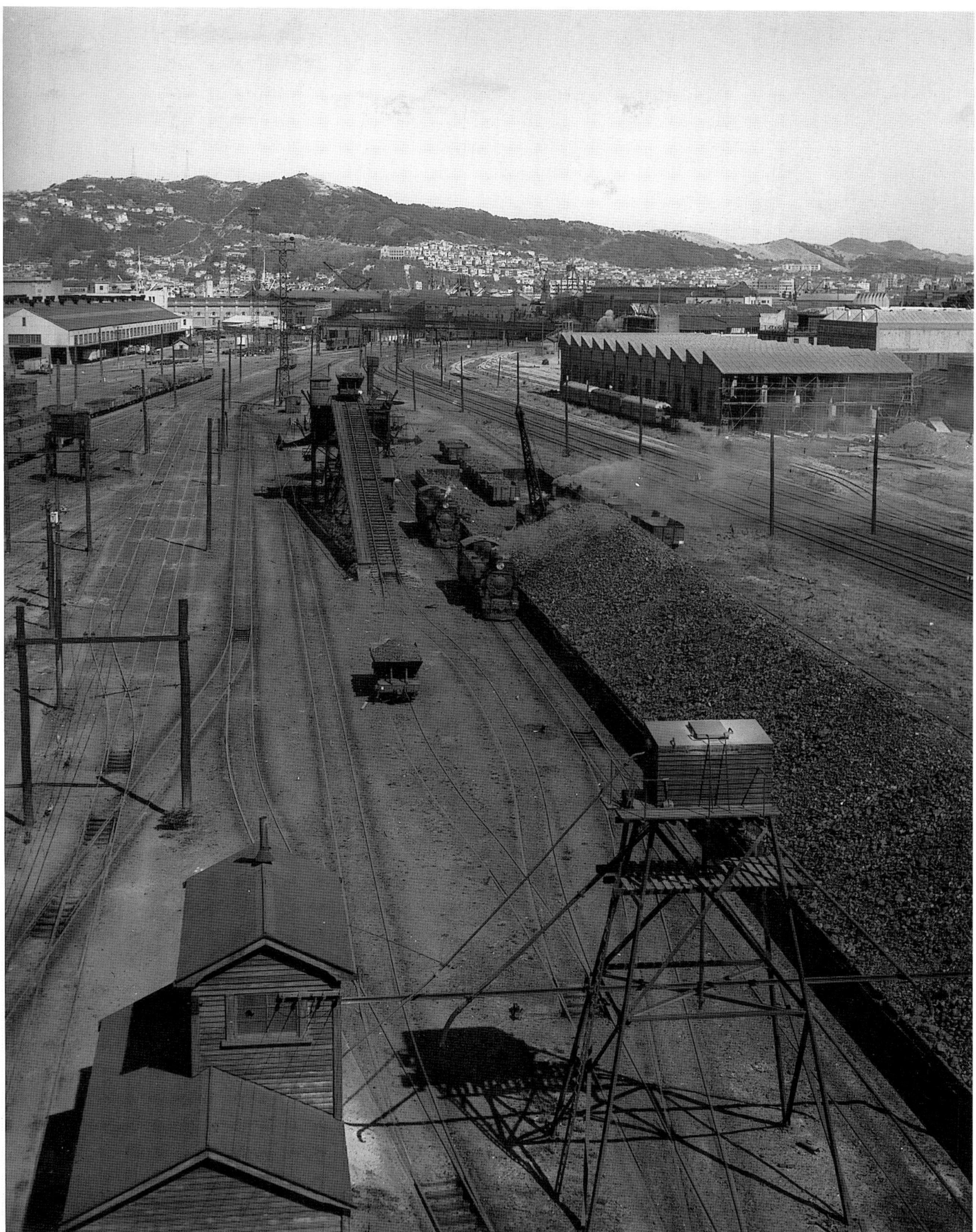

A view of Wellington railway yard before steam ended in the region in 1955 upon the electrification of the Hutt Valley lines that year. Servicing facilities for resupplying steam loco coal stocks are prominent in this view, while a water tank is in the foreground. A pair of Ww tank engines are next to the coal heap, while further over a three-car electric multiple unit, for the time being in use on the Wellington–Paekakariki run, can be seen next to the shed being built for them. NZR

Night steam

The last regular steam workings in New Zealand were the overnight Christchurch–Invercargill expresses in 1971. These scenes capture the atmosphere of steam night workings.

▲*Stop at Gore on a cold night in August 1969.* MARK COLE

▼*3.30 am on a Saturday morning in 1970. JA 1256 can be heard but not seen by the sleeping population of Oamaru as it howls off. Train 189 should have been shunted up to the platform by this time, preparing for a 3.40 am departure for Dunedin.* B.J. MCKENZIE

▲*JA 1260 drops its fire at Oamaru after a northbound run.*

▶*JA 1240 takes water at Ashburton during its haulage of train 189.*

▼*Decoking a steamer.* B.J. MCKENZIE

A Dx diesel heads a freight train near Waiouru on the North Island Main Trunk on a snowy winter's day on 4 June 1974. NZR

until September 1978; and lastly 35 articulated twin-unit, two engine (156 kW each) 88 seater "Fiat" type introduced between 1955 and 1958 and used widely during the 1960s. From 1967 they were gradually phased out and the last one in the North Island ran between New Plymouth and Taumarunui in February 1978, and the last one in the South Island ran between Christchurch and Greymouth in September 1978. Examples of the "Rimutaka", "Standard" and "Vulcan" railcars have been preserved in rail society museums, but no 88-seater "Fiat" type were made available for preservation. Although the "Fiats" saw their end as railcars, fourteen were converted into Ac class locomotive hauled carriages between December 1977 and January 1979 and painted an unique grass green colour.

A positive note came in March 1979 with the announcement that a $33 m contract had been awarded for 44 two-coach electric passenger units for the Wellington suburban lines to replace 40-year-old stock. This order was the largest rolling stock order ever placed by New Zealand Railways. The successful tenderer was the Hungarian firm of Ganz-Mavag, in association with General Electric of Britain, which would supply the traction motors and other major electrical components. They were placed in service between August 1982 and March 1983 and represented a significant improvement over the older English Electric units. The new units are lighter and seat more passengers at 148 against 128, and are capable of higher speeds. The carriage stock on the Auckland suburban services also needed replacement, but after a Budget announcement that new carriages would be purchased, the Government changed its mind and no new stock was bought. Also introduced at this time was the DF class, a General Motors 1230 kW diesel with all six axles driven for maximum haulage capacity at slow speeds.

Technically, during the 1970s there was growth in the use of pre-stressed concrete sleepers in place of traditional hardwood sleepers and treated pine sleepers. Pre-stressed concrete sleepers, despite being much heavier, are more durable and have a longer life than wooden ones. Nylon insulators between the base of the rail and the fastenings prevent interference with electric track circuits and the problem of a harder, less yielding ride is overcome with the use of a rubber pad between rail and sleeper. In association with concrete sleepers came the increased use of continuous welded rail. Present day rails weigh 50 kg per metre and are laid initially in 76.8 m lengths. When they have properly bedded in, after about six months, they are welded together to make continuous welded rail. Good ballasting is required with ballast up to the top of the sides and ends of the sleepers to help stop any tendency of the track to buckle from severe temperature changes. Speed restrictions are imposed in hot weather in areas where heat buckling is known to be a problem.

The 1980s

In February 1979 the then general manager of the Railways, Trevor Hayward, issued a discussion paper entitled *Time for Change* against a background of sharp increases in operating losses in each of the two preceding years. This paper set out the situation regarding the various services that the Railways were operating and where they were most profitable. Three basic principles were enunciated: the development of commercially sound services; continuation of services of proven social benefit with a spelling out of their costs, and the ending of services which have no clear commercial or social justification. This paper served to foreshadow the general developments that were to take place in the 1980s.

Included in the services that services whose continuance was not found to be justified were most remaining branch lines in the South Island and many small stations throughout the country. Branch lines that soon disappeared were the Clyde to Cromwell portion of the Otago Central Branch in April 1980; the Hokitika to Ross portion of the Greymouth to Ross line in November 1980; the Ngakawau to Seddonville portion of the Seddonville Branch in May 1981; the Mossburn and most of the Kingston Branches in December 1982; the Kurow Branch in June 1983 and the Rewanui Branch by early 1985.

In 1980 a review of country stations recommended the immediate or eventual closure of nearly 200 small stations and sidings, bringing the total number of stations and sidings open for goods and/or parcel traffic to fewer than 300, less than a quarter of the total that existed in 1958 and less than half that of 1973. To put this into perspective however, at the end of the 1970s, some 60% of stations produced only 2% of freight revenue. Typically these stations handled less than 200 tonnes of freight a year.

A more positive development was the electrification of the North Island Main Trunk. The NIMT is the prime traffic artery between Wellington and Auckland, along the way directly linking Palmerston North and Hamilton, the section between Auckland and Hamilton having the heaviest density of the whole rail network. The proposals for electrification from the early 1950s were resurrected and in 1980 the Government established a project team to finalise design criteria and estimate financial returns for electrification between Te Rapa (Hamilton) and Palmerston North. The hilly nature of the terrain was the reason for choosing this part of the line to begin with. The amount of traffic that could be handled over the whole NIMT was dependent on the maximum tonnage and the time taken to traverse certain critical sections of the line, in particular the Raurimu Spiral. This had grades up to 1 in 50 and curves as tight as 150 metres in radius, representing an equivalent grade on the straight of 1 in 42. The most powerful NZR diesel locomotive—the 2050 kW DX—could haul a train of 720 tonnes up this grade at a speed of just 27 km/h, so a primary aim of the project team was to increase the traffic capacity, by increasing train loads and speeds on this section.

The 412 route kilometres between Te Rapa and Palmerston North required some 500 km of overhead structures, taking into account sidings and overlaps. Spaced every 60 metres, some 8,500 catenary masts were involved. The Wellington suburban system and the former Lyttelton and Otira systems used 1,500 Volts DC. However, for the North Island Main Trunk the Railways chose 25 kV, 50 Hz AC. There were several factors in favour of this system. If the 1,500 Volt DC system had been used high currents would be needed—comparable locomotives of 4,500 kW would draw 3,000 amps compared to 300 amps with AC. This means the DC system requires rectifier sub-stations at every 10 km along the line, while the AC system only needed a simple 50 Hz power connection every 90 to 150 km.

At some stage the electrification may be extended southwards from Palmerston North to connect with the Wellington suburban system at Paraparaumu. Locomotives travelling inter-section will then need to be dual system. Although the new electric locomotives with their shorter rigid wheelbase (three two-axle bogies, compared to two three-axle for most diesels) are able to travel faster around curves, in several places it was

Guard's vans disappeared during the 1980s and the last one ran behind a freight train into Wellington at 11:30 p.m. on 30 May 1987. This scene shows one of the older type on a train at Ferniehurst in 1968. COLIN DASH

▲One of the six locomotives acquired for the electrification of the Christchurch–Lyttelton line in 1929, Ec 7, is seen at Heathcote on 25 August 1970, 25 days before the ceasation of electric operations on this line. This locomotive is now preserved at Ferrymead. B.J. MCKENZIE

◀The 925 kW 1-Do–2 Ed class arrived in 1938–39 for use on the Wellington electrified lines. The first was built by the English Electric Company and the following nine of the class by NZR workshops. Here Ed 109 is seen with a workshops staff train on the Gracefield Branch on 16 January 1964. MARK COLE

▼Ew 165, one of seven of this 1,340 kW Bo-Bo-Bo type locomotive acquired for the Wellington region in 1952 near the end of its days is seen with an empty return service to Wellington from Paekakariki near Mana on 17 March 1982. MARK COLE

◀*Four of the five Toshiba built Eo locomotives supplied in 1968 sit at Arthur's Pass awaiting a return to Otira. These locomotives were built for the Otira–Arthur's Pass section as replacements for the original locos built for the opening of the Otira tunnel in 1923.*
B.J. MCKENZIE

▼*A roller-coaster effect is suggested as one of the 22 new class 30 locos, 30-059 on a Sunday afternoon Wellington to Auckland express freight, runs through the Bunnythorpe dips on 26 February 1989.*
MARK COLE

The DA was the standard locomotive of the 1960s in the North Island, but all had been withdrawn by the end of the 1980s (apart from those rebuilt as DCs). Here DA 1487 heads express 626 out of Wellington in the late 1960s. NZR

necessary to ease sharp curves so that trains could travel at a more constant speed over the line. In conjunction with the electrification it was also necessary to improve clearances in several tunnels, either by lowering track, enlarging the bores or opening out ("daylighting") the tunnels into cuttings. Major civil engineering works produced four new deviations, in the process bypassing or eliminating ten former tunnels and replacing the former viaducts at Mangaweka, Hapuawhenua and Taonui.

As some of the new earthworks were in the Tongariro National Park, care was needed to minimise the amount of environmental intrusion. In fact the total number of wayside masts and poles were actually reduced, due to the installation of underground optical fibre cables for communications, doing away with telephone poles. The 406 km fibre-optic cable was a notable installation at the time, and capacity on it has since been hired to a telecommunications operator.

Early in 1984 the announcement of the type of electric locomotives to be used on the Palmerston North to Hamilton section was made. The 22 new locomotives, built by Brush Electrical Machines of England, are known as the EF class and are the most powerful ever to run in New Zealand. They are triple bogie type Bo-Bo-Bo with a 500 kW traction motor on each of the six axles, giving a continuous power rating of 3,000 kW at 42 km/h. The Bo-Bo-Bo design was chosen over the alternative Co-Co design so as to give a good spread of the load on bridges and viaducts. The total weight is 108 tonnes and the maximum axle load is 18 tonnes. Regenerative braking is fitted so that when drifting downhill the traction motors are switched to generating power which is converted on board to 25,000 Volts AC and fed back into the system. Unlike a diesel-electric locomotive, electric locomotives can exceed their continuous rating for short periods as there is an almost unlimited power supply from the overhead wires. Four substations feed power into the line. Work on constructing the catenary started in the second half of 1984, and delivery of the first of the new electric locomotives took place in 1986.

Other technical developments in the first half of the 1980s were the delivery of a new track evaluation car designed and built by the Plasser Company (Austria/Australia) and said by them to be the most advanced in the world at the time. Denoted EM 80 on account of its 80 km/hr top speed, the 12 metre long car is able to accurately measure specific data on the rails and evaluate it so as to identify potentially dangerous portions of track. Parameters that need examination are; the top of the rail to establish if any low points needing packing exist; the height or cant between the two rails, so that on curves the trains will "bank" ; the twist in the rails; the gauge between the rails; and the degree of curvature or versine for each rail. Deficiencies in any one of these factors may in themselves be acceptable, but in combination they could lead to derailments. Some new wagon types, with a higher ratio of loaded to empty weights, had proved to be rather susceptible to derailment when empty.

In 1984 the first new locomotives to be built by NZR since 1967 were unveiled in the form of the DSJ class diesel shunting locomotives. These were single engine versions of the 24 twin engine 670 kW DSG shunters delivered from Toshiba in Japan between March 1981 and September 1983. These locomotives were intended for heavy train haulage in the yards at Auckland, Napier, Palmerston North, Wellington and replacing 0-6-0 shunting locomotives denoted as classes DSA, DSB, and DSC, the first of which went into service in 1959. A total of 40 of the new DSJ locomotives were planned to be built at the Addington shops to replace all the DSA and DSB shunters, but in fact only five were built as the need for shunting locomotives decreased.

In December 1983 a new inter-island ferry, the *Arahura* ("pathway to the dawn") arrived in Wellington as a replacement for the aged *Aramoana*. The new ferry was designed jointly by NZR and the maritime consultants Burness Corlett & Partners of Basingstoke in England, and built by Aalborg Vaerft A/S in Denmark. Just five months passed from the laying of the keel in October 1982 to the launching of the ship in March 1983. Externally the most notable features are a bulbous bow, designed to reduce wave height and increase speed through the water, as well as a large funnel, the absence of conventional masts and an innovative bridge design. The *Arahura* accommodates 900 passengers in a relatively luxurious interior, for the first five years with a distinctly Scandinavian decor.

On 30 July 1981 a new benchmark for the Railways came with the introduction in Parliament of a Government Bill to turn the Railways from the department they had been for 105 years into a corporation. The new corporation was to remain subject to a Minister of Railways, who would have ultimate control over matters such as the opening and closing of lines, the introduction or reduction of significant activities and passenger services. Around these broad political constraints the new corporation would have much more commercial freedom in areas such as tariff fixing and would be free from much Treasury scrutiny on expenditure. The new corporation came into being on 1 April 1982 and was steered by a seven-person board empowered with all the provisions of the former Railways Act 1949 necessary to run the Railways. For staff the change initially made little difference as the existing conditions of employment remained the same. Financially, however, the corporation did represent changes. Firstly provision was made for the cost of the "social services" that the Railways provided in the form of passenger services and certain branch lines to be paid by the Government as a subsidy. Secondly provision was made for the debt that the Railways had accumulated to be converted into equity capital, reducing the interest payments on accumulated debt that represented a significant percentage of total losses. It was claimed that the Railways could thus become a profitable enterprise once again.

A few months after the Railways Corporation came into being, on 16 December 1982, the then Minister of Transport introduced into Parliament the Transport Amendment Bill which effectively served to deregulate land transport in New Zealand. Among other things the restrictions on competition between road and rail which had existed since the beginning of the 1930s were to be removed over a three-year period, beginning on 1 January 1984. This, it was claimed, would result in substantial savings to transport users and the "net economic benefit" to the nation was put at between $15 and $22 million. These savings were to arise through greater efficiency of road in carrying certain categories of freight, especially those involving traffic that transferred between modes. Some of the savings would be in the form of "non-transport" costs such as warehousing, high inventories, packaging and damage. The minister, George Gair, estimated that removing the 150 km restriction on road–rail competition would cost the Railways 12-18% of their existing freight traffic. Total freight revenue was expected to drop about 25%. This loss was estimated to involve a reduction in staff numbers of between 1,500-2,000. In fact in the next few years revenue and staff numbers were to be reduced by a much greater extent, as had been prophesied at the time by opponents of deregulation.

To cope with deregulation, the Railways Board appointed the American consultancy firm of Booz, Allen and Hamilton Inc.—reputedly for a $1 million fee—to "review the effectiveness and efficiency of the present operations". This report was completed in December 1983 and released to the public on 30 March 1984. It described the compilers' views on how a commercially viable rail transport system could be built in a deregulated land transport industry. The most controversial aspect of the report was probably the recommendation for large-scale staff shedding. The report did not advocate a drastic reduction in the network; rather it concluded that substantial capital investments in conjunction with productivity gains would be required if the NZR freight business was to be profitable.

The message was that without significant changes a multimillion-dollar annual operating deficit would be the result within a decade. Electrification of the NIMT should proceed and productivity improvements should be made in a number of areas. These included: freight centre consolidation and reductions in smaller stations; increased utilisation of locomotives; modernisation of the wagon fleet eliminating many four-wheel wagons and replacing these with more bogie flat wagons; a changeover to automatic couplers on all wagons; workshop modernisation and consolidation; installation of further CTC signalling systems; increasing train lengths; eliminating guard's vans; and operating higher horsepower locomotives in multiple with strengthened drawgear.

Standard railcars RM 32 and RM 31 with a Sunday evening service to New Plymouth cross the Waikanae River bridge on 6 December 1964. MARK COLE

The overnight Auckland–Wellington "Northerner" introduced in 1975 lasted in this form for 12 years. DX 5229 in the "clockwork orange" climbs through Muri with the hot water bottle (steam heating van) and the train of yellow cars in tow on 30 October 1982. MARK COLE

▲Two of the 35 "Fiat" type articulated railcars enter Arthur's Pass across Rough Creek bridge in January 1974. ROY SINCLAIR

▶A double set of "Fiat" railcars in "Blue Streak" livery on an Auckland–Wellington run at Mangaonoho on 8 April 1969. NZR

Wellington's two electric locomotive classes were finally withdrawn in the early 1980s. Here EW 1805 heads a southbound freight train out of NIMT tunnel no. 2 in June 1967. R.J. McGAVIN

On passenger services the option preferred was to reduce service levels, maintaining services between main centres but replacing provincial services with buses. Regardless of whether or not services would continue in entirety or in part, several operating improvements were recommended, including greater adherence to timetabled arrivals, shortened schedules, combining passenger functions into one business unit, co-ordination of the reservations and ticketing systems by a single system, increased marketing, and including parcel and mail capacity. On road services, recommendations were for more co-ordination with rail, improved amenities and better buses, with improved maintenance centres in some areas.

Several aspects of the report were adopted in the next four years—elimination of guard's vans, longer trains, reduction of workshop capacity, more bogie wagons, and particularly the streamlining of operations to reduce staff. In the five years from March 1982 to March 1987, total employees were reduced from 20,834 to 14,919.

The Eastown railway workshops at Wanganui were closed in October 1986, and in the following years the Addington (Christchurch) and Otahuhu (Auckland) workshops were also closed, leaving just two major workshops, at Woburn and Hillside, both with drastically reduced staff numbers. All the smaller workshops at regional centres were closed or down-sized.

The Railways were re-organised on the basis of four business groups: Railfreight Systems; the Passenger Business Group which operated the Intercity trains and coaches, the Cityline commuter services and the Speedlink parcels service; the Property Group which managed the corporation's land and buildings assets; and the Interisland Line which ran the three Cook Strait ferries.

On the positive side of things, the electrification of the North Island Main Trunk between Te Rapa and Palmerston North was completed ahead of schedule on 24 June 1988. The electric locomotives could now run over the whole electrified section, allowing the DX class diesels to be re-allocated to other parts of the country, including the South Island. The first transfer of DX locomotives to the South Island took place in February 1989.

At the end of 1987 a new concept in long distance passenger trains with the upgrading of the Christchurch–Greymouth express, which was re-timetabled and renamed the "TranzAlpine Express". The cars feature seven large tinted 1 m x 2 m observation windows along each side in place of the previous 14 small windows, wall to wall carpet, grey lambskin covered seats arranged in bays of four with snack tables in between and an internal sound system. Onboard catering replaced previous refreshment stops at Springfield and Otira. Following very positive results, the same service was introduced on the Christchurch to Picton run on 25 September 1988, the train being renamed the "Coastal Pacific Express. The new Intercity livery of blue with a longitudinal stripe of white, red and white became standard also for the "Southerner" and the "Northerner". Although sleeping cars and dining cars were removed from the latter in 1987, a new video car was introduced on this overnight run.

In March 1989 a new look inter-island ferry service was announced, with the renaming of Searail Ferries as the "Interisland Line". Accompanying the new name was a change from the hitherto lime green paint scheme to white with a longitudinal band each of green and blue on the sides, plus a dolphin logo on the funnels outlined with green and blue lines. The interiors were refurbished and included for the *Arahura* a movie theatre, restaurant, shops and conference facilities.

In November 1989 a new look passenger service between Wellington and Napier was announced, with the "Endeavour" being re-launched as the "Bay Express", based on the successful tourist orientated trains the Coastal Pacific and TranzAlpine Expresses.

By the end of 1989 a computerised reservation and ticketing system had been installed together with a digital telephone exchange system in Auckland, Wellington and Christchurch. The new computerised system included the installation of terminals in travel agencies throughout New Zealand. New corporate uniforms for front line staff of Intercity were unveiled in late 1989. These featured summer and winter variants, and were intended to provide an image similar to that of airline stewards and hostesses.

From 1988 onwards, a new system of train control known as "Track Warrant Control" began to be introduced. This in time replaced all tablet system working and most single line automatic signalling installations, enabling reductions in operating costs. Like the tablet system, a "Track Warrant" is required to occupy a system, but in addition the warrant may also contain specific restrictions or instructions to the particular movement authorised. Track Warrants are normally prepared by Train Control Operators, using a computer system so to prevent Warrants being prepared for conflicting movements, and transmitted by radio or other means. Locomotive Engineers are not allowed to receive Warrants while moving, to reduce the possibility of error. As with the tablet system, the main safety risk is that the Engineer will go beyond the authorised section of track. New red and purple signals were installed at crossing loops in Track Warrant areas. These are worked by track circuits and indicate stop or proceed settings, based on the point settings, but do not in themselves give authority to proceed.

In 1989 trials began of "Road-railer" vehicles, which through the use of changeable wheel sets could be run on either road or on rail. These enabled transport of goods for part of the route on the road hitched behind a truck, and for part on the railway as a freight wagon. These vehicles were used for a while on routes such as Auckland–(rail)–Rotorua–(road)–Hastings, but were not successful enough to come into general use.

Another development about the same time was the

*The appearance of a locomotive on the Johnsonville Branch is rare, two locomotives on separate trains extremely so. Here D*SC *438 and D*E *514 are seen with work trains at Ngaio in October 1973.* G.T. RADCLIFFE COURTESY NZR&LS

In a a scene dated by the FM guard's van behind the locomotive, DH 2839 heads a shunt at Panmure (Auckland) in October 1981.
REID McNAUGHT

use of remote controlled locomotives, which was eventually applied to virtually all shunting locomotives. As part of the drive for higher productivity, one person with the remote control equipment could act as driver and shunter. Nearly all the remaining rigid-frame DS, DSA and DSB shunters were withdrawn, leaving DSC, DSG, DSJ and DH class shunters to be fitted with remote controls. Also gone by the end of the 1980s were virtually all the older main-line diesels of the DA, DB, DG, DI and DJ classes. Still in service were 85 DA class locomotives which had been rebuilt to the DC class, and 10 DB class rebuilt to the DBR class. In the short-sighted fashion characteristic of the time, none of these withdrawn locomotives were "stored serviceable" for future traffic growth, so when traffic grew some years later, second-hand locomotives had to be bought from Australian railways, or even hired from enthusiast groups.

Branch lines to be closed during the 1980s were the Rewanui Branch in 1985, the Otiria to Okaihau Branch in November 1987, and the Makareao Branch in June 1989. Despite all these changes to improve efficiency, the losses of the Railways Corporation mounted, as 30% of freight traffic was lost to the road operators, and freight rates had to be reduced to keep the remaining traffic. In 1988-89, the overall loss was a record at $263 million, including massive restructuring costs. By September 1990, 7251 employees had taken voluntary severance, at a total cost of $251 million.

The 1990s

After a decade of major change, the 1990s brought even more change. On 28 October 1990 the rail operations and the Cook Strait ferry services of the Railways Corporation were transferred to a new company—New Zealand Rail Ltd. This was set up as a debt-free company required to pay its own way, and in the 1990-91 financial year it made a net profit of $51 million. The Railways Corporation remained the owner of land and buildings, the InterCity coach fleet and its Speedlink parcel service. The InterCity coaches were sold in mid 1991 to a consortium of private long-distance coach operators and Speedlink was sold to New Zealand Post Ltd. These sales by no means recouped the previous Corporation debt, most of which was written off. A major programme of land disposal saw most station buildings sold, whether or not they still had rail passenger services. There was a continuing rationalisation of facilities along the operating lines, so it become normal for there to be no staffed station on 100 kilometres or more of main line. By 1992, N.Z. Rail had only 5,500 employees. The Middlemarch to Clyde section of the Otago Central Line was closed in April 1990, and regular trains on the Thames Branch ceased in June 1991.

There were some positive initiatives. The "Silver Fern" railcars on the daytime Wellington–Auckland service were replaced by the locomotive-hauled "Overlander" in December 1991, providing a greater passenger capacity. The three railcars were then used to reintroduce Auckland–Tauranga and Auckland–Rotorua passenger services. Unfortunately the Rotorua service was only able to reach the outskirts of the town, as the station had been sold and the last 2 km of track removed. The "Capital Connection" commenced running in April 1991, providing a commuter service from Palmerston North and the Horowhenua to Wellington. And a new, more attractive, blue and yellow colour scheme was introduced for locomotives to emphasise the "branding" of the new organisation.

By now it was clear that the National Government which had taken power in November 1990 was intending to sell N.Z. Rail. The sale took place in September 1993, to a consortium including Wisconsin Central, a U.S. regional railroad, and other financial partners in-

The first branch line casualty of the 1990s was the closure of the 172 km of the Otago Central Line beyond Middlemarch in April 1990. Fortunately the Dunedin City Council came to the rescue of the first 64 km to Middlemarch so that visitors and locals are able to enjoy the spectacular scenery of the Taieri Gorge. TONY HURST

cluding the Fay Richwhite merchant bank. To avoid Treaty of Waitangi claims, the land needed for railway operations remained in public ownership, to be leased for $1 per year to N.Z. Rail.

The new owners of N.Z. Rail decided to capitalise on the by now glamour image of the TranzAlpine Express, and on 18 October 1995 they launched the new company name of Tranz Rail, with the freight operation renamed Tranz Link, the long distance passenger trains as Tranz Scenic and the commuter trains as Tranz Metro. Passenger cars and the Wellington suburban multiple units received a new lighter blue livery with the new name. The same locomotive blue livery was kept, but in 2001 the first locomotive was unveiled in a new black and yellow colour scheme, colours claimed to be particularly visible to reduce level crossing accidents.

A recent analysis of the 1993 privatisation by investment analyst Brian Gaynor revealed that of the nominal $328 million sale price, $221 million was actually borrowed money which was added to the debt of N.Z. Rail, and that $100 million was returned to the investors in 1995. The original buyers then received a further $190 million in May 1996, when Tranz Rail owners sold shares in a public offering and the company was listed on the New Zealand and New York Stock Exchanges. These massive returns to the original consortium were rather ironic, as the necessity of new investment capital was said to be one of the reasons why the Government needed to sell Tranz Rail. The share price on listing was close to $7.00 but with declining profits this also declined and as at mid 2001 it stood at around $4.00.

The sale of N.Z. Rail came at a time when the N.Z. economy was improving, and after several years of low freight tonnages (the worst year was 1991, with only 8.25 million tonnes moved), freight volumes began to increase again. The first corresponding move to increase locomotive power was with the DF class. These locomotives had a mismatch between a comparatively low-power (1230 kW) diesel engine and 86 tonnes of adhesive weight, which meant they could haul heavy trains, but not at the faster speeds that were required. All 30 locomotives were therefore rebuilt between 1992 and 1996 to become the DFT class. The main change was the incorporation of a turbocharger to increase the engine power to 1800 kW, which makes them able to nearly match the DX class on load capacity. There was also a proposal to rebuild the DX class with turbochargers for increased power as they received their half-life overhauls. A prototype, DXR 8007, appeared in 1993 with a number of other changes as well, including a new cab that quite changed the appearance. However, it was decided that this amount of rebuilding was not economic, and the rest of the DX class is now expected to get much less radical alterations upon major overhauls.

As mentioned, Auckland suburban trains missed out on new stock in 1979, and by the early 1990s the locomotive-hauled carriages were really showing their age, at a time when road congestion was starting to encourage patronage to grow again. Fortunately, when the suburban lines in the Australian city of Perth were electrified in 1991 some comparatively modern Diesel-Multiple Units were available second-hand that could be very easily adapted to run in Auckland, without change of gauge. Nineteen two-car sets were purchased, and they first entered service in July 1993. In July 1994 Saturday suburban services were re-introduced on the south line, after a gap of 26 years. These new trains encouraged another look at extending the rail tracks back to the main Queen Street shopping and business area. In 1993, it was hoped to have the 800 metre link ready in two years, but in 2001 construction of the underground terminal station near Britomart Place had only just commenced, the delay the result of Auckland local body politics.

The long dominance of the Rail Ferries on Cook Strait passenger and car transport was threatened in late 1994, when it was announced that Sea Shuttle would be introducing a competing fast ferry that would cut more than an hour off the 3 hour schedule. There was a quick response from N. Z. Rail with the announcement that they would be introducing their own "Lynx" fast ferry. There was unprecedented traffic through Tory Channel for the 1994-95 summer as the two new ferries joined the three conventional ferries, but the Sea Shuttle vessel was unreliable, and its service ceased after three months. The "Lynx" service stopped for the winter months, but returned during each of the following summers. It offered a 1 hr 45 min crossing for a slightly higher fare than the regular ferry, and significantly boosted Marlborough tourism.

Tranz Rail didn't want to spend money on new locomotives or carriages, so it went looking for second-hand ones. Twenty-five locomotives were acquired from Queensland Rail from 1995 onwards. The intention was to rebuild a significant number of them to a DC equivalent, but the DQ class which resulted did not fulfil expectations, and at the time of writing there were only 4 in service, running coal trains between Middleton and Lyttelton, and banking freight trains north of Dunedin. Twelve of this class were sold to Tasrail, another member of the Wisconsin Central "family" that Tranz Rail has shares in. Another batch of 10 locomotives came from Western Australia in 1998; so far two of them have also gone to Tasrail, the rest being stored. Second-hand carriages were bought from Britain, but although 64 were bought, only eight were converted for the "Capital Connection", with the remainder, like the Westrail locomotives, looking fairly abandoned at Hutt Workshops, although West Coast Railway plans to buy another 25 of them.

As a public company, Tranz Rail was under pressure to make continuing profits and maintain its share price. Further maritime deregulation, allowing overseas shipping companies to carry domestic New Zealand traffic between ports, increased the pressure of competition. Both Tranz Rail and its Wisconsin Central parent had decreased profits during the 1997-98 Asian economic crisis, and the first consequence was a boardroom coup at Wisconsin Central which deposed Ed Burkhardt as chairman, and he later lost this position at Tranz Rail also. The new Tranz Rail board brought in Michael Beard to run Tranz Rail, with a strongly profit-centred approach. As part of this, Tranz Rail was

Left: At the time of going to press the 10 year experience of Silver Fern railcars running regular passenger services between Auckland and Tauranga seemed doomed to end. Here the "Kaimai Express" is seen leaving Hemopo not far from the Kaimai Tunnel entrance. DAVE NELSON COURTESY BOB STOTT

Below: A two-car Diesel Multiple Unit ex-Perth stops at Puhinui Station in West Auckland on 11 October 1999. A.K. SIM

Two DX locomotives in the Tranz Rail livery adopted in 1995 head a train of refurbished ex-British Railways carriages, now used on longer distance Tranz Metro runs. The train, for "Toast Martinborough" patrons, is seen exiting the southern entrance to the Rimutaka tunnel. TONY HURST

to cut back to its core business, by selling off or outsourcing all other activities, and make further reductions in staff numbers. The rail operations were to concentrate on 34 key traffic routes, for containers, box wagons for Freight Forwarders, and bulk cargoes.

The export of West Coast coal from Lyttelton gradually increased, especially after Solid Energy, the successor of the former State Coal Mines, abandoned its attempt to build a coal loading jetty at Granity.

A completely new bulk traffic developed in the 1990s as Dairy Factories amalgamated and the distances between farms and factories increased. Tranz Rail had moved small quantities of milk in Northland and the Bay of Plenty, and was then successful in winning the contract to shift milk from a collecting point in Hawkes Bay to the Kiwi Co-operative Dairy Whareroa factory near Hawera. The first train of bulk milk tanks ran in August 1997, and now four trains run daily to Whareroa during the season, two each from Oringi and Longburn. A 16 wagon train can carry 800,000 litres of milk, and is a full load for a pair of DFT locomotives on the Westmere bank.

In 1999 Tranz Rail and the Port of Tauranga combined to operate an "inland port" near Southdown in South Auckland. Dedicated trains moved containers to and from ships calling at Tauranga. This has been so successful that Ports of Auckland is now planning a similar service with a Palmerston North depot.

The sixth of the Cook Strait 'Ara' series ferries, the *Aratere*, was ordered from the Vigo yard of H. J. Barreras, a Spanish shipbuilder, in 1997. The *Aratere* had a different appearance to her predecessors, with a funnel on each side of a wide upper deck to maximise space for trucks, and a smaller passenger capacity. When put into service in February 1999, it had more than the usual "teething" problems. In June 1999 the now surplus *Aratika* was sold to the Philippines. Resource management act approval for a new ferry terminal at Clifford Bay, south-east of Blenheim, was obtained at this time, but the new management of Tranz Rail put this project on hold. Its future revival may depend on whether it is possible to carry rail wagons on a fast ferry.

Another attempt to compete with the Cook Strait ferries came in May 1999, when *TopCat* began what was intended to be a year-round fast ferry service. Again there was increased traffic in the Marlborough Sounds, and there was local concern about the intense wash from the fast ferries. After considering the danger to small boats and the damage to foreshores, the Marlborough District Council imposed speed restrictions on all ferries, which added 30 minutes to the fast ferry schedules. This was one of the factors which led to the failure of the

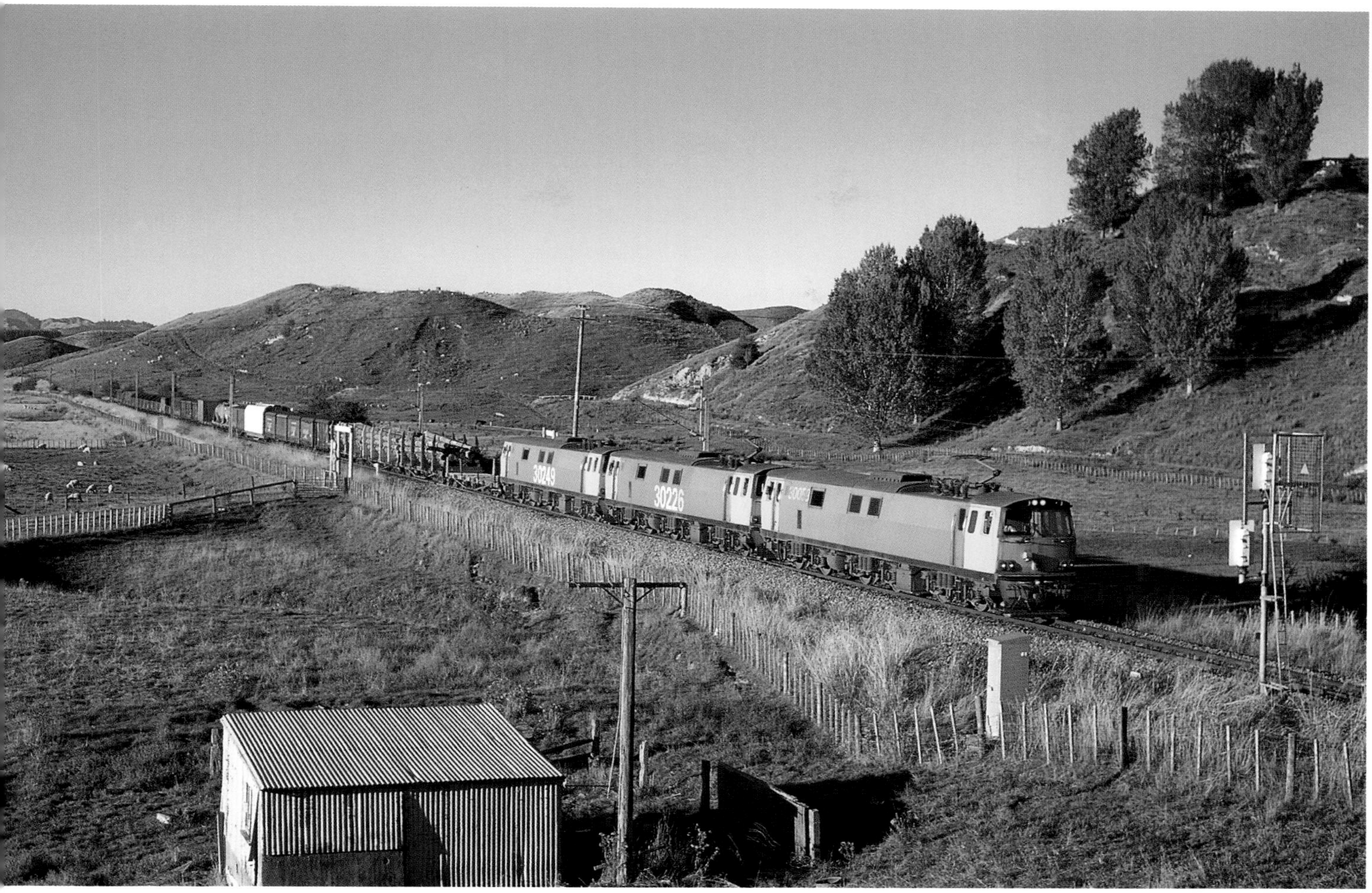

Above: Three Ef *class electrics (or "toasters") head a southbound freight train near Hunterville in the central North Island.* TONY HURST
Below: Turbo-charged DFT *7239 +* DC *4692 with freight train 142 on the Whangarata Bank on 23 November 1999.* A.K. SIM

The two South Island glamour trains: Above: The "Tranz Coastal" (introduced as the "Coastal Pacific Express" in September 1988) heads along the rocky coastline near Kaikoura where road and rail share a narrow space between the hills and the beach; and Below: Next to a classic West Coast telegraph pole, two DX locomotives head the "Tranz Alpine" (introduced in November 1987) past the tranquil waters of Lake Brunner with Mt Alexander in the background. TRANZ SCENIC

Left: In the short lived NZ Rail livery, the prototype Dxr*, 8007, and to date the only example, sits next to the prototype* Dft*, 7008, in Wellington yard in May 1994.* TONY HURST

Below: The "Milk Train" climbs Westmere Bank just out of Wanganui. TONY HURST

company running *TopCat* in November 2000. Tranz Rail then brought in a larger catamaran for the "Lynx" service, and announced that it would operate it all year round. There was a shortage of capacity early in 2001, causing a backlog and public complaints, as Tranz Rail cut costs by taking the *Arahanga* out of service. *Arahanga* was brought back into service for a short time in March during major repairs to the *Aratere*, but then in May it was sent to India to be broken up.

In November 2000, Tranz Rail introduced the "Shuttle Train Service" concept, trying to reduce the number of locomotives needed by smoothing out peaks in traffic. Simultaneously, 4-wheel wagons were banned from all regular services, although there are still some running in particular dedicated services.

Technical developments during the decade included the fitting of a new ZTR wheelslip control system to the DC, DBR and DQ classes to increase their haulage capacity by up to 20% and the introduction of a barcode system to track every movement in a consignment of goods from pickup to delivery.

At the time of writing, the future of many rail services is in doubt, as Tranz Rail attempts to increase profits by running only the most profitable freight services, by making Tranz Link more separate and mode-neutral—demonstrated by the Tranz Link fleet of trucks, which stood at 226 in mid 2000 (including some owner drivers)—and selling all passenger services. Another controversial decision was to shift the Tranz Rail headquarters to Auckland's North Shore, as if to avoid contact with actual railway operations.

What future in the new century?

Until 1993 the main railway system in New Zealand was part of the public sector, owned and controlled by the Government. The sale to private sector investors was a mixed blessing: while the involvement of an experienced American short-line operator was positive, that of Fay Richwhite—whose only concern was short term capital profit maximisation—was not. It demonstrates that the pressure for increasing operating profits is not compatible with long term planning and capital investment in equipment and infrastructure.

Tranz Rail now appears to be retreating almost to a niche operator, running mainly container and bulk trains, and selling off other services. For smaller quantities of freight the "mode-neutral" stance of Tranz Link does not sound good for rail.

It isn't yet clear what combination of ownership and operation will develop, but it seems rather likely that the completely privatised rail model will not last a decade. Whether for Auckland and Wellington suburban passenger services, or for new line construction, such as a branch line to Marsden Point, there are major problems in providing public funds that support the operations of a private company. The State's road construction financing agency Transfund, while empowered to finance railway lines as well as roads, so far has not provided any of its annual billion dollar budget for railways. Tranz Rail has made clear that it is not interested in providing the capital to invest in significant enhancements to the network. In fact it is looking for areas it can withdraw from, with the Gisborne and Rotorua lines under most threat. The whole area of wagonload freight is under threat, as Tranz Rail tries to minimise shunting. This reduces the ability of smaller firms to benefit from rail transport, as Tranz Rail increasingly orientates itself towards its largest customers.

Moving containers by an hydraulic truck on New Plymouth wharf, with DSG 3020 at the train end. TONY HURST

Tranz Rail is applying some new ideas to its primary interest of fixed schedule trains, such as shifting containers by forklift rather than shunting wagons. One of its prime aims is to improve wagon utilisation, at any given time 2/3 of the wagon stock is sitting in yards. While it may run well within its niche area, with the current export boom leading to record total tonnage, this leaves the question as to how it can share one rail infrastructure with other operators, and who will control the system. Wellington–Paraparaumu suburban train services have just been increased, making it even more embarrassing if a Tranz Rail freight stalls when climbing south from Paekakariki and thus delays 'units' belonging to the new Metro operator.

In Auckland too many popular destinations are not served by the existing rail corridors. The ridiculously long time it has taken to even begin getting rails back to Queen Street shows the difficulties in extending traditional rail in an urban area. If the local authorities take control of the Auckland rail infrastructure then they can look at new options for rail services. The existing

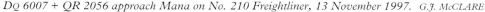

DQ 6007 + QR 2056 approach Mana on No. 210 Freightliner, 13 November 1997. G.J. McCLARE

Above: The Interisland Line freight ferry Arahanga *sails out of Wellington Harbour heads.* TONY HURST
Below: The newest inter-island ferry, Aratere. TRANZ RAIL

DMUs could be replaced by Light Rail vehicles, with tracks extended to destinations such as Manakau City Centre and the Airport. In countries such as Germany, Light Rail successfully shares rail tracks with trains, so this offers an economical way of using the rail corridors for a wider range of destinations. Negotiations are currently underway for Tranz Rail to sell the Auckland network, with Central Government now negotiating with Tranz Rail.

The Australian operator West Coast Railways, the preferred bidder for the Tranz Scenic long-distance passenger services, has announced that some services will close. The hope is that with the remaining services it will continue along the lines of the successful marketing of the "TranzAlpine", which required 12 carriages and 3 vans to cope with the demand on Boxing Day 2000. With the increased patronage that such marketing brings, West Coast Railways may then even consider reintroducing services that it has said will end.

The inability of a private company to make the investment required to make rail properly contribute to the development of New Zealand is hardly surprising, it is why governments ran NZR for so long. What is needed is a model that gives rail some equality with road, which has the advantage that the government lays down new highways, and then charges trucks a proportion of the cost as they use them, rather than charge them the entire cost before they can leave the depot.

There is no disputing that rail transport is more fuel efficient than road, and there are national economic savings that result from less fuel oil being imported. With environmental factors also there can be no disputing the desirability of rail over road. Considerably less disturbance to the environment is involved with a railway, both in regard to the amount of physical space taken and the amount of atmospheric pollution created. Most motorists are well aware of the increased traffic congestion that has occured over the last 15 years or so, but it seems few of them reflect why. Obviously few people stop to consider that the cost to the country of having no railways would be an enormous increase in the number of heavy trucks on the roads, adding to traffic congestion, road wear and exhaust pollution. On a pure conventional accounting basis, such facts do not show up on profit and loss statements, yet they are real costs that railways save the country. It was rather ironic that in the same week as the intended cessation of five long distance passenger trains was announced, the land transport authorities announced they were considering an increase in the size of trucks allowed to be run on the country's highways, from 44 tonnes to 62 tonnes.

The price of deregulation and privatisation is a heavy one, and is likely to spark moves for re-regulation and re-nationalisation in the next few years. Whether this happens in time to save the closure of most remaining branch lines and secondary lines as well as handling facilities, is however, rather doubtful. One can only hope.

The third livery change in 10 years: the first locomotive to be painted in the new yellow and black colours, DC 4323, at Hutt Workshops on 31 May 2001. At the time of writing two further locomotives had been so painted. REID McNAUGHT

CHAPTER TWO

Life on board

In the early days passenger carriages, like all other aspects of railways infrastructure and rolling stock, were basic. All were short four or six wheeled (two or three rigid axled) affairs and their bodies were made of wood. Nearly all were built with longitudinal seating. They were rough riding and suitable only for slow speeds. Passengers wanted comfort and refreshment stops after spending any length of time inside a carriage for which 30 km in an hour would be a good rate of speed.

The advent of the private enterprise Wellington and Manawatu Railway Company in 1886 brought major advances—bogies, electric lighting, comfortable upholstery even in second class and dining cars were innovations of the company. By the turn of the century most new cars of the government railways were of a standard 44ft (13.4 metre) bogie design with end platforms, although wood was still the predominant construction material. Padded seat bases were added to the longitudinal seats of second class cars in 1899, toilets were announced in 1900 and foot-warmers for South Island cars in 1901.

By World War 1 steam heating equipment was being fitted, and gangways and gates were being fitted to all stock. The dining car disappeared in 1917 as an economy measure and did not reappear until the 1970s. In the 1930s cross seats generally replaced longitudinal seating and SKF roller bearings were fitted as from 1931, which would eventually eliminate journey delays caused by overheated axle boxes. Exterior steel panelling made its first appearance and open platforms were replaced with vestibules. In 1938 the first of a new design of 56 ft (17 m) cars were placed into service. Apart from multiple units, railcars, and the "Silver Star", these carriages in one form or another have carried passenger traffic ever since.

The introduction of the Fiat railcars 1955 to 1958 was to be the only significant development during the next three decades. For second class fares these offered reclining seats to all passengers, something which up until then had been the preserve of first class passengers. With the upgrading of three of these railcars into "Blue Streaks" in 1968 and 1969, a hostess service providing light refreshments on board was introduced.

The 1970s saw buffet cars introduced on the "Southerner" between Christchurch and Invercargill and on the "Endeavour" between Wellington and Napier. The major advance however, came with the "Silver Star", a luxury overnight train between Wellington and Auckland in September 1971. The appeal was to the businessman wanting an overnight hotel on wheels, and featured comfortable twin or single roomettes with a dining car. However the service did not see out the decade.

At the other end of the scale, another experience which did not see out the 1970s was the "goods train

Left: An early NZR four-wheel first class carriage (complete with smokers compartment) and a six-wheel second class carriage at Mangaonoho. The rigid axles would have made the difference in comfort betweeen the two rather small. A.P. GODBER

External and internal views of an early NZR 44-ft second class bogie carriage built in 1894 at Addington workshops with longitudinal seating and gas lighting, and without toilets, taken in 1963 with what seems to be a Sunday school outing. NZR

Above: A guard checks tickets of passengers on a train on the Nelson section in the 1950s. NZR

Opposite above: The interior of the lounge car on the North Island Main Trunk "Daylight Limited" of the 1920s. NZR

Left: Elegance on rails: the interior of an NIMT dining car between 1900 and 1917. NZR

Right: The interior of a first class car in the 1920s. NZR

Above: A 47 1/2 ft passenger car, one of two built in Petone workshops in 1927 for the royal tour that year of the Duke of York (later King George VI), this one being used in the South Island. After this use it was hired out to tourists for a period before becoming the South Island Ministerial Car. The North Island car was longer. NZR

Below: One of two passenger cars built for the tour of the Duke of Gloucester in 1934, this one being used in the North Island. It was refurbished for use by Queen Elizabeth II's royal tour of 1953. In between times it was used for trips by the Governor General. NZR

Above: One of the standard steel panelled 56 ft passenger cars from just prior to World War II. This example was built in 1938 and converted from a second class car to a first class car in the 1950s by installing a 2+1 seating arrangement instead of the 2+2 seating arrangement, thus reducing the number of seats from 56 to 35. NZR
Below: Interior of a North Island Main Trunk first class car built in 1940. NZR

▲*A train hostess chats with mum and the kids on a short distance train in the 1950s.* NZR

▶*Although dowdy by today's standards, this was royal accommodation during the 1953–54 Royal Tour.* NZR

◀*The interior of a main trunk sleeping car compartment in the 1950s, the seats converting into beds.* NZR

with car attached", generally referred to as a mixed train. For those who wanted to view the scenery at a leisurely pace and did not mind lengthy stops at stations while goods wagons were attached and detached, they often provided the only passenger services to many places.

The 1980s saw mixed fortunes—the "Endeavour" and "Northerner" both lost their buffet cars, and the latter also lost its sleeping car accommodation in 1987, the last such train to have sleeping cars. The same year, however, the next major improvement was introduced with the "TranzAlpine Express". The old red cars on the Christchurch-Greymouth run were converted into big window panorama cars with on-board catering, comfortable lambskin covered seats and a commentary on features of interest along the route. The previous 14 small windows along each side were replaced with seven 2 metre x 1 metre picture windows. The external livery was changed to blue sides, with a red band through a longitudinal white stripe, replacing the red which on grounds of economy has been the dominant colour for most of this century. The success of this service and the subsequent "Coastal Pacific Express" between Christchurch and Picton and the "Bay Express" between Wellington and Napier indicates that at last a new market has been developed fot the long distance passenger train.

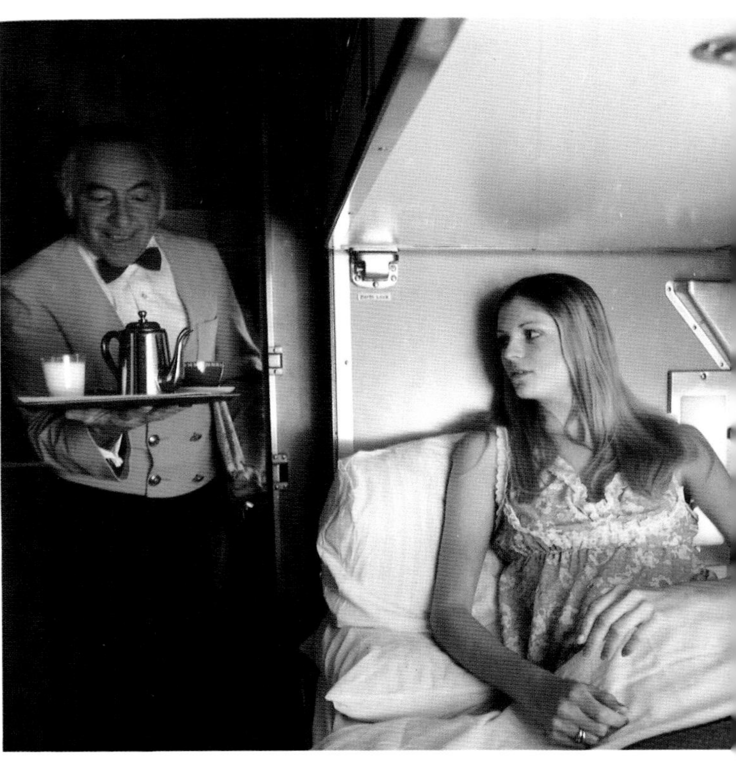

Above: Breakfast in bed was a feature of the "Silver Star" overnight express. NZR

Right: Airline style seat service from a hostess wearing an early 1970s uniform on the "Silver Fern" daylight railcar. NZR

Above: The end-of-train observation car used on the "Overlander" and "Bay Express" North Island trains where passengers can either amuse themselves with their own entertainment, socialise or watch the scenery out of the large windows.
Below: The Café Counter where refreshments en route can be obtained. With the end of the famous "Railways Refreshments Stops", the last being at Kaikoura in September 1988, this is essentially the sole opportunity for alimentation on long journeys. TRANZ SCENIC

CHAPTER THREE

Down at the station

The railway station has played a dominant role in the lives of many people over the years. To quote well known railway historian the late J.D. Mahoney: "The railway station was one of the most important places in New Zealand cities and towns. It was something of a community institution. Every community set a lot of store by being on the railway, and by having a significantly large and dignified station. All roads led to the railway station, and its platform would be thronged with citizens as the trains arrived and departed. Everyone travelled on the train and everyone was down at the station some time to welcome or farewell friends or relatives, or just to be part of the action. The station was the place where holiday trips began, and resort stations like Rotorua were places where holiday makers arrived. The station was also remembered as the place from where you left for family occasions, joyful ones of weddings and anniversaries, and sad ones of bereavement. Football, cricket and other sports teams arrived and departed from the local stations as did bands, theatre companies and territorial soldiers en route to camp. Generations of school children all over the country used to travel to school on the train. Farmers and their families rode from their local station to town on market days, and bushmen and coal miners from their settlements to shops and entertainment."

Like the early railway lines, the early stations were built with a minimum of capital expense and were invariably made of wood. Apart from main city stations, concrete and brick did not become standard building materials until after World War 2. In the old days the station was one of the most important buildings in small towns and the station master had a status equal to that of the policeman, bank manager and headmaster. In recent years the majority of stations on lines that remain have been closed and many have disappeared altogether along with their sidings, goods sheds, engine sheds, water vats and coal bunkers.

▲*Electric locomotive Ec 11 draws up at Opawa Station with a 3.15 pm Christchurch to Lyttelton suburban train on 20 November 1957.* NZR

◀*At the newly opened Wellington Station, K 926 sits at platform 8 with the 3 pm overnight express to Auckland in 1937.* NZR

▶*A "Wairarapa" type railcar approaches Belmont Station on the now closed Melling–Haywards section of the Hutt Valley Line in 1953. There were no passengers to pick up this day.* NZR

An aerial view of Auckland Station, opened in 1930, with the freight yard on the left and the causeway of the 1930 Westfield deviation at the top. A Dc hauled suburban train can be seen at one of the platforms. This is the third Auckland Station building; the first two were located in Queen Street behind where the Chief Post Office now is. The decision to resite the station from Queen Street to Beach Road, a good 10 minute walk from the business district, clearly resulted in much less suburban traffic than is the case in Wellington. One interesting episode in the history of the station was its appearance in the film Merry Christmas Mr Lawrence *starring David Bowie when it was made to resemble a building in Japanese occupied Malaysia in World War II.* NZR

New Zealand's finest railway station is clearly that of Dunedin. This building is the city's fourth station, being built between 1904 and 1906. The architect was George Troup (later Sir George Troup), a Scottish immigrant who designed many provincial stations as well as a number of the viaducts on the Hawkes Bay line. The materials used included granite, bluestone from central Otago and white stone facings from the Oamaru area. The design includes two towers and many ornamental features. At one time the station was a hive of activity with passenger trains departing to Palmerston, Mosgiel and to Otago Central as well as the Main Trunk expresses.

CHAPTER FOUR

Bush tramways

From the later part of the nineteenth century until the middle of the twentieth century a large number of primitive railways, known as bush tramways, were built to facilitate the felling and removal of native trees to the nearest sawmills, and sometimes from them to NZR railheads. These were invariably rough affairs with light rails, temporary road-beds, sharp curves and steep gradients. Often the gauges were narrow to allow even tighter curves. Once the timber in a particular area had been felled, the rails would be lifted and laid to the next area to be worked.

On these tramways, the total length of which at their peak rivaled that of the NZR network, an incredible variety of motive power would be found. The simplest just used horses. The most sophisticated came close to NZR standards. In the nineteenth century locomotives were imported from Climax and Heisler of the USA, and Fowler, Peckett, Sharp, Stewart and Co. and Kerr Stuart of Britain. The New Zealand builders of A. & G. Price in Thames also provided many locomotives. In the diesel era the motive power often consisted of conversions of trucks, vans and cars. Most of the tramways were built around the Rotorua area, in the central North Island, on the West Coast of the South Island and in parts of Southland, all being heavily afforested areas of the country to the present day.

Gradually as roads improved and the felling of native forests was phased out in favour of the usage of exotic timber planted in the 1930s, the bush tramways disappeared. The last of the significant tramways was that at Mamaku on the Rotorua branch, which closed on 19 October 1974.

▲ *A Heisler locomotive and an ex-NZR C class seen near a Westland sawmill in the early 1960s.* BOB STOTT

Opposite: Climax locomotive number 1650 with empty logging bogies poses on the big timber viaduct on the Ellis and Burnand Ltd.'s tramway from Ongarue into the King Country. Several ladies enjoy the view on the viaduct.

▼*Later in the day 1650 crosses the viaduct again with nine large logs in tow.* ALEXANDER TURNBULL LIBRARY

▶The tractor used on the Taringamotu Totora Sawmills tramway in the King Country in the early 1960s. This was a conversion of a steam locomotive, repowered with a Fordson motor.

Sanding the track by hand. TONY HURST

▶An A. & G. Price C type locomotive at the Taringamotu sawmill on 19 October 1960. J.A.T. TERRY

◀*The Price C locomotive makes its way between the sawmill and the railway station at Taringamotu (on the North Island Main Trunk) on 19 October 1960.* J.A.T. TERRY

One of the ontraptions used to aul timber over nother Ellis and urnand tramway, en at Manunui in ay 1969. TONY URST

The Lake Brunner Sawmilling Company's tramway at Ruru in Westland appears to be the last genuine steam worked bush tramway in New Zealand and closed in 1962. Here the company's Barclay 0-4-2T is seen underway. Original features included the cylindrical smoke arrester and the pushed-out back of the cab to allow more elbow room. J.A.T. TERRY

DF's 6041 and 6110 with a northbound express freight cross the Okarahia Viaduct on the Main North Line on Saturday 4 March 1989. The train was overtaken by the Coastal Pacific Express at Ferniehurst. The No. 1 tunnel is visible to the left, while the No. 2 tunnel is out of sight around the bend. B.J. MCKENZIE/IMAGE ENGINEERING

PART TWO

The system

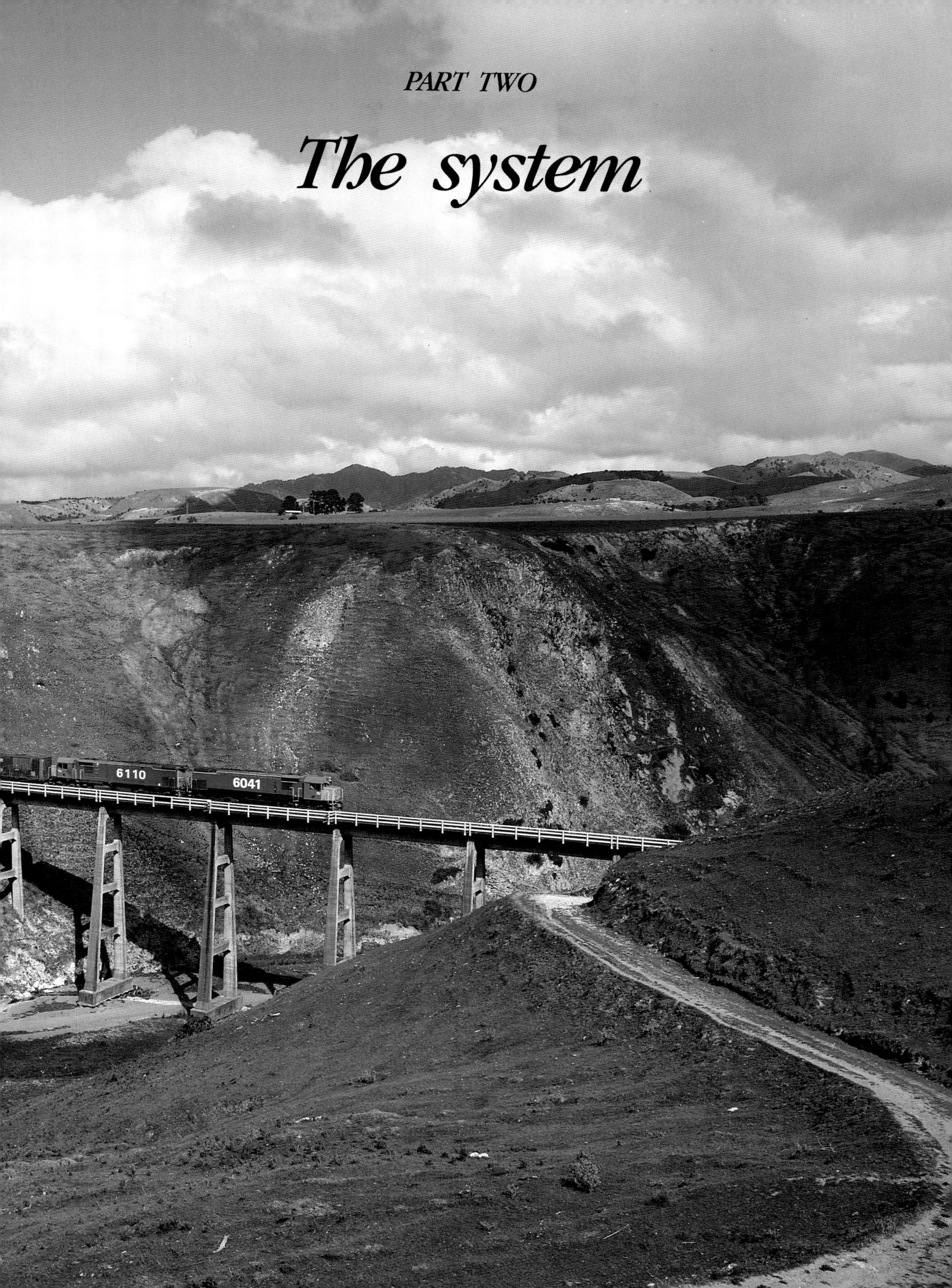

CHAPTER FIVE

Northland

The tourist brochures may claim that Northland is the "winterless north", but the combination of easily eroded landscape and substantial rain made railway construction and maintenance difficult. A major reason for the slow progress of some of these lines was that most work had to stop for winter, during which floods and slips undid much of the work done. In 1920 some 600 men were working on seven railway construction projects in North Auckland. Small numbers of men without mechanical aids made little progress, yet these small projects were not worth mechanising. Gordon Coates, a North Auckland M.P. who became Minister of Public Works in 1920, moved to consolidate railway construction at a smaller number of sites, and introduced steam-shovels and other mechanical aids which could make better progress through the soft and slipping ground.

The rows of hills and long branching harbours made it difficult to run railways in anything like a direct route. The passenger services north to Northland were doomed as soon as the Auckland Harbour Bridge offered a direct road route north, although the local mixed trains outlasted the railcars by nearly a decade.

Okaihau Branch

This line, intended to go to the "Far North" centre of Kaitaia, branched off the line from Opua to the south at Otiria Junction. Construction started in 1910 and the line was opened to the town of Kaikohe on 1 May 1914. From this point on the construction process was a classic case of a government unwilling to spend enough to make adequate progress, yet unwilling for political reasons to stop. Work was slowed by the First World War, by floods, and by the "Great Flu" of 1919. The line to Okaihau, only 13 km from Kaikohe, and 270 metres above sea level, was opened on 29 October 1923, and construction continued slowly down the hill to Rangiahua, near the Hokianga Harbour. Beyond Rangiahua two routes to Kaitaia were being considered, a shorter route of about 30 km with two tunnels to go through the Maungataniwha Range, or a 40 km route around the hills.

Below: A DF/DA combination lead an excursion train near Portland on 5 February 1984. TONY HURST

Left: The railway line through the main street of Kawakawa was the best known feature of Northland's railways. Here two DAs pull an excursion train through the town on 5 February 1984. MARK COLE

Below: The same train between Maromaku and Otiria Junction. DAVE SIMPSON

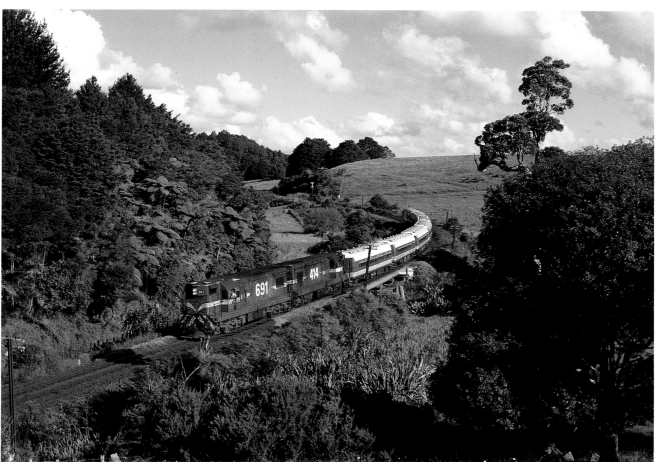

When work ceased because of the Depression the rails had reached Rangiahua, although the station buildings there had not been built. In 1936 the new Labour Government considered all the railways on which construction had stopped. With increasing motor traffic, a railway to Kaitaia no longer seemed a priority, and the steep and winding section between Okaihau and Rangiahua was little use by itself. The decision was made to salvage all the material past Okaihau, which was to remain the railhead. Mixed trains, connecting at Otiria with the Northland Express, provided passenger services on this line until the introduction of railcars in Northland in 1956, which ran right through to Okaihau. This excellent service only lasted a decade; in 1967 the railcars were withdrawn, and it was back to mixed trains, which provided a local service until 1974.

Okaihau was on the main highway, and was an important goods transhipment point, while Kaikohe was the commercial centre of the area. Traffic at Okaihau fell away rapidly when the old 64 km limit on competing road transport was increased to 160 km in 1977, and scheduled goods trains ceased on 12 August 1983, although shunts ran when required from Kaikohe, and several excursions ran to Okaihau after this date. With further decreases in traffic, NZR closed the whole line past Otiria on 1 November 1987. Although there has been much talk of possible forestry development in the area, with the current Tranz Rail attitude to investment in new infrastructure it seems there is now little chance of any revival of rail in this area.

Opua Branch

This line is the successor to a horse drawn tramway opened in 1868 to take coal from the mines at Kawakawa to Taumarere wharf. It was built in standard gauge (1435 mm) and originally used horse traction and wooden rails. Two locomotives, some wagons and rails were obtained second hand from the abortive Auckland and Drury Railway in 1871. The railway was purchased by the government in 1876 and re-gauged to 1067 mm by 1877. On 7 April 1884, an extension to a deep-water wharf at Opua was opened, and the spur to the Taumarere wharf was closed. The linking of the Kawakawa section to Whangarei is described below.

The Opua express from Auckland ran three times a week until 1956, when it was replaced by a daily railcar service which ran to Okaihau instead. However, mixed trains continued to run to Opua, although oddly enough they did not connect with the railcars. The mixed trains outlasted the railcars; the last mixed between Whangarei and Opua ran on 18 June 1976. By 1984 there were no regular freight trains past Kawakawa, as the only traffic to Opua was on the increasingly rare occasions that an overseas cargo ship called.

The Kawakawa–Opua section was last used by NZR in 1985, and at the end of that year was leased to the Bay of Islands Tourist Railway. This private venture now operates steam-hauled trains along this scenic 12 km route, which includes the famous run along the middle of the main street of Kawakawa. The line between Kawakawa and Moerewa was closed in 1993 and the rails removed.

North Auckland Line (Auckland–Whangarei–Otiria)

Northland got a very small share of the Vogel rail construction boom, just a very short line from Whangarei to coal mines at Kamo, and the conversion of the Kawakawa tramway into a 1067 mm gauge railway. Efforts to link these lines as part of a North Auckland Line had no immediate effect, but in 1894 the Whangarei line was extended north to Waro, and in 1899, with the railhead 30 km north of Whangarei at Waiotu, a parliamentary bill authorised the link from Kawakawa to the Whangarei section. It took another twelve years to build the 44 km to join the two sections. The slow progress was due to the difficulties of access and working in areas that turned into mud in the frequent rain, and also because the resources put into railway construction in North Auckland were spread over so many projects. Three of the Wb 2-6-2T locomotives, built by Baldwin (USA) in 1898, were the main power of the isolated Whangarei section.

Two alternatives were considered for the railway route north from Auckland. A route approximately following the present North-Western motorway was considered before the more circuitous route south-west to New Lynn, and then north through Henderson and Waitakere was finally chosen. The railway was opened to Henderson on 21 December 1880, and on 13 July 1881 the formerly isolated Kaipara–Helensville railway was linked to Auckland, making Helensville the railhead. During the early part of this century, an intensive suburban service developed between Henderson and

Left: The "with car" goods trains from Whangarei were not very long by the time they reached Opua in the Bay of Islands. This photo from 18 March 1970 shows a DA with a flat wagon, passenger car and guard's van near Opua. NZR

Right: Two DGs with a north Auckland freight train near Ahuroa on 19 March 1964. NZR

Auckland, with some trains travelling on to Waitakere or Helensville. Diesel multiple-unit cars now provide a suburban service as far as Waitakere, and there are currently plans to double-track part of this route for greater capacity.

A fairly easy section to Kanohi was opened on 3 May 1889, but it took another eight years to complete the next 5 km section. This difficult section included grades of 1 in 44 northbound and 1 in 46 southbound, and the constricted Makarau tunnel, which required its floor to be lowered before modern diesels could be used in Northland. Beyond Makarau, the route ran through a series of narrow valleys running east or west, so a succession of tunnels were necessary on the way north. The poor road access made it difficult to work far in advance of the railhead. This slowed progress, and meant that only a short section could be worked on at a time. Nine short sections were opened from 1900 to 1913, taking the line to Topuni, 130 km from Auckland, but still 80 km from Whangarei.

World War I had the effect of slowing construction, but work continued on some of the tunnels. After the war a concentrated effort was put into this line, and the sections from Whangarei to Portland and from Kaiwaka to Huarau opened in 1920. The final obstacle was the Golden Stairs Tunnel, of 600 metres. The first attempt at digging this tunnel was abandoned, and its southern portal can still be seen, although it is partially buried. There is a myth about this tunnel, that the Public Works Department (PWD) started to dig the tunnel "the wrong way", and diverted a stream to try and hide the evidence. In reality, the PWD was finally learning to take geological advice when tunnelling, and the second tunnel was dug with much less difficulty. The complex geology of Northland had given the PWD engineers many problems. The final section was opened on 29 November 1925, completing a link from Auckland to Opua and Okaihau.

The numerous curves and short but sharp gradients on this line meant that passenger services were never very fast, and this became more obvious as the competing roads were improved. The thrice-weekly "Northland Expresses" of the early 1950s took 5 hours 20 minutes from Auckland to Whangarei, while the railcars introduced in November 1956 eventually cut this to 4 hours 10 minutes. This was not bad for 207 km of rather curved railway, but once the Auckland Harbour Bridge opened in 1959, and gave a 30 km shorter road route, the writing was on the wall for these services. All railcar services were withdrawn in July 1967. Carriages were attached to some goods trains to provide a service for certain isolated areas. One author (Tony Hurst) once caught the 5.30 am mixed from Whangarei to Opua, making a connection from the 1.15 am "Herald" NZR bus from Auckland. Passengers were conspicuous by their absence, except for a few local travellers near Opua, but this train provided a vital service for newspaper readers, with single copies and small bundles thrown by the guard from his van, and a few stops for larger bundles and other parcels traffic. The last of these mixed trains in North Auckland ceased in 1976, leaving no passenger trains north of Helensville. In 1980, the daily passenger train each way between Auckland and Helensville was withdrawn. Waitakere is now the northernmost NZR passenger station.

The coal-fired J class 4-8-2's handled both passenger and goods trains in the later years of steam, assisted by the ubiquitous Ab's. The last regular steam services

View from the carriage of a mixed train from Whangarei to Opua in 1969. TONY HURST

were in 1966. DG and DB diesels took over from steam, as the DA class were not allowed north of Helensville until the track was lowered in the Makarau Tunnel in 1968. The Makarau Tunnel still had insufficient clearance for DC locomotives, so DA locomotives continued to work in Northland long after they had been taken out of mainline service elsewhere. The last DA working in Northland was in February 1989. They were replaced by DFs, with DXs also authorised to run to Whangarei. Now both DXs and DCs can run right through to Otiria. The major traffic from Otiria is logs, with short ones to the chipmill at Portland, and long ones for export. Logs also come from Wellsford, while fertiliser is carried there from Whangarei. The chips from Portland are taken the short distance to Port Whangarei by rail, as there were environmental objections to road transport. There is still some meat from Moerewa, and dairy products from Kauri, north of Whangarei, and Maungaturoto, further south. China clay from Kamo is loaded in Whangarei. Another traffic used to be Waikato coal for the cement works at Portland, but this traffic was lost when coal began being barged from Greymouth about 10 years ago.

Dargaville Branch

In 1922, work started on a line from Waiotira Junction to Dargaville. The first few kilometres were through very unstable country, and construction was very expensive. The 22 km section to Kirikopuni was opened on 15 May 1928. There had been a proposal to have a railway north from here to Kaikohe, but by 1928 this line was seen to be totally unnecessary, as there was already a railway via Whangarei. At Kirikopuni was the notorious "balloon loop", the result of political pressure from the local M.P., Gordon Coates, who was by then Prime Minister. Kirikopuni station was located 2 km north of the direct line to Dargaville. All trains ran on the "balloon loop" north to Kirikopuni and then back to within a few hundred metres of where they had been before, until it was finally bypassed in 1943. By 1930, the line was at Tangowahine, only 16 km from Dargaville, but the Depression stopped construction until 1935. Trains started running to Dargaville in 1940, but the line was not formally opened until 15 March 1943, because the old station by the wharf was closed to eliminate a number of level crossings, and a new station had to be built.

Mixed trains ran to connect with the Northland Express, and later with the railcars. The last mixed train ran in March 1967, a few months before the railcars were withdrawn from Northland. For many years the main traffic was coal to, and container loads of products from, the Northern Wairoa Co-operative Dairy Company at Dargaville. Squash (the vegetable) for export was also a significant traffic. Ab and J class steam locomotives worked the line until the mid 1960s. DA class diesels worked the line until 1988. In 1998, with the Dairy Factory about to be closed, the line was "mothballed" after damage from slips and derailments.

▲Dx 5074 rounds the foreshore near Whangarei with a Waitangi weekend excursion in 1984. NORM DANIEL

▼A line that must now be on the endangered list is the Dargaville Branch. Here DA 86 takes the daily goods working back to Waiotira along the bank of the northern Wairoa River on 10 June 1982. MARK COLE

A mixed train from Dargaville with Ww 573 in front arrives at Waiotira Junction in 1950. NZR&LS

It was re-opened on 17 April 2000 for log traffic, initially using DJ 3096 from the Tranz Rail Heritage Fleet. Whangarei-based DBR diesel locomotives are now generally used.

Donnelly's Crossing Branch (Kaihu Valley Railway)

The Kaihu Valley Railway Company was formed in 1883 to build a railway north from Dargaville, to bring down timber from the kauri forests. The company took until 1889 to build the 25 km to Opanake, by which time the company was in financial difficulties. The government therefore took over the line in 1890. The line was extended the short distance to Kaihu in 1895, and there was a substantial timber traffic from the Kaihu district for about the next 25 years. In 1908, construction started on a further extension northwards. It took fifteen years to complete the 12 km to Donnelly's Crossing, including four years in which no work was done because of the First World War. A timber tramway north of Kaihu would have been more appropriate, and would have not have diverted money and effort from much more important lines needed to link up the isolated sections of New Zealand Railways.

The mixed trains on this line were generally worked by F class locomotives, and four six-wheel carriages handled the passengers until two bogie carriages arrived in 1933. The line was upgraded for Ww locomotives by the time Dargaville was linked to the main line in 1943. The traffic hardly justified a larger locomotive, as the timber was exhausted, and the main traffic was bulk inwards goods such as fertiliser. Passenger traffic lasted longer than in many other areas, even in 1958-59 there were 4375 passengers, about 15 per train based on the thrice-weekly mixed. In this rather isolated area, the slow pace of the mixed train was still acceptable. The line closed on 19 July 1959, although the Dargaville shunter took wagon-lot goods to Kaihu for some months after this.

Onerahi Branch

Whangarei was established in the upper reaches of the Whangarei Harbour, and by the 1890s it was realised that ships could no longer reach the wharves near the town. Accordingly, in 1899, a 4 km. railway was authorised, to link Whangarei to deep-water wharves at Onerahi. It took from 1902 till 1904 to build a 323 metre long bridge, with a central lifting span, across the Whangarei Harbour. This timber truss was known as the "Gull Roost", for reasons which can be guessed. Construction work on this line halted between 1906 and 1910, and it was 1911 before it was finished. There was considerable traffic to and from the Auckland steamers for about 15 years, but once the Auckland - Whangarei railway was completed in 1925, traffic fell drastically, and the line was closed completely in 1933.

Marsden Point proposed lines

"Political" railway construction, in which a group of labourers were set to establishing a railway formation, but without sufficient resources to make much progress, was a common feature of the first seventy years of railway development in New Zealand, and Northland had more than its share. An extreme case was a proposed line to Waipu Cove, branching off the main line a few kilometres south of Whangarei. The line was surveyed in 1914, but construction did not start until after the First World War. In 1920, 25 men were working on this line. By 1924 it was obvious that branches were no longer needed to serve every farming area, and the Waipu line was abandoned before any track was laid. Oddly enough, such a line might have come into its own fifty years later. By then, Marsden Point, near the originally proposed route, was a deepwater oil port, and two proposals were made that would have required rail access. One was to convert the Marsden B Power Station to use Waikato Coal, since after the oil shock of 1973, it was not economic to run it on oil. The other was to use Marsden Point as a forestry export port, and a 14 km. rail link was proposed as part of this development in 1979.

After a long hiatus, the forestry port has now been approved, but without a rail link. If the port goes ahead without rail access, then the woodchips and much of the log traffic will be lost to rail, and both the Otiria and Dargaville lines would probably close. It is unlikely that Tranz Rail would fund the whole cost, so the future of rail in Northland depends very much on whether other parties, such as central or regional government, will pay a share of the cost.

Kaipara–Riverhead

This short line was literally a cross-country line. It linked the east coast Waitemata Harbour with the west coast Kaipara Harbour, giving better communication between Auckland and the Kaipara district, as far north as Dargaville. It was opened in 1875, and the Kumeu - Riverhead end was closed in 1881, made redundant by a rail connection from Auckland to Kumeu. The remainder of the line became part of the North Auckland line.

CHAPTER SIX

Auckland and Waikato

Onehunga Branch

The 3.3 km branch line from Penrose Junction to Onehunga was part of the first line to be constructed in the North Island. Originally, in 1864, the Auckland Provincial Council empowered the appointment of a railway commission for the purpose of constructing a £100,000 railway from Auckland to Drury, 35 km, with a branch from Penrose to Onehunga. The gauge was to be 4'8½" (1435 mm) with rails weighing 26 kg/metre. Construction began in 1865 but with the money all spent two years later, work came to a virtual standstill with only a few km of track having been laid, amid protracted disputes between the provincial councillors, engineers and contractors.

With the advent of the Vogel era, a railway was authorised in 1870 between Auckland and Tuakau with the branch to Onehunga. One of the contracts entered into with John Brogden and Sons in August 1872 was for a 66 km railway from Newmarket to Mercer, while a subsequent contract dated 19 July 1873 included the Auckland-Newmarket and Penrose-Onehunga lines.

The 13 km line from Auckland to Onehunga was completed in December 1873 and thus became the first of the "Vogel Railways" to be brought into use. The first train to leave Auckland station, then located near the present intersection of Anzac Avenue and Beach Road, departed on 24 December 1873 amid little public excitement. The first train consisted of 0-6-0 saddle tank locomotive *Ada* (later one of the F class) with a short train of 6 tonne, 6 wheel passenger cars.

By 1882 there were five trains daily each way between Auckland and Onehunga, which were allowed 35 minutes each way, with stops at Newmarket, Remuera, Green Lane, Ellerslie, Penrose Junction and Te Papapa. Through train services from Auckland began to diminish after the advent of electric trams in 1903.

The last through passenger train from Auckland ran on 28 July 1950 consisting of a Ww steam locomotive plus five passenger cars. However, a shuttle service between Onehunga and Penrose Junction continued until 1973. The branch today, truncated, serves industrial users in the Onehunga area.

WAB 769 heads a train of suburban carriages in the loop at Remuera Station on 5 March 1955. The signal box and station building have been preserved. All the houses seen in the area to the right, however, have long since made way for the southern motorway. NZR

A unit train of imported steel coils from Auckland to the steel mill at Mission Bush, headed by two DAs, nears its destination in 1969. NZR

Waiuku and Mission Bush branches

Originally recommended by the Railway Commission of 1880, construction of the 18.8 km branch to Waiuku took many years to get underway. Until the early 1900s the only progress had been one rather cursory survey in response to numerous petitions from pressure groups. In 1912, with the election of W.F. Massey as Prime Minister, the line received attention from the top, it being in his constituency. Authorisation was received for work to proceed in 1912 and the first sod was turned in February 1914 at Waiuku. Unlike most other railway construction projects, the outbreak of war did not stop the works, which continued steadily. The first section from Paerata (on the North Island Main Trunk) to Patamahoe was completed in 1917. On opening this section, Mr Massey predicted that the line would be one of the most profitable in the Dominion and even predicted the need for suburban trains from Auckland. Post-war shortages of materials delayed completion of the Patamahoe to Waiuku section until May 1922. A special passenger train was run from Auckland for the opening on 10 May 1922 consisting of two Ww class locomotives and 16 cars as from Paerata.

The first 4.3 km section from Paerata to Helvetia was relatively steep, but from there gentle undulations applied as far as Glenbrook. From there the line descended through a long cutting and continued to a summit under the Shakespear Road bridge. From there it was one long downgrade to the terminus at Waiuku. The only signalling was at Paerata where, in the mid 1920s, power signalling and interlocking was installed. A metallic circuit telephone was completed between Paerata and Waiuku in 1925-26.

From the beginning two daily return goods trains with passenger cars attached were run. These connected at Paerata with passenger trains headed north and south. Experiments to improve the service in 1929-30 did not last long with the advent of the Depression and services along with staff were cut.

Following World War II, passenger services were short-lived after buses and private cars considerably reduced patronage. The end of passenger services came on 17 July 1948. In the early days of the branch, timber from felled native bush was one of the main products hauled over the line. In later years inwards goods traffic consisted mainly of coal for the Waiuku Dairy factory at Fernleigh along with machinery and other goods for the farming community. Outwards traffic until about 1954 was mostly livestock.

Locomotives used on the line until around 1950 were one of either the Wf, Wg or Ww class tank locomotives. With the closure of the locomotive depot at Waiuku, Ab's, coal burning J's, and oil burning Ja's became regular power for the next 15 years. From 1965, DB diesels replaced steam traction.

Closure of the line came on 1 January 1968. This had actually been a recommendation of the 1952 Royal Commission, but the branch lingered on for a decade and a half. From the beginning, traffic on the branch had never lived up to expectations. In its last decade of existence the line saw minimal maintenance. The last train to Waiuku was run by the Railway Enthusiasts Society from Auckland on 31 December 1967, headed by two DBs.

It was not, however, the end of railway services in the district. In the 1960s construction of a large steel mill complex at Mission Bush had begun, a few kilometres from the Waiuku township. A new 5.5 km spur line was built from Glenbrook to the mill at Mission Bush and the old line from Paerata to Glenbrook was extensively upgraded. Traffic over the new line opened on 7 October 1968 includes inwards coal from Huntly and lime from Hangataki, with trains of steel coils to Mt Maunganui for export. Double headed DAs were the normal power for several years, yielding in the 1980s to double headed DCs, which now haul four trains a day each way.

The 7.7 km section from Glenbrook to Waiuku soon reverted back to nature. Its rescue and rebuilding is the story of the Glenbrook Vintage Railway.

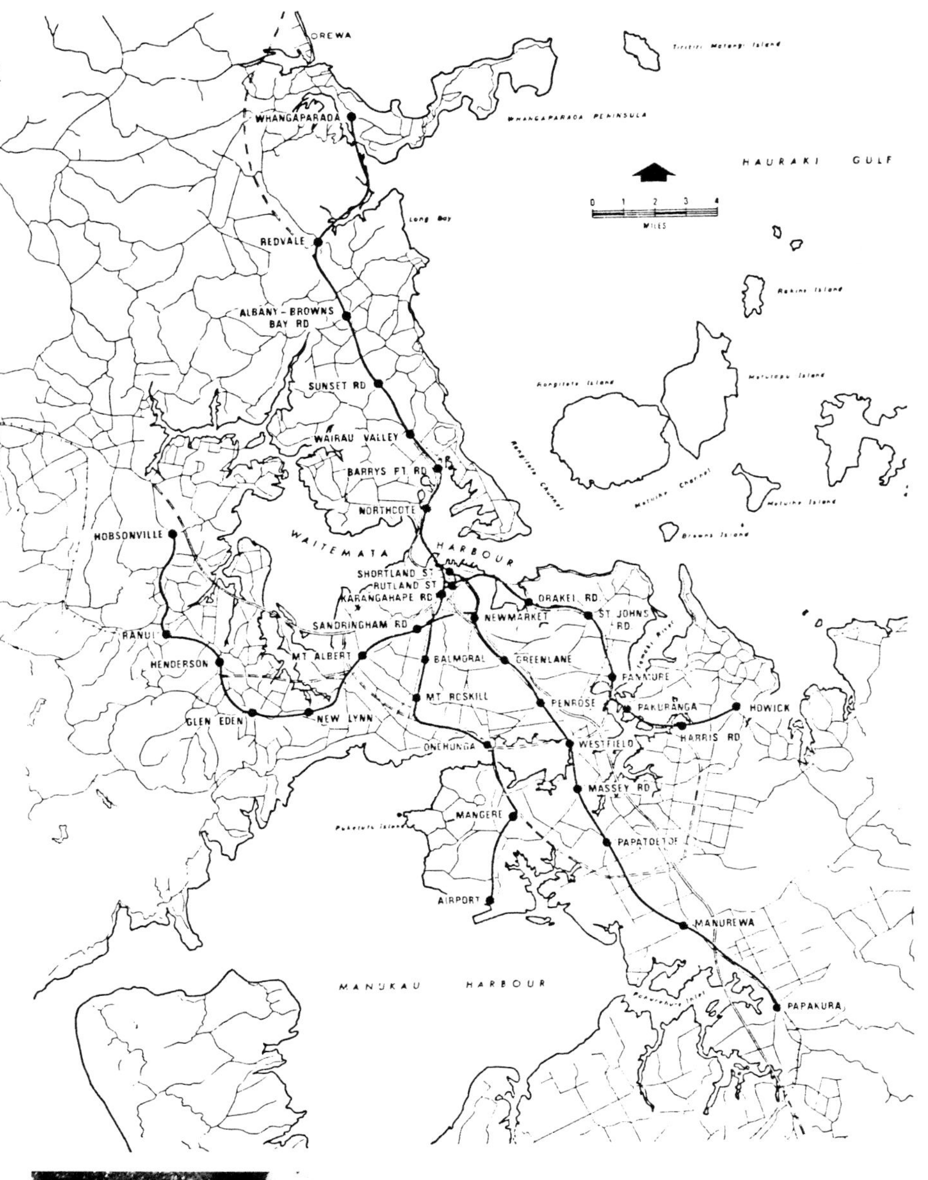

◀ *In 1969 the Auckland Regional Authority set up a working party to report on a planned rapid rail transit system for the Auckland region. The report released in 1972, would have involved a network (using the standard NZR gauge) with an aggregate length of about 126 km. In July 1973 the Authority accepted an offer from the Government to electrify the line from Papakura to Auckland and to build an underground loop under the city centre. Further reports were announced and design work reached an advanced stage, until eventually the project died when the Government in 1976 decided not to make any money available for the project.*

▼ *Streamlined J 1212 steams up the Parnell bank with Train 15 in tow on 19 September 1946. An unidentified locomotive assists at the rear.* THE LATE W.W. STEWART

Glen Afton Branch

In 1910 the need for a bridge over the Waikato River at Huntly for both road and rail and for a branch line to serve the exploitation of extensive coal deposits in the Awaroa district several km west of Huntly was urged on the Government. Provision for the first 5 km of the line was contained in the Railway Authorisation Act of that year. Work on both the rail-road bridge and the railway started in 1911. The bridge comprising eight 30.5 metre and two 12.2 metre spans of Australian hardwood on steel and reinforced concrete piers was completed in October 1914 and included an extension at the east end to carry the railway over the main highway. This bridge carried both road and rail traffic until November 1959, when a new road bridge was opened a short distance upstream. In 1911 the annual report of the Public Works Department contained a proposal for an extension of the railway about 7 km in the direction of an easy saddle which would open up valuable coal bearing country and then later a further extension of the line in the direction of Waingaro and Raglan counties could be made. As it happened the first extension (Rotowaro to Glen Afton) was built gradually between 1915 and 1924 but the second extension did not eventuate. The hill section from Rotowaro (Maori for "coal lake") to Glen Afton was relatively difficult to construct and was delayed at one stage by large slips caused by four months of continuous wet weather. The biggest job was the very large "summit" cutting just before Glen Afton. Grades on this hill section were as steep as 1 in 50 with 150 metre radius curves.

As few of the mines were close to the final stages of the railway, several short private lines branched from NZR sidings at Rotowaro, Pukemiro and Glen Afton, over which 10 locomotives at various times ran. The longest of the private lines was from Renown Siding near Rotowaro to the State Mine at Waikokowai, 5 km north. Another relatively long private tramway was a rope incline from near Glen Afton to the McDonald Mine.

Normal locomotives to run over the branch until the mid 1960s were Ab's and Bb's. Non-NZR locomotives used for transporting coal from the mines to the railway included ex-NZR 0-4-2T C 132 (now preserved on the Silverstream railway), ex-NZR F 185 now preserved at Pukemiro, two 0-6-0T Pecketts, and an 0-4-0T Barclay, now preserved at Motat in Auckland.

DB diesels began running on the line in February 1966, and the last recorded run of a steam locomotive was on 29 September 1967 when an Ab replaced a DB which had failed. With the upgrading of the Waikato river bridge, DA diesels began running as from April 1972. Shortly thereafter on 23 June 1972 passenger trains, which mainly transported mine workers, ceased. Goods traffic west of Rotowaro ceased about 1975 as coal from the mines began to run out. There is still reasonably heavy coal traffic from Rotowaro, most of it destined for the Mission Bush steel mill some 60 km further north, which began running as from 31 October 1969. In December 1996 the coal loading point was shifted east to a site near the old Renown Collieries siding, as coal was to be mined from under the Rotowaro town and station area. Coal is also loaded at Kimihia, on the east side of the NIMT north of Huntly.

The former section from Rotowaro through Pukemiro to Glen Afton became the site of the Bush Tramway Club's museum operations as from 1977. This runs trains over about 5 km of the former NZR road-bed, the last 2.5 km to Glen Afton being no longer usable.

*Opposite: A. & G. Price built B*B *167 hauls a miners' train on the Glen Afton branch, September 1957.*
*Above: B*B *625 hauls empties to the Wilton Mine at Glen Massey on 20 June 1957.* DEREK CROSS

Glen Massey Branch

Like the Glen Afton Branch further north, this 10.6 km long Waikato branch was built to serve coal traffic. The genesis came with an application from the Ngaruawahia Co-operative Coal Company Ltd for a private siding at Ngaruawahia in April 1908. In January 1910 the company Waipa Railway and Collieries Ltd submitted details of a proposed private railway from Ngaruawahia to Glen Massey. The private siding was ready for use in May 1912 and was used in the supply of construction materials for the branch which initially ran the 8.2 km to Glen Massey. The branch was opened to this terminus in March 1914, by which time a weighbridge had been installed at the Ngaruawahia private siding and coal transport commenced. The company owned a Barclay 0-6-2 side tank locomotive imported in 1912, but this proved inadequate for the 1 in 40 grades on the line and was joined by a 2-6-2 side tank locomotive formerly owned by the Wellington and Manawatu Railway Company and classified by NZR as Wh 449. Some former WMR clerestory carriages were also acquired to run a regular Saturday passenger train known as the "Wilton Express".

The mine at Glen Massey was all but worked out by 1930 and the company went into liquidation. However, a new coal seam was located about 3.5 km south and a new company—Wilton Collieries Ltd—was formed to operate the new mine. The new company acquired the railway line in November 1930 and extended it 2.2 km. The coal was carried in skips from the mine on a 610 mm gauge cable incline to the railhead, 1.6 km away. Two Wd class 2-6-4 side tank locomotives were brought from the Railways Department, the second being necessitated following the crash of a runaway train on 28 March 1933, which wrecked the original 0-6-2 Barclay tank locomotive. This locomotive was left in the creek at an S-bend where it fell near a place called Windy Point for many years.

By 1935 some 70,000 tonnes of coal was being transported over the line annually, half of it for the Railways Department. The daily output was 400 tonnes and three return trips a day were made. As from 12 August 1935 the Railways Department took over train working on the line and Ww and Bb class locomotives were to remain the standard power on the branch until it closed on 19 May 1958. Although NZR worked the line, it remained in State Mines Department hands from their take-over of the mines in 1935 until the end. With deteriorating track, sharp curvatures, steep grades and 22 bridges on the line, the speed limit in the last few years was down to16 km/h with 10 km/h in some places. The best known feature of the line was a 91.5 metre long, 18.3 metre high timber trestle bridge about half way between Ngaruawahia and Glen Massey.

A scene on the then State Coal's 3.3 km private line, known as the Kimihia Branch, near Huntly on 10 March 1952. The locomotive is a 4-6-4T Wg, built by NZR (Hillside) NZR

Above: Bb 222 approaches Pukemiro with a Huntly–Glen Afton miners' train on 22 December 1965. This was to be the last regularly steam-hauled passenger train in the North Island. J.A.T. TERRY

Cambridge Branch

This branch was a long-term survivor of the many rural branchlines built in the 1880s and 1890s to serve rural communities, and which closed in the 1950s and 1960s. Part of the 19.3 km line from Ruakura to Cambridge still survives, to serve a dairy company and a freezing works which rail containers over the line.

The branch was opened on 8 October 1884 when some 100 passengers travelled on the first train, which was hauled by an F class tank locomotive. At that time Ruakura Junction was an isolated spot in the middle of a swamp, accessible only by rail. Some 2 km from Ruakura at Newstead the line crosses a 98 m long, 15 m high nine span bridge to reach Matangi (Tamahere before 1906); 6 km of former swamp lie between this point and Bruntwood. Then 2.2 km beyond here is Hautapu and after another 5.4 km, the line ended at Cambridge.

Regular passenger trains ended on 9 September 1946. However, the busiest passenger traffic in the line's history was on 7 February 1950 when the Empire Games rowing events were held at Karapiro. Three trains carrying 1500 people left Auckland for Cambridge. The last steam locomotive to run over the line was Ab 733 on Monday 26 June 1967. The old station building at Cambridge was demolished in 1973, but freight was still handled at Cambridge until 1999, when the line was cut back to Hautapu.

Below: A NZR built Dsc twin bogie diesel shunter from the mid-1960s on the Newstead bridge on the Cambridge Branch with a local shunt. DAVE SIMPSON

CHAPTER SEVEN

Bay of Plenty

Thames Branch and the East Coast Main Trunk

The discovery of gold in the Thames area in the 1850s indirectly created the first impetus for a railway between Thames and the Auckland area. The gold fields being quartz rather than alluvial created a need for coal to power pumping machinery for underground mines and to power the rock crushing batteries. At first coal was transported by barge from North Auckland fields but the vagaries of tides and the weather made this form of delivery unreliable. In 1872 the Auckland Provincial Council recommended a rail connection to Thames and the following year a survey was made despite the opposition of the Maoris who at one stage drove the surveyors off their land by force. Hopes for a start to the line were maintained for the next five years when in 1878 the cost of the 54 km proposal was put at £178,000.

At the northern end the Prime Minister, Sir George Grey, turned the first sod at Thames, but 18 months later the line was one of the many victims of the 1880 Royal Commission on the railways. The Commission felt that the line from Thames to Hamilton should be completed only between Hamilton and the junction of the branch line than being built to Cambridge, and the proposed link from Grahamstown (Thames) to Te Aroha was unnecessary in view of the existence of good water connection between the two towns.

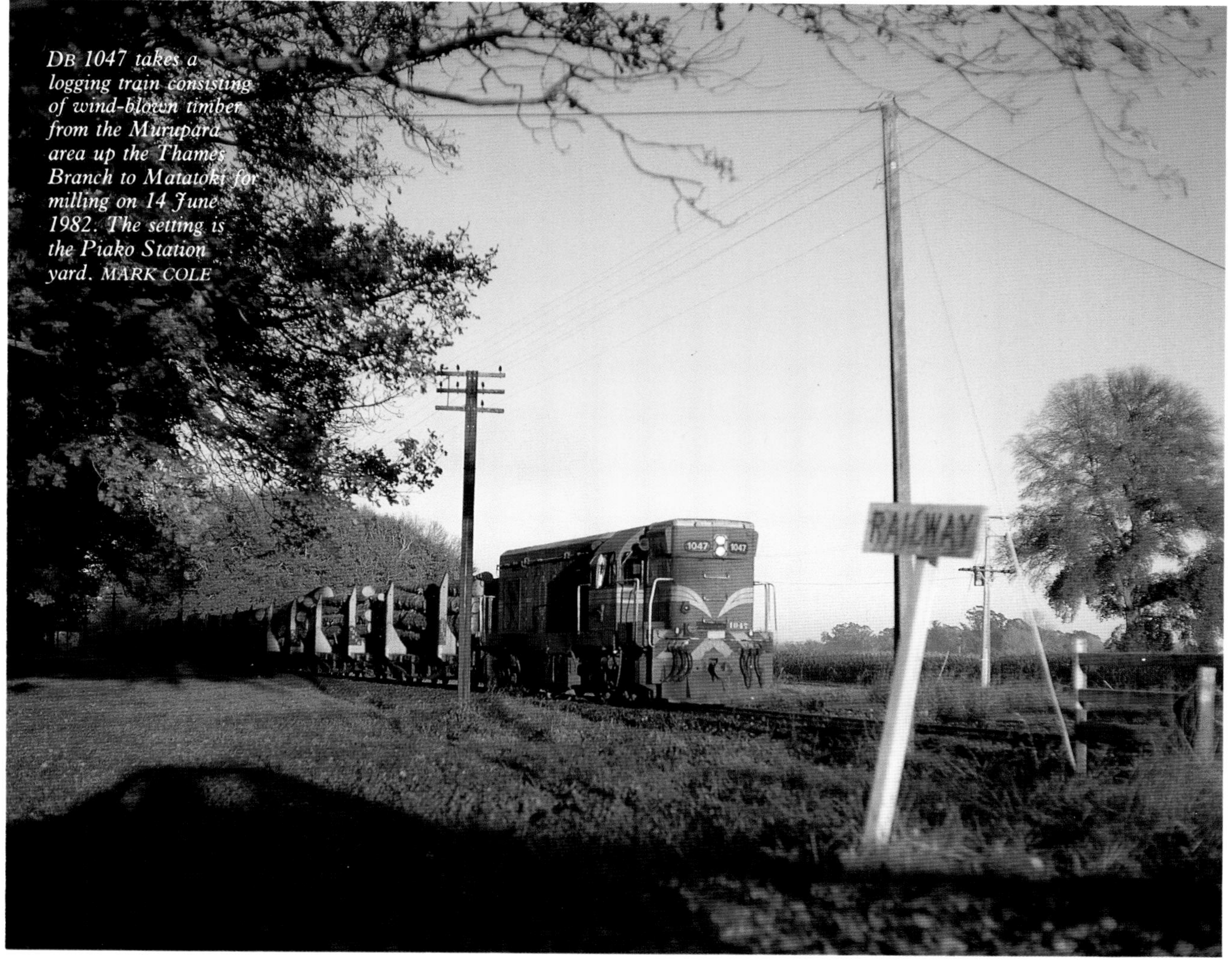

DB 1047 takes a logging train consisting of wind-blown timber from the Murupara area up the Thames Branch to Matatoki for milling on 14 June 1982. The setting is the Piako Station yard. MARK COLE

A Taneatua to Auckland express is seen at Te Aroha on 9 July 1957. NZR

At the southern end progress was held up by the need to bridge the Waikato River. The work was in the hands of a bridge engineer from Canada, B.M. Beere, but work was delayed until most of the ironwork had arrived from England. Finally completed in 1883 the Waikato River bridge was the first iron lattice girder bridge in New Zealand.

Despite the Royal Commission report, work continued on the line to Thames although rather more slowly. The section to Morrinsville was opened on 1 October 1884 and from there to Te Aroha on 1 March 1886. Having got that far work ceased for over five years. The delay was in part due to the financial crisis that hit the colony in 1888 resulting in the suspension of almost all railway construction and in part to the doubts of the then Government as to the worth of a railway between Te Aroha and Thames.

With a new Liberal Government elected in 1891, work on the line past Te Aroha was energetically pursued. Construction was at times hampered by swamp conditions and by floods but the first section of 24 km as far as Paeroa was opened for traffic just before Christmas 1895.

The complete line to Thames was officially opened 19 December 1898 when the Minister of Railways drove the F class tank locomotive which headed the official train through a tape held across the line by the wife of the Chairman of the Thames County Council, Mrs T. A. Dunlop, and Miss Belle Scott, daughter of the Mayor of Thames.

On completion of the line a daily mixed train was run each way to Frankton Junction and an additional mixed daily from Thames to Te Aroha. The through service to Auckland was provided by a further three times a week mixed train that connected with the recently introduced "Rotorua Express". The railway provided competition with the river boats from Thames and Te Aroha to Auckland, and initially the river boats held their patronage mainly due to the timetables and the fares that the railway charged. Locomotives used on the line were the "F" and "L" class and other small tank locomotives until about 1908. The pending completion of the North Island Main Trunk prompted urgent motive power acquisition for the Auckland region, and seven Baldwin locomotives - four "N" class 2-6-2 and three "Q" class 4-6-2 were assigned for use on the line but could not actually run over it until the Waikato River bridge at Hamilton was strengthened. The local engineering firm of A. & G. Price Ltd. at Thames also provided power for the line. In 1904 they produced the first of the 123 steam locomotives they were to produce for NZR, a Wf 2-6-4T, put into service on 1 September of that year. Nine more were built by 1906 and in December 1907, Prices delivered the first of their four cylinder A class Pacifics, although they could only haul trains across the bridge at Hamilton after December 1908. Additional power came in the form of "T" class 2-8-0's and K class 2-4-2's - two of the latter, together with J's released from other areas by the coming of newer locomotives, became regular sights on the Thames line.

1908 saw the development of regular passenger trains on the line in place of the usual mixed trains. Up until the completion of the North Island Main Trunk, the only passenger train south of Auckland, apart from suburban trains, was the "Rotorua Express", introduced on a daily basis in 1902. In December 1908 a second afternoon express was introduced between Auckland and Frankton together with connecting trains to Cambridge, Waihi and Thames. As more of the compound "A" class arrived the 237 km journey was cut to 6 hr 45 min - not fast enough to divert much traffic from the cheaper and more direct services provided by the Northern Steamship Company. During the 1920s this express service had been supplemented by an additional passenger train that connected with the Auckland to Wellington Expresses at Frankton. This service was notable for being the last regular working of the ex-Wellington and Manawatu Railway Company's Ud class 4-6-0's, withdrawn in 1928, and the first Auckland region railcar—the Sentinel-Cammell steam railcar imported in 1925.

Passenger traffic declined during the depression and war years and in 1947 passenger accommodation was withdrawn. Diminishing goods traffic on the line north of Paeroa to Thames saw goods trains reduced to just one a day. South of Paeroa to the Bay of Plenty, however, was a different story.

In 1959 railcar services were introduced from Auckland to Te Puke, utilising the recent "Fiat" railcars, and which replaced the three times a week Taneatua Express. South of Te Puke to Taneatua rail passenger services were replaced by buses. The railcar service lasted until August 1967 when it was withdrawn.

Motive power on the Thames line in the 1920's and 1930s was predominantly A and Ab 4-6-2's, at first supplemented by Ww 4-6-4T's and Bb 4-8-0's. The large J class 4-8-2's were introduced during the War years on the Bay line, but the Ab's saw steam out between Paeroa and Thames. In the diesel era the DSC shunters, DBs and DBRs became the usual motive power.

On 20 July 1959 a new direct connection at Paeroa from the Frankton-Thames Line to the Paeroa-Taneatua line was opened so as to avoid the need for Bay line trains to reverse at Paeroa. This saved some 15 minutes in time and reduced the distance from Frankton to stations on the Bay line by some 5 km.

On 6 May 1979 however, eight months after the opening of the Kaimai deviation and the closure of the section from Paeroa to Apata, the Thames Branch was realigned back to almost the original formation. The Toyota car assembly plant at Thames was a major source of traffic, but as local assembly wound down, this traffic was lost. In July 1991 the line was mothballed, with the chance of revival if forestry traffic developed. This did not happen, and most of the line was lifted in 1995-96, although a short length from Morrinsville to a dairy factory at Waitoa survived until 2000, but apparently never carried traffic after 1991.

The firm of A. & G. Price Ltd. at Thames is still in operation at Thames, its last locomotive to be produced was a 15 tonne 0-6-0 diesel-hydraulic shunter delivered to Borthwicks Feilding works in 1969.

Paeroa—Tauranga via Waihi

The first part of this line to be built was the line from Paeroa to the gold-mining town of Waihi, construction of which started in March 1900, soon after the completion of the railway to Thames. The main obstacle on this 20 km line was the Karangahake Tunnel, 1006 metres long through hard rock. The headings in this tunnel met in September 1904, and the line to Waihi was opened on 9 November 1905. Small tank engines, such as the rebuilt L class 4-4-2T locomotives, were used to work the Waihi branch.

At this time, the government was investigating a number of alternative railway routes to the Bay of Plenty. A route from the Mamaku summit on the Rotorua line was investigated, but proved to be inferior to an extension of the Waihi line. The fact that a Mamaku - Te Puke route was taken seriously is an indication of how poor the mapping of the more inaccessible parts of New Zealand was at this time. In 1909, the government adopted a plan for an "East Coast Main Trunk" (ECMT) railway, to link Auckland with the Bay of Plenty, and to eventually connect with Gisborne. The first sections of this railway to be authorised were from Mt Maunganui to Te Puke and on to Paengaroa, and then in 1911 an extension from Waihi to Athenree was

An Auckland to Taneatua express crosses the Karangahake double deck road-rail bridge over the Ohinemuri River on 12 February 1956. NZR

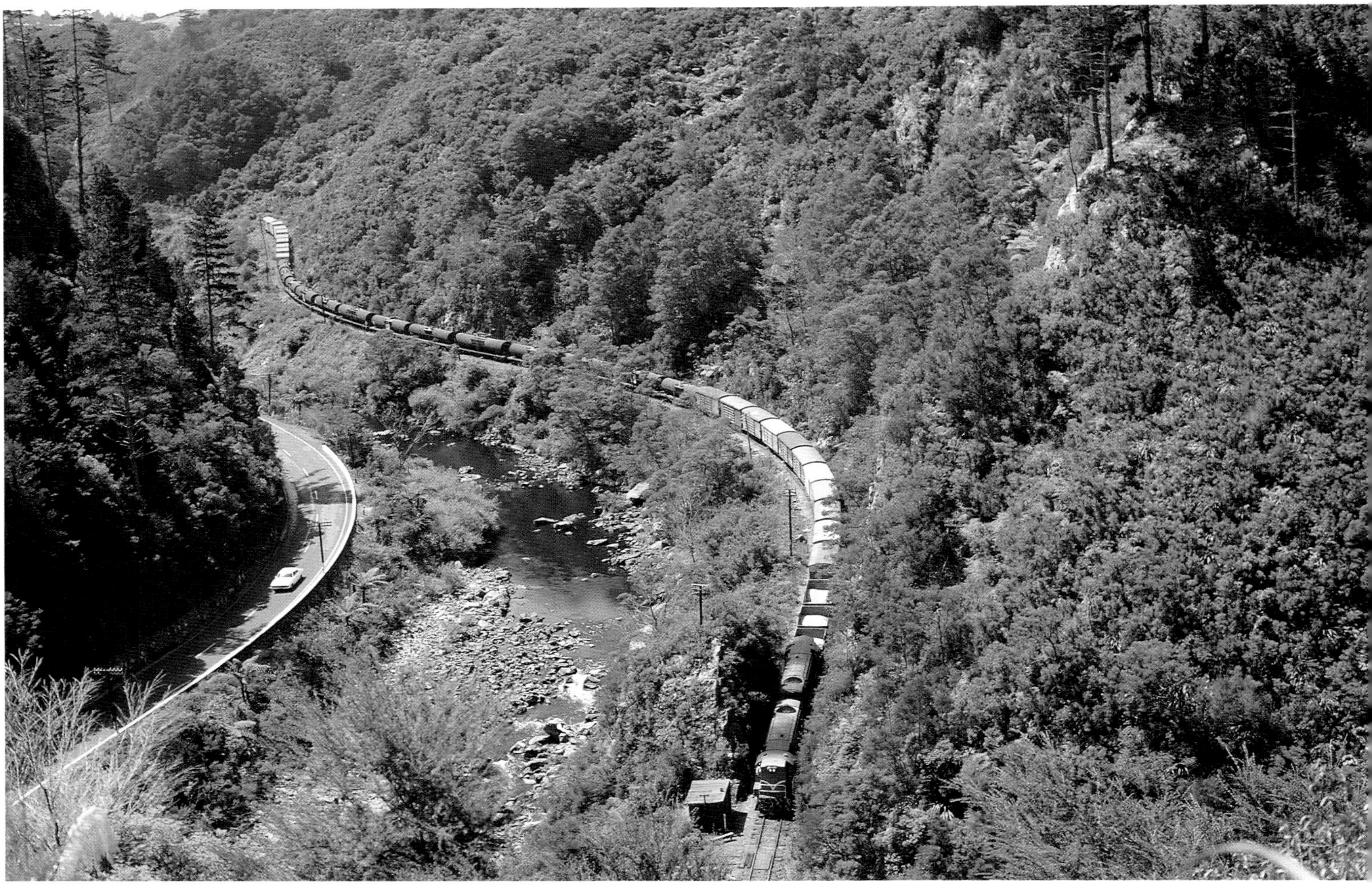

▲*In February 1978 two DI's make their way through the Karangahake Gorge near the entrance to the 1,006 metre Karangahake tunnel.* NORM DANIEL

▼*JB 1213 heads through the Karangahake Gorge with the last steam hauled goods train on 17 October 1967.* J.A.T. TERRY

Another view of JB 1213 on the last steam run through the Karangahake Gorge.
J.A.T. TERRY

authorised, as the first section of a Waihi–Tauranga line.

The ECMT construction was competing for resources with a number of other lines around the country, and progress at first was slow, with two periods when construction was halted completely. By 1920, the formation was nearly complete for the first 14 km to Athenree, but tracklaying could not commence as the bridges were not complete. The Public Works Department (PWD) workshops at Mount Maunganui had burnt down in 1919, and this had caused long delays in supplying bridge girders for all the Bay of Plenty lines.

In 1924, the PWD started a goods service to Athenree, and the next 9 km to Katikati was nearly complete. Also in 1924, the government let a contract to the English firm of Armstrong Whitworth & Co. for the 26 km section from Katikati to Te Puna. This change of policy indicated some dissatisfaction with progress on railway construction by the PWD and a hope that more rapid and possibly cheaper progress could be made by the greater use of machinery.

Armstrong Whitworth completed their section in four years, although they had some problems getting adequate foundations for bridges. This experiment did not lead to the use of contractors for later railway construction, but mechanised methods were increasingly used by the PWD.

The completion of the three long bridges near Tauranga by 1925 had joined Te Puna to Mount Maunganui and the line to Taneatua, so the PWD was able to hand over the last section of the route to Tauranga to NZR on 18 June 1928, and the Tauranga–Taneatua line on 2 September 1928.

The first NZR passenger service in 1928 took a full 12 hours between Auckland and Taneatua, but after a year the track was consolidated, and the "Taneatua Express" was introduced, on a daily 10 1/2 hour schedule. Because of the 1930s Depression, and wartime and later coal shortages, these expresses were only running on two or three days a week for most of their life. Ab and later J class steam engines worked passenger and freight trains in the Bay of Plenty until 1959.

In 1959 a faster daily railcar service was introduced, but only to Te Puke. This service only lasted only eight years. Largely because of the circuitous rail route from Auckland to the Bay of Plenty, it was one of the services cancelled in 1967, in the first cutbacks resulting from mechanical problems with the 88-seat articulated railcars.

Traffic on the first sections of the Bay of Plenty line had been light, which partly explained why light rails were used on the Waihi-Tauranga section. For the first decade, the freight traffic was handled by two daily mixed or freight trains to Taneatua, and another daily mixed to Tauranga. By the late 1930s, forestry development, especially from the new pine plantings, and more intensive dairying, was boosting traffic.

Work on a direct railway link from Pokeno, south of Auckland on the NIMT, to Paeroa began in 1938. About 27 km of formation had been completed when work stopped in 1940 because of the Second World War. This project would have reduced the distance between Auckland and the Bay of Plenty by nearly 80 km, but would not have improved the difficult stretch between Paeroa and Tauranga. By the time resources were again available, the situation had changed, and direct passenger routes were less important than better-graded routes for freight, so the Kaimai Tunnel line was eventually constructed instead. However, a short cut-off at Paeroa was installed in 1959, so trains to and from the Bay of Plenty no longer had to reverse there.

The massive boost to freight traffic on this line that followed the completion of the paper mill at Kawerau in 1955 put particular stress on the Paeroa - Tauranga section, with its 1 in 50 grades, and light rails which prevented the use of Da diesel locomotives. The rated loads for westbound trains were 265 and 345 tonnes for Ab and J class steam locomotives, and 600 tonnes for the 2-Co-Co-2 Df class diesels (not to be confused with the later Co-Co DF class), that were introduced to the Bay of Plenty line about 1960. It would not have been sensible to lay heavier track for the few years before the Kaimai Tunnel was opened, so as an interim measure, a fuel oil tank was installed at Tauranga in October 1965, and oil-burning Ja and Jb steam locomotives were assigned to the Bay of Plenty run. The arrival of DB and DI diesels, and a temporary traffic decline saw steam end in November 1967.

Pairs of DB and DI class diesels worked most trains

Above: An original DF on a goods train approaches Tahawai on the former Paeroa–Tauranga line on 3 August 1971. NZR

Right: A driver's cab view of the approach to the old Karangahake tunnel. DAVE SIMPSON

on this route from their introduction between 1965 and 1967 until the last through train ran on 12 September 1978. The section between Paeroa and Katikati was then closed, but Katikati to Apata was kept open for a period as a siding for kiwifruit shipments. Today, the only part of this route in use is the section between Waihi and Waikino operated by the Goldfields Railway.

Kaimai Tunnel route to Tauranga

In the late 1950s the forestry industries of the Bay of Plenty were booming, and the railway between Paeroa and Tauranga was becoming a real bottleneck. Mount Maunganui was also becoming an important port for forest products and other traffic from the Waikato and the Rotorua districts. Because of the circuitous rail route, much of this traffic to Mount Maunganui was travelling by road, and the big trucks were unpopular, especially when passing through towns. A Commission of Inquiry in 1962 concluded that the best answer was a rail tunnel through the Kaimai ranges, to provide a direct route from Hamilton and Kinleith to Mount Maunganui, and to shorten the route from Auckland. It recommended that at a later date the Mamaku route to Rotorua be replaced by a less steeply graded route from Paengaroa, to the east of Tauranga.

The difference between the Paeroa–Pokeno scheme of the 1930s and the Kaimai Tunnel scheme of the 1960s was that the first emphasised the shortest route, important for passenger traffic, and saw the Bay of Plenty as subsidiary to Auckland. The Kaimai scheme was to reduce the ruling grade for cheaper freight haulage, and was a response to the increasing role of Mount Maunganui as an export port. Work on the 25 km deviation, which includes an 8.85 km tunnel, began in 1965, with an estimated cost of $10.5 million.

A number of geological and geophysical surveys were made to try and find the best tunnel route through the complex volcanic rocks. It was 1969 before a tunnel route was chosen, and the actual tunnelling started. The tunnel proved to be very difficult to construct, with four men being killed by a cave-in near the western portal in January 1970. A 900 kW Jarva tunnelling machine bought for this project proved to be of little use, and could for many years be seen rusting away near the western portal. It was June 1976 before the headings met, and the tunnel and deviation was finally opened on 12 September 1978. The final cost was $69 million, reflecting both the difficulties of the work, and 10 years of inflation.

Initial gross tonnage on this line was 4 million tonnes/year. This new route has kept railways competitive for much of the Bay of Plenty traffic, over twenty trains per day pass through the tunnel, mostly hauled by pairs of DC locomotives, and weighing up to 2000 tonnes. As well as the forest related traffic, there is fertiliser and general traffic from Mount Maunganui.

Mount Maunganui is also used for steel traffic to and from the N.Z. Steel mill at Glenbrook, as more efficient handling and lower wharf costs justify a much longer rail haulage than would be needed if Auckland was used. A recent development has been dedicated

Whakatane Board Mills locomotive, FA 41, built by NZR (Addington) in 1893, is seen with a train of logs at Awakeri at the start of the 10 km private line on 13 July 1956. DEREK CROSS

traffic between the Port of Tauranga and its Metroport in South Auckland, linking Auckland customers to container ships calling at Tauranga. This currently uses 22 dedicated container trains running each weekend, and in mid-2001 weekday trains were being introduced.

After 24 years with no regular passenger services to the Bay of Plenty, The "Kaimai Express", using the Silver Fern railcars tranferred from the Notrh Island Main Trunk was introduced in December 1991. It was initially a morning service from Tauranga, returning from Auckland in the evening. In mid-2000, the service was changed to morning from Auckland, and lunchtime return from Tauranga, to enable the railcars to also provide a commuter service between Hamilton and Auckland, known as the "Waikato Connection".

Mt Maunganui Branch

This branch has had a chequered career, and has been left derelict twice, before recovering to be the hub of rail traffic in this area. A wharf was established at Mount Maunganui by 1910, for the unloading of railway construction material, and Mount Maunganui became the main PWD locomotive depot, with D, L and R class tank locomotives. Until 1924, this was the main railhead, and goods and passengers for Tauranga used the ferry across the harbour.

The PWD kept this branch when the main line was handed over to the NZR in 1928. At the time, the PWD was expecting that their workshops would have a continuing role providing steelwork for railway and other construction. The Depression from 1930 onwards resulted in the virtual closure of the workshops, and the branch had no regular traffic from about 1934 onwards. In 1942, the wharf end of the branch was lifted, and relaid to the RNZAF base, at what is now Tauranga airport. This was again virtually abandoned after the war.

The decision to use Mount Maunganui as the export port for paper from Kawerau resulted in the revival of this branch, with trains again running from August 1955. The branch was relaid with heavy rails, and finally handed over to NZR in January 1958. A new marshalling yard was built at Te Maunga, the junction station, but in recent years all mainline trains have run into Mount Maunganui, so it is effectively operated as part of the ECMT.

In the mid 1980s NZR was negotiating with the National Roads Board on a combined road and rail bridge across the Tauranga Harbour, to shorten the distance between Tauranga and Mount Maunganui, but these negotiations were not successful, and the bridge was built for road traffic only.

East Coast Main Trunk (Tauranga–Kawerau)

As mentioned above, the first section of the line east from Mount Maunganui was authorised in 1909, and this 21 km section to Te Puke was opened on 16 October 1913. Work continued during the First World War,

Two DAs with a logging train on the Murupara Branch in the early 1970s. NZR

but temporary bridges were necessary because of steel shortages. In 1915, work commenced on the line from Mount Maunganui to Tauranga, which required a 448 metre bridge across an arm of the Tauranga Harbour.

In October 1918, just before the war ended, passengers could reach Matata, 61 km east of Mount Maunganui, by rail, and the approach to the Tauranga Harbour bridge was complete. However this bridge, and the link to Tauranga, was not finished until 1924. The temporary bridges further east were then replaced by permanent steel bridges, and work started on the section to Taneatua.

The Public Works Department commenced a goods and passenger service to Taneatua in February 1926. The final handing over of the Tauranga - Taneatua section to New Zealand Railways occurred on 2 September 1928, following the completion of the Waihi - Tauranga section.

In March 1953, the decision was made to site a large paper mill at Kawerau. Work on a 14 km branch from Hawkens Junction on the ECMT to the mill site started on 12 April 1953, and by August the rails had reached Kawerau. The first train arrived at Kawerau on 26 October 1953, only six months after work started.

Once the mill commenced production in late 1955, this branch became the major source of traffic in the eastern Bay of Plenty. The tonnage of "other goods" carried on the ECMT east of Mount Maunganui grew from 90,000 tonnes in 1954/55, to 315,000 tonnes in 1959/60 and 520,000 tonnes in 1964/65. The importance of this line is now officially recognised by the East Coast Main Trunk being defined as terminating at Kawerau, rather than Taneatua. Currently the main traffic is export logs and newsprint, of which more than half is exported through Mt. Maunganui, and the remainder travels to destinations throughout New Zealand.

The easy grades between Kawerau and Mount Maunganui have enabled very long trains to be operated on this section. A 2700 tonne test train was operated on this route back in 1970, and trains now regularly exceed 2000 tonnes.

Murupara Branch

This branch, built to tap the forests of the Kaingaroa Plateau, was the last major extension of the NZR network. Work begun in 1951 on a line south from near Edgecumbe to Murupara on the edge of the Kaingaroa plateau. It was originally intended to build a pulp and paper mill near Murupara. Before very much work had been done however, it was decided to build the mill at Kawerau, where geothermal steam could provide a cheap source of energy. Another factor was that the climate of Murupara, especially the winter mist and fog, did not encourage the idea of siting a large town there. The route was therefore altered, so that the Murupara branch ran from Kawerau to Murupara, rather than directly from the ECMT. Major earthworks were required to limit the ruling grade against loaded log trains to 1 in 60. Heavy earthmoving machinery enabled these earthworks to be completed quickly, and prefabricated track sections were then laid at the rate of 3 km per week. The first logs were loaded at Galatea, 48 km from Kawerau on 4 April 1955.

Steam locomotives were not allowed through the forest areas, and De 506, a Bo-Bo diesel electric locomotive, was used for construction and the first log trains. A regular service to the terminus at Murupara, 57 km from Kawerau, started on 15 January 1957. Both this line and the Kawerau branch were operated by the Ministry of Works (the successor to the PWD) until 1 July 1957, although it appears that NZR locomotives were used. DG locomotives were put into service on this line about the time of the handing over. From October 1963 onwards, there was a long period in which a pair of DAs were standard, hauling 1500 tonne log trains. The annual tonnage of logs carried increased from 730,000 tonnes in 1960 to 1.126,000 tonnes in 1965.Until the opening of the Kaimai tunnel in 1978, Kawerau had a "captive" group of DAs, which were not allowed to work trains on the light rail sections east of Tauranga.

Competitive pressure from the large off-highway log trucks has made it necessary for NZR to search for more economical operating methods. After a period of long trains, typically a trio of DC locomotives hauling 53 USL bogie log wagons, Tranz Rail is now considering using shorter trains with a single DFT, which will require a turntable at Murupara. In the last few years the traffic on this line has increasingly been export logs to Mount Maunganui.

Taneatua Branch

This line was intended to be part of the East Coast Main Trunk to Gisborne, but Taneatua has proved to be the eastern terminus of railways in the Bay of Plenty. The

J 1211 with an excursion train climbs the Mamaku Bank on 23 April 1989, Lake Rotorua in the background. G.B. CHURCHMAN

ECMT is now defined as Hamilton–Kawerau, and Taneatua is now on a branch line. The line across the Rangitaiki Plains follows a southerly route, to avoid areas which were swampy when the line was built, and therefore misses the large town of Whakatane. A private line was built from Awakeri to the Whakatane Board Mill, just over the river from Whakatane, but the line has never provided a public freight or passenger service.

A small amount of work was done on the line past Taneatua about the time the line to Taneatua was opened, but in 1929 the effort was shifted to the Rotorua –Taupo line, and nothing was done during the Depression years. Survey work past Taneatua started again in 1939, but ceased in 1940 because of the War, and never resumed.

Traffic between Gisborne and the Auckland district was transhipped here, but this traffic ended after the deregulation of road transport. Another main source of traffic was the Rangitaiki Plains Co-operative Dairy Company at Edgecumbe. The Edgecumbe Earthquake of 2 March 1987 caused some spectacular damage to this line in and around Edgecumbe station.

In October 1999 Tranz Rail took over the operation of the former private railway connecting Awakeri to the Whakatane Board Mill. However, after this traffic shifted to road, all regular freight on this line ceased in May 2001, and the line is likely to be mothballed. The most recent traffic to Taneatua was fresh vegetables, and this section of line is also not currently being used. Its prospects of future traffic are not good, as although there will be logs coming out of this district, they are more likely to be trucked to the large log yard near Kawerau.

Rotorua Branch

The 50.5 km line from Putaruru to the scenic thermal terrains of Rotorua involves a steep ascent through attractive forest over the Mamaku Ranges on grades of 1 in 35.

The original undertaking to build the line came from a private company, the Thames Valley and Rotorua Railway Company. Authorisation for the line was granted under the District Railways Act 1877 and the Railway Construction and Land Act 1881. The original route proposed was to be via Putaruru and Lichfield (south of Putaruru) to Rotorua, but giving evidence before the Public Accounts Committee in 1885, a Mr J. Stewart, engineer of the company, said that the junction for the line to Rotorua would be at Putaruru and the branch would run from Putaruru to Lichfield.

On 21 December 1885 the uncompleted section of line from Morrinsville was taken over by the Government, although the company continued the construction and the line to Tirau (then known as Oxford) was opened on 8 March 1886. The section from there to Putaruru and Lichfield was opened on 21 June 1886. Although at the time of purchase no work was underway from Putaruru to Rotorua, the Public Works Statement for 1886 reported that a survey was underway and contract plans for the first 13 km would be ready by April. During March 1887 a contract for the formation and platelaying for the section as far as Ngatira (12 km) was let. Earthworks on the new section were classed as heavy, and a gradient of 1 in 35 was needed.

At the Rotorua end, 8 km of the line were set aside for Maori labour and several formation sections were let, which progressed satisfactorily. In his 1888 report the Minister of Public Works said that the first contract from Putaruru to Ngatira had been completed, but as there was no traffic it was not proposed to open it. The intervening distance between Ngatira and Ngongotaha had been surveyed for contract. A survey was also in progress for a 10 km road to connect the proposed station at Okohiriki (Mamaku) with the Oxford-Ohinemutu road. Apart from completion of the road survey it was not intended that any more work in connection with a Putaruru to Rotorua line be done

▲*JB 1218 lifts train 284 out of the Tarukenga yard and onwards up the hill to Mamaku on 3 May 1956.* THE LATE DEREK CROSS

◀*K 900 approaches Putaruru on the Kinleith Branch on 19 February 1957.* NZR.

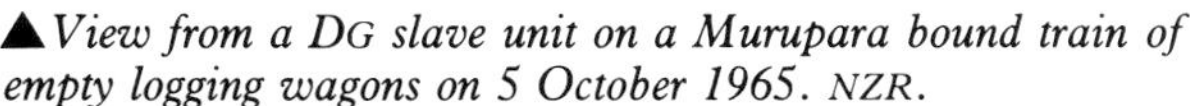

▲*View from a* DG *slave unit on a Murupara bound train of empty logging wagons on 5 October 1965.* NZR.

▶KA *953 on a goods train from Frankton to Kinleith is seen between Putaruru and Lichfield on 25 May 1966.* J.A.T. TERRY

▼*A view of Kawerau yard on 5 October 1965.* NZR.

at that time.

In his 1889 report the Minister of Public Works said that no work had been done since his last statement, that £70,000 (the cost beyond Putaruru) was not being utilised and he recommended that work be recommenced to complete the line up to the Saddle which would then link up with the proposed 10 km road to connect with the present (Oxford-Rotorua) Ohinemutu road. This would reduce the coach journey to 18 km and it would then be possible to travel from Auckland to Rotorua in one day instead of two.

During February 1890 a contract for 17 km beyond Ngatira was let to a Daniel Fulton, this being known as the Kaponga section. In 1891 it was reported that work on the Kaponga contract was well advanced and it was proposed to abandon the scheme for the 10 km road connection and to extend the railway a further 7 km to intersect the road from Cambridge to Rotorua. Daniel Fulton completed his contract in December 1891 and a contract for the extension to Tarukenga was let in January 1892. As the distance to Rotorua would only be 14.5 km from the completed railway and the formation work of about 10 km at the Rotorua end was completed, it was decided to complete the railway to Rotorua.

The line from Putaruru to Tarukenga (36.7 km) was opened on 24 November 1893, thus enabling tourists to reach Rotorua from Auckland in one day. In June 1894 a contract for the completion of the Rotorua station buildings was let to a Mr A. Gardiner for £2,823 and this contract was completed on 31 January 1895. The line had actually been completed two months earlier and opened to traffic on 8 December 1894 when the first train into Rotorua was drawn into Rotorua by two 'J' class locomotives.

Of interest are the brick vats at Tirau, Ngatira and at Lichfield, said to be relics of Thames Valley and Rotorua Railway Company. Maximum engine loads for certain classes of locomotives over the Mamakus have been as follows: Old J (2-6-0) – 80 tonnes, J (4-8-2) – 220 tonnes, K (4-8-4) – 260 tonnes, DA & DC (A1A-A1A) – 380 tonnes, DX (Co-Co) – 640 tonnes.

The first express train service to Rotorua began on 8 December 1894. It ran just once a week from Rotorua at 9.00 am on Mondays and 8.00 am on Tuesdays from Auckland, taking 8 hr 40 min, an average speed of less than 30 km/h. In winter time when traffic fell away, the express was discontinued altogether and replaced by a mixed train providing three slow services each way each week.

In December 1903 dining cars were introduced on the Rotorua Expresses between Auckland and Putaruru. These were the first dining cars on which catering was provided by the Railways Department instead of by private contractors. The service lasted until 1917 when wartime conditions brought about their withdrawal. Late in 1917 the Rotorua Express, now down to a 7 hour schedule, was combined with the Thames Express (due to manpower shortages) thus extending the run to 7 hr 40 min. Then in June 1919 a coal shortage saw all provincial expresses cancelled, and the only rail connection for a period was a mixed train taking 12 hours. But the express was back in December 1919 and the speed limit was raised to 80 km/h in 1925 resulting in journey times being reduced to 6 hr 50 min down and 6 hr 40 min up. The famous Ab class locomotives were now used on the trains and publicity of the period extolled the attractions of the "Thermal Wonderland of New Zealand".

In May 1930 the express became the "Rotorua Limited" with a six hour schedule and the passenger cars (Aa class) were the first in New Zealand to be steel panelled with enclosed entrance vestibules. Two observation cars with lounge chairs were also built but after a trial during this depression period were withdrawn and converted to ordinary coaches. These cars were numbered Aa 1686 and 1687.

The "Limited" was soon dropped from the title but the service remained. During World War II passenger loadings built up but larger locomotives in the form of the new J and K classes were available to help out. With drastic coal shortages the service was reduced to three trains a week. In 1951 further cuts reduced the service to two trains per week. Railway Road Services was now offering five or six trips a week each way between Auckland and Rotorua over a newly improved highway.

On 9 February 1959 articulated "Fiat" railcars took over the service. This provided a boost to passenger services with a 5 hr 10 min journey time, but like other provincial services it made a loss and on 11 November 1968 the service was ended.

In 1988 it was announced that the site of the Railways Travel Centre including the Rotorua Station was to be redeveloped, and the yard at Rotorua was lifted during 1989, with a new freight yard being created near Koutu. This proved to be an unfortunate decision, as in December 1991 a railcar service to Rotorua was reinstated, using former "Silver Fern" cars. For a while there were two services each way daily, but in April 1995 the afternoon service was restricted to Friday and Sunday, and in November 1996 it ceased completely. In 2000, the timings were adjusted, to enable the introduction of a Hamilton–Auckland commuter service using these railcars.

Meanwhile freight traffic had been declining, as most forestry traffic went by road rather than rail. In 1994, the "Bay Raider" service was introduced, to carry freight between Auckland and Hawkes Bay via Rotorua, initially using "road-railer" wagons and later containers, but this ceased in 1999. At the time of writing, no regular freight trains had run to Rotorua since 10 June 2000. The future of rail services to Rotorua is very much in doubt, complicated by the imminent sale of the Tranz Scenic part of Tranz Rail.

Kinleith Branch

As mentioned, the Thames Valley and Rotorua Railway Company had built the railway south of Morrinsville as far as Lichfield. The section from Putaruru to Lichfield (8 km) was opened in 1886 but lasted in its original form for only 11 years. By 1906 the Taupo Totara Timber Company had built a tramway to transport timber from Mokai near Taupo to Putaruru, including the NZR formation from Putaruru to Lichfield. This 82 km private tramway lasted until 1946 by which time most of the native forests in the area it served had been removed.

The Government of the day realised that the line had a wider potential and decided in September 1946 to acquire the first 29 km of the line from Putaruru to Kinleith. Accordingly this section was opened again on 9 June 1947 under the control of the Public Works Department which used the geared steam locomotives bought from the Taupo Totara Timber Company. The line was not suitable for carrying the heavy traffic that would be generated after the development of the Kinleith pulp and paper mill - it had grades of 1 in 36 and curves as sharp as 60 metre radius as well as being laid with light rail. Major works to reconstruct the line began in 1949 with the section from Putaruru to Lichfield, where the grade was reduced from 1 in 44 to 1 in 70 and to ease the curves from 201 m radius to 322 m radius. Some 57,500 cu. metres of spoil was involved in the realignment and the line was handed over to NZR on 12 June 1950. The Tirau to Putaruru section of the Rotorua Branch, where the 1 in 40 to 1 in 50 Taumangi Bank included 150 m radius curves, was also realigned to improve the ruling grade.

Much more work was involved with the Lichfield to Kinleith section. The grade was reduced from 1 in 36 to 1 in 63 in the southbound direction, while major deviations were made to reduce the sharp curvature. The rebuilt line was opened as far as Tokoroa in 1951 and in October of the following year it was completed right through to Kinleith, just one year before pulp and paper production began at the mill.

The Kinleith mill is today a major source of Tranz Rail traffic, with most trains now going directly to Mount Maunganui.

Taupo proposals

One of the earliest routes proposed for the North Island Main Trunk was via Taupo and Napier, but after one look at this route by the surveyors it was abandoned. Just before the First World War, the Taupo Totara Timber Company, which operated an 82 km timber tramway south from Putaruru to Mokai, just north of Lake Taupo, tried to get parliamentary support for a scheme to lay a branch to Taupo, for passengers and general freight. The proposal eventually lapsed, partly because of a competing proposal to build a line from Rotorua to Taupo, and partly because of difficulties with the acquisition of Maori land in the Taupo district.

After much local agitation, work started on a line from Rotorua south towards Taupo in 1929. Only a few kilometres of formation had been constructed when work was stopped by the Depression. One of the reasons for the lack of railway development in this area was that much of the volcanic plateau was unable to be used for livestock farming because of trace element deficiencies which were only discovered and cured about 1950.

A railway extension southward from Rotorua was seen as a natural continuation from the Paengaroa - Rotorua line proposed by the 1962 Commission of Inquiry, but since this scheme was abandoned, there has been little likelihood of a Rotorua - Taupo line being built. The Paengaroa - Rotorua scheme was very much alive in the early 1970s, and would probably have gone ahead if the timber from the southern Kaingaroa forest had gone north to a mill in the Rotorua or Tauranga areas, but the logs were instead sent east by road to a mill north of Napier.

In 1946, the Government took over the Taupo Totara Timber Co line, to convert the northern part of it into a heavy-duty railway to the mill being built at Kinleith. There was talk of the line being reconstructed south of Kinleith and extended to Taupo, but this proposal disappeared after the 1949 election. The proposal was revived several times, but the traffic offering has never been sufficient.

A third proposal raised in the early 1980s, and still a possibility, is for an extension southwards of the Murupara line through the Kaingaroa forest to Taupo. This would be too circuitous a route for most traffic to Auckland or the Waikato, so it would be mainly used for logs to the Kawerau pulp mill, and wood and wood products, especially plywood, from Taupo to Mount Maunganui. This plan seemed to be viable about the mid-1980s, until deregulation and restructuring made NZR lose interest in any new capital expenditure. This situation is even more the case with Tranz Rail, who with their present owners are highly unlikely to want to invest capital to build significant railway extensions, nor do the forest owners seem very interested in such an extension.

A DB shunts at Hikutaia on the Thames Branch in April 1978.
DAVE SIMPSON

CHAPTER EIGHT

North Island Main Trunk

For many railfans the words North Island Main Trunk cannot fail to stir emotions. The 680 km line linking Wellington and Auckland is New Zealand's busiest and most important and not only has it seen the most powerful locomotives—steam, diesel and electric—to run over New Zealand rails but the history of its trains and townships is somehow intertwined with New Zealand's national identity. In addition the line courses through some of the North Island's finest scenery.

The building of a main trunk railway between Wellington and Auckland was a fundamental plank in Vogel's 1870 "Great Public Works" policy. At that stage it was no more than a dream—no definite route was specified, no survey had been made. Inter-provincial trade was carried out by coastal vessels. There had been virtually no penetration into the remote interior. In 1872 the Minister of Native Affairs, Donald McLean confessed that the King Country was a part of the colony over which the Government "had no practical control". The hostility of the local Maori tribes sealed off the King Country.

By 1880, not much had happened to achieve the trunk railway. A north western railway out of Wellington had been commenced but then suspended. A privately owned wooden tramway from Foxton to Palmerston North had been taken over by the Public Works Department and converted into a steel railed line, a railway had been opened from Palmerston North via Marton to Wanganui and further lines opened in Taranaki, and in the Auckland district the line through Mercer had been extended into the Waikato as far as Te Awamutu (160 km) on the border of the King Country.

In 1882 more amicable relationships between the Government and the Maniapoto chiefs of the King Country resulted in both chiefs, Wahanui and Rewi,

A WAB hauls a Auckland–Wellington "Daylight Limited" near Taumarunui in the 1930s. NZR

A construction train on the Raurimu Spiral circa 1906. NZR

withdrawing their objections to the railway and in fact they made a gift of the railway reserve through their tribal domain. The same year the passage of the North Island Main Trunk Loan Act authorised the raising of £1 million, subject to a survey being approved by the General Assembly, for which £10,000 was allocated. Four reconnaissance surveys were made of the routes that had been surveyed by John Carruthers nine year earlier. John Rochfort and his party were assigned the "central route" from Marton or Feilding northwards to Te Awamutu; Charles Wilson Hursthouse, a Waipa-Mokau line from Te Awamutu to Waitara in Taranaki; Robert West Holmes and Morgan Carkeek, a line from Stratford to Te Uira 32 km south of Te Awamutu; and George Phipps Williams, a line from Te Awamutu or Cambridge south-eastwards to Hastings.

The survey party led by John Rochfort, a civil engineer with 33 years experience in England and New Zealand, set out from Marton in June 1883 on the first of four treks over the central route during the following 16 months. He found that the line from Marton to the head of the Hautapu Valley, at what is now Waiouru, provided a near-natural river-grade allowing a ruling gradient of 1 in 70. From the Karioi district he found a table land some 22 km long, generally poor in quality but heavily timbered, a part of which would be traversed by the railway and would necessitate "bad crossings" of the Manganui-o-te-Ao and Managatote (Makatote) depressions, the former 30 metre and the latter 60 metre deep. From Waimarino, Rochfort's route descended over 50 km to Taumaranui. There was another ascent of 45 km northwards to the Poro-o-Tarao summit from which the descent to Otorohanga occupied 51 km. From there onwards to Te Awamutu any very sharp gradients were relatively short. He indicated with reasonable accuracy the total length of his line to be between 338 and 354 km.

Following completion of the reconnaissance surveys by the four parties, a select committee of the House of Representatives resolved in 1884 "to recommend the central route from Marton to Te Awamutu as the best for the North Island Main Trunk Railway". The conditions necessary to the raising of the Main Trunk loan having been met, the first sod was ceremoniously turned on 15 April 1885 on the bank of the Puniu River south of Te Awamutu. Those in attendance included the Maniapoto chiefs Rewi and Whanaui and the Premier, Robert Stout.

The first contract to be let was for the 2.25 km section which included the piercing of the 1 km Poro-o-Tarao tunnel through the Mokau-Ongarue watershed and its immediate approaches, sited remotely some 77 km south of the Te Awamutu railhead. The intention was to begin with this work so as to avoid delays in continuing beyond the summit once the easier work to the tunnel was completed. However, the tunnel proved very arduous and its construction lasted for 6 years. As the route of the line went through country of difficult access

▲*Goods train no. 456 was not overly long on 21 April 1961, seen here passing through Hihitahi with KA 934 on the front.* J.A.T. TERRY

▼*KA 960 heads a goods train up the Raurimu Spiral on 15 January 1963. Raurimu Station and township can be seen in the background.* J.A.T. TERRY

*The old line through the Square in Palmerston North was particularly associated with the steam era. K*A *935 arrives at Palmerston North with the Night Limited.* OIL PAINTING BY THE LATE P.J. BAKER

and where there was no European settlement, it was necessary to build roads to certain parts to facilitate the carrying out of the works and limited use was made of some rivers such as the Wanganui River. Construction did not proceed very far when reductions in the vote for the Main Trunk line in 1885 delayed construction work and represented the first of a number of delays during the first 15 years of the project resulting from the vagaries of political and economic pressures. Nevertheless by 1887 the line had been opened to Te Kuiti, 42 km south of Te Awamutu and at the southern end from Marton, 30 km had been opened for traffic.

The heaviest earthworks and most difficult engineering lay in between. The crossings of the deeply cut gullies of the Makohine, Manga-te-weka and the Toi Toi were to require high viaducts. Substantial viaducts were also required at Makatote, Hapuawhenua, Toanui and Manganui-o-te-Ao.

In the 1890s much pressure was exerted to have the route of the line deviated through Taranaki and two more select committees of the House of Representatives would be convened before it was ultimately resolved in 1900 that there would be no deviation of the route from that originally surveyed. Gradually the line was completed over the next 8 years.

By October 1906 the rails from the Taihape section had reached Turangarere. The deadline for completion of the line had been set as November 1908, and to ensure that this was met, the Minister of Public Works, Hall-Jones, almost doubled the workforce of 1300 men, with 600 men being put on the central section. In December 1906 came the first use of mechanical power with the introduction of a steam-navvy to engage in excavation work, although it could only move along rails and thus its usefulness was restricted. By December of the following year all looked to be on schedule. Following a bet between Hall-Jones and the resident engineer at Ohakune, F.W. Furkert, that the railway would be complete three months early by August so that Members of Parliament and other dignitaries could travel overland to visit the United States "Great White Fleet" in Auckland, strenuous efforts were made to complete the viaducts and earthworks. The Taonui and Hapuawhenua viaducts were complete by April 1908 and the Makatote on 10 July 1908.

On 3 August 1908 the rails from north and south met at Manganui-o-te-Ao. On 8 August 1908 an 11 car parliamentary train completed a 20 hr 30 minute journey over the complete line from Wellington to Auckland. The state of the track in many parts of the central section was temporary and many improvements were required before it could be considered complete. On 6 November 1908 the last spike was ceremoniously driven home at Manganui-o-te-Ao by Prime Minister Sir Joseph Ward. Through trains began running the following day, initially a two day service between Wellington and Auckland, until through overnight Main Trunk expresses were introduced on 14-15 February 1909.

With the completion of the construction works in the central North Island the final step was the acquisition of the Wellington and Manawatu Railway's line between Wellington and Longburn, 135 km, which was formally handed over on Monday 7 December 1908 at a luncheon in the Wellington Town Hall.

With the development of traffic over the complete Main Trunk, it became obvious that many gradients and curves needed easing and that more powerful locomotives were needed. The latter saw the building of the compound "Pacific" A Class 4-6-2 locomotives built for the opening of the Main Trunk, and then the X "Mountain" class 4-8-2 locomotives used between Taihape and Taumarunui. Later in the 1920s came the experiments with the unsuccessful 4-6-2 and 2-6-4 Garratts and in the 1930s the 4-8-4 K's and Ka's. In the diesel era the Main Trunk saw the A1A-A1A class DA diesel-electrics introduced as from 1955, which in turn gave way to the powerful Co-Co class DX diesel-electric locomotives in 1972. Most recently the Palmerston North to Hamilton section has seen the most powerful locomotives yet used in New Zealand—the class 30 electric, now classified as the EF class.

The continual move to improve alignments so as to eliminate severe curvature, gradients and other operational difficulties saw plans adopted in the 1920s for two major deviations at Auckland and Wellington—the Westfield Deviation and Tawa Flat deviations respectively. The Westfield deviation was intended to avoid the steep grade up the Parnell Bank to Remuera and Newmarket Junction. This would also eliminate the bottle-neck with the combined suburban traffic and Main Trunk traffic crawling up through the single tracked Parnell Tunnel. The 14 km deviation included a 3 km causeway through Judge's Bay, Hobson Bay and the Orakei Basin. It also involved a 596 metre double tracked tunnel at Purewa. The highest point on this deviation was only 24 metre compared with 81 metre at Remuera on the original line. Work on the deviation together with the new Auckland Railway station began in the summer of 1924-1925. In September 1929 the down line was opened for single-line working of through goods traffic, and the following year, in May 1930, the up line was opened. Like other metropolitan railway construction of the period such as the Hutt Valley branch in Wellington, the whole 16 km from Auckland to Westfield was devoid of level crossings, all intersections of rail and road being furnished with overbridges or underpasses.

After World War Two, traffic had significantly increased and the pressing needs for improvement included track duplication between Tawa and Plimmerton, with deviations to improve the winding section around the Porirua Inlet and the replacement of the original single track timber-truss bridge across the entrance to the Paremata Inlet. Work on the Tawa to Plimmerton deviations started in 1950 with the duplication of the Tawa to Porirua section and by October 1961 traffic was running over the entire deviation to Plimmerton.

Major improvements were also needed at Palmerston North, where even before World War I, facilities were clearly inadequate to cope with the traffic, coming not only from north and south but also from Taranaki in the east and Napier in the west. A plan to improve traffic flow in 1914 was dropped following the outbreak of war. The next active move came in Gordon Coates's eight-year plan of 1924, proposing a devia-

KA 945 with goods train 456 arrives at Ohakune from the south on 3 September 1964. This locomotive has now been preserved by Steam Incorporated. R.J. MANN

The Raurimu Spiral

While the NZR network contains many great feats of civil engineering, undoubtedly the best known is the spiral at Raurimu. The problem of how to descend from National Park on the central plateau to the Raurimu Flat below, a drop of 218 metres in under 6 km of direct distance, was what faced early surveyors. The general slope of the land is from the south-east down to the north-west and two narrow bedded streams flow north – the Piopiotea to the east and the Makaretu to the west. At the time of the early surveys in the 1890s the terrain, like most of the central region, was covered in tall, dense rain forest. Accordingly it was all the more remarkable that R.W. Holmes, a senior engineer with the Public Works Department, worked out this ingenious configuration in 1898, which avoided an earlier proposal of a 19 km alternate route involving nine viaducts. The spiral as built rises 71 metres in 3.6 km of track, incorporating two tunnels, 384 metres and 96 metres long, one complete circle and three horseshoe bends. The sharpest radius of curvature at the lower horseshoe bend is 198 metres, while the radius of curvature in the higher horseshoe bends and the circle is 200 metres. Most of the spiral is on a 1 in 50 gradient, while the average gradient between Raurimu and National Park is 1 in 52. The spiral has the effect of doubling the "line of sight" distance between these two stations of 5.6 km to a rail distance of 11 km. Ascending on board a train, the spiral provides an interesting viewing experience as the track just travelled over appears to one side below while the track about to be travelled over appears to the other side above. Viewed from the highway at the level of Raurimu, a train will appear from one side, disappear from view, re-emerge some minutes later in the opposite direction, disappear again and finally re-emerge travelling in the original direction, either higher or lower than it was initially. NZR

The Turangarere Loop

Some 23 km north of Taihape and 16 km south of Waiouru is another striking civil engineering feature of the North Island Main Trunk. Like the Raurimu Spiral, it bears the stamp of R.W. Holmes who located it in 1888. Like the Raurimu Spiral it considerably lengthens the rail distance so as to achieve a modest 1 in 70 gradient between two points of sharp altitude change in a short "line of sight" distance. The Turangarere Loop closely follows the course of the Hautapu River. Electrics 30-140 and 30-186 with train no. 700 on 28 February 1989. MARK COLE

The "Scenic Daylight", the successor to the steam hauled "Daylight Limited", heads through Mangapehi in the late 1960s.

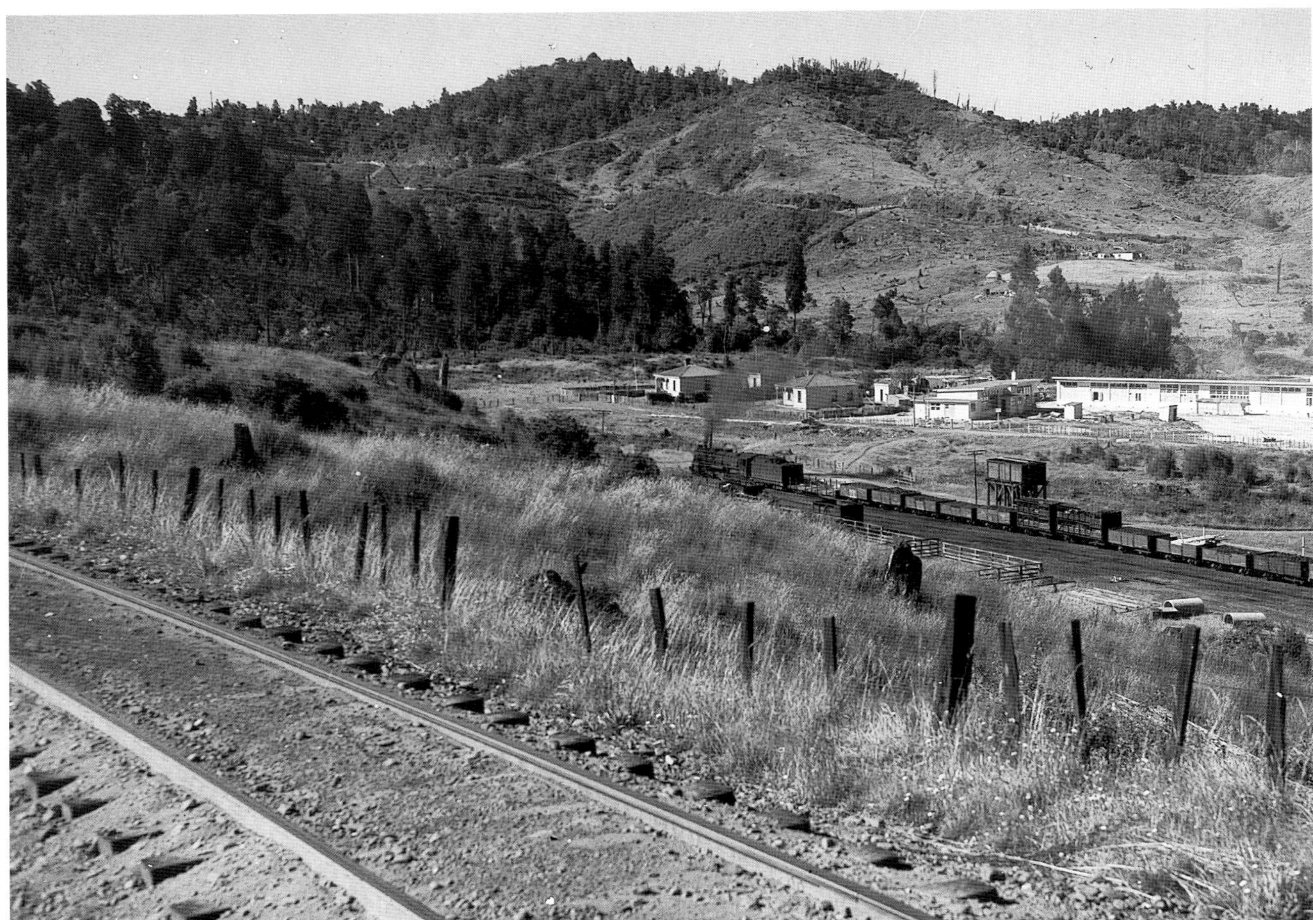

With a goods train comprising wagons of coal, timber and livestock, a KA pulls away southbound from Raurimu Station yard in the 1950s. After travelling through the bottom loop it will shortly pass over the track in the immediate foreground in the opposite direction. NZR

tion from the line through the Square at Palmerston North to Milson, with a new Palmerston North Station and yard. A start was made on this project in 1926, although it was initially a low-key job. Work was stepped up in 1928 and the number of men engaged increased to 204. However, on 18 April 1929 the Minister of Public Works, E.A. Ransom, ordered the works stopped on the grounds that the capital expenditure was no longer justified by the rate of traffic increase. Work resumed again in 1938 under the first Labour Government, but was halted again after the outbreak of World War II. Not until 1957 did the project get underway again. In 1959 the first stage was completed with the laying of the 12 km of single track from Longburn to Roslyn. Next followed the new marshalling yard, goods shed, locomotive depot, the deviation to the Woodville line and the new passenger station. The new deviation and station was opened officially on 21 October 1963. Another small but significant improvement at Longburn was the replacement of the old Longburn Bridge on a 2 km deviation to a new crossing down river so as to allow maximum speed of approach. This had been opened on 18 October 1960.

By far the largest and most expensive deviations on the Main Trunk, however, have been those over the central section between Marton and Horopito built since the 1960s. The first of these was the Mangaweka deviation. This replaced the tortuous section of track involving five tunnels, the most northerly of which was known as the "Black Hole". This was built on a curve of 180-metre radius and very close to the cliff face above the Rangitikei River. The cost of maintaining the 9 km section and inconvenience of operating it, together with the ageing of the high steel viaduct over the Mangateweka Gully from 1903, led the Railways in 1961 to seek better ground on the opposite river bank. Major engineering features of the new deviation include the 181 metre long, 77 metre high North Rangitikei Viaduct, the 181 metre long 72 metre Kawhatau Viaduct, a 100 metre high embankment across Blind Gully, and the 315 metre long, 75 metre high South Rangitikei Viaduct. The deviation has a maximum gradient of 1 in 100 and the pre-stressed concrete viaducts involve minimal maintenance. The work was due to have been completed in 1977 but following the collapse on 5 May 1975 of the steel truss false-work used to launch the hollow box superstructure onto its twin shaft concrete piers, the works were considerably delayed. Eventually the new deviation was opened on 18 November 1981 and four days later a 20-car special excursion passenger train ran over it. Features of the new viaducts include the existence of wind and earthquake absorbent laminated rubber and steel pads placed between each pile and the base of each upright pier. Another device is a steel torsion bar designed to control the degree of rocking during an earthquake. One bar is fitted to the base of each pier leg to prevent the possibility of cyclic acceleration, without which the viaduct could sway so much as to topple sideways.

In 1985 significant deviations were brought into service at Mangaonoho which eliminated two tunnels ("Moa" and "Kiwi"), Taihape which eliminated the 115 metre "Hedgehog" tunnel on a twisting section of track, and at Hapuwhenua, where a new, graceful, curved concrete viaduct replaced the old steel viaduct. Also eliminated were the 208 metre Hapuwhenua tunnel immediately to the north of the viaduct which was daylighted, and the former 122 metre high, 34 metre long Taonui viaduct.

To the north between Waimiha and Mangapehi, work had begun on replacing the old Poro-o-Tarao tunnel in 1974. The old tunnel was in bad condition because of ground movements and clearances inside the tunnel were very restricted. The new 1.3 km long tunnel opened in 1980 contained ample clearance for overhead catenary. Construction of it was nevertheless hindered by the same unstable ground conditions that brought about the demise of the first tunnel.

The purpose of the new deviations, apart from reducing gradients and easing curvatures, was to increase clearances for the electrification works that began in 1981 and which were completed on 24 June 1988. This coincided with a period when road transport deregulation produced a 20% decrease of total rail traffic, so this $400 million project was seen by many as a white elephant, which only served to add to the corporation's large debt burden. Until 1993 the electric locomotives were not even normally trusted with passenger trains. They now haul both the day "Overlander", which replaced the "Silver Fern" railcars which were transferred to the Tauranga and Rotorua services in 1991, and the night "Northerner". Now that overall rail traffic is again increasing, the electrification is much more appreciated, and there is little doubt that the 410 km of catenary utilised by the powerful class EF electrics enhances the status of the "Trunk" as New Zealand's most important traffic artery. Recent developments are linked to the use of rail as an extension of overseas shipping, with the Port of Auckland using a dedicated container wagon service to and from an "inland port" at Palmerston North. Tranz Rail is also moving to standard trains, comprising either 28 container wagons or 22 of the new-generation box wagons, linking Auckland with the South Island.

Raetihi Branch

The 13.7 km branch line from Ohakune on the Main Trunk to Raetihi was a politically inspired railway, like so many others. It was built to fulfil an election promise, being opened on 18 December 1917 at which time it was proclaimed as being the start of a new line to Wanganui. The line was authorised by Parliament in 1911 with Rangataua as the intended junction. This was changed in 1913 to Ohakune, so making the station and its settlement "Ohakune Junction".

There was little remarkable about the line. It ran on a steady downgrade from the junction except for one short uphill length of 1 in 45 south of Makaranui. Heading towards Ohakune there was a short length of 1 in 45 near the junction. One of the stations, Rochfort, was named after well known surveyor, John Rochfort. Passenger services ended on 16 December 1951. With most of the bush areas milled out there was no real need for the line, but it lingered on until 1 January 1968. Locomotives which worked the branch included Wf and Ww tanks and A, Aa and Ab Pacifics.

On their delivery run to Te Awamutu BA 552 and A 423 climb between Erua and National Park on 26 September 1970. J.A.T. TERRY

▲*A view of the old Mangaweka viaduct on 21 April 1961 with* K*A 945 heading no. 155 goods.* *J.A.T.* TERRY
▼*A* D*X heads a southbound freight over the Toi Toi viaduct in October 1987.* DAVE SIMPSON

▲*Mt. Ruapehu provides a fine backdrop for a southbound* D*x* *crossing the Manganui-o-te-Ao viaduct, not far from the highest point on the NZR network (815 metres above sea level).* B.J. MCKENZIE

▲*A view of the 79 metre high Makatote viaduct in diesel days.* TONY HURST

▼*A few days before the erection of catenary masts, a double* D*x* *combination on train 616 climbs the grade across the newly opened new Hapuawhenua viaduct on 4 September 1987.* MARK COLE

CHAPTER NINE

Taranaki and Wanganui

Marton–New Plymouth

The Marton–Wanganui section of this line was built between 1876 and 1878 as part of the Foxton and Wanganui Railway. Linking Foxton with Wanganui was not an end in itself, since both were ports, but was the easiest first step towards a trunk line from Wellington to Taranaki. The line was built as cheaply as possible, and this included a series of steep grades as the line climbed in and out of the Turakina and Whangaehu valleys. As early as the 1890s, when the routes for the North Island Main Trunk were being considered, these grades were seen as a substantial obstacle, but it was not until 1936 that work on a deviation commenced. The realignment included two long tunnels, and during their construction it was found that the tunnel linings were being pushed inwards by the surrounding ground. These problems later resulted in a Commission of Inquiry. It found that the methods being used in major tunnels were still too rough and ready. There had not been adequate preliminary investigations of the ground being tunnelled, and the tunnel shape was an unsuitable one for soft ground. The new line was eventually brought into use on 6 December 1947.

To the west of Wanganui, the section to Kai Iwi, opened on 28 June 1879, includes the 1 in 35 Westmere Bank, which still establishes the ruling gradient for this line. The line was opened to Waverley, 57 km from Wanganui, on 23 March 1881.

Meanwhile, work had started in 1876 on a line south from Lepperton, on the New Plymouth–Waitara Railway. Although this line climbed to an elevation of 343 metres at Waipuku, this summit was reached by a nearly straight route, with grades no steeper than 1 in 50, and no major engineering works. On 20 October 1881, this line was opened to Hawera, 76 km from New Plymouth, and only 43 km from the other railhead at Waverley. The depression of the 1880s slowed construction somewhat, but Taranaki was more fortunate than most areas in that the railway to Taranaki was close to completion, and work continued, a situation which was repeated in a later depression with the Stratford–Okahukura Line. It still took nearly four years before the last section, which included the Manawapou and Tangahoe viaducts, was opened on 23 March 1885, to complete the Foxton–Palmerston North–Wanganui–New Plymouth railway.

In the following year, this line was linked to Wellington by the opening of the Wellington and Manawatu Railway. A twice weekly mail train took a total of 14 hours 50 minutes for the 404 km.

These trains linked with New Plymouth–Onehunga steamers to provide the fastest route between Wellington and Auckland. By 1901, the mail trains were running every day except Sunday, and taking only 12 hours 50 minutes. By then, the travel time between Wellington and Auckland was just over 24 hours, providing the weather was favourable for the steamer.

Tank locomotives were the main power on this line, first the Wa and Wb 2-6-2T's, then the Wd and Wf 2-6-4T, and later the Ww 4-6-4T. In 1925 with the introduction of Ab class 4-6-2 tender locomotives, the existing express schedule of 12 hours between New Plymouth and Wellington was cut to 9 hours 38 minutes. There were also three mixed trains and a single freight train south from New Plymouth daily. A local passenger train between Wanganui and New Plymouth was introduced in 1926 to replace one of the mixed services. A limited load and an Ab locomotive enabled these "Taranaki Flyers" to have schedules of about 41/2 hours.

The Standard railcars introduced in April 1939, initially ran an evening service between New Plymouth and Wellington. On 31 October 1955 these railcars took over all regular passenger services on this route, on schedules of about 7 hours 15 minutes. In 1972 they were replaced on the morning service by the three "Blue Streak" refurbished 88-seater railcars, while ordinary 88-seater railcars ran the evening services, by then only running on Fridays and Sundays. The last railcars to run between Wellington and New Plymouth were those on the last " Blue Streak" services on 30 July 1977.

From about 1955 until 1966, K and Ka class 4-8-4's displaced from the NIMT by new diesels were concentrated at Wanganui and New Plymouth. Their most spectacular workings were double-heading freight trains up the Westmere Bank, and the running of the holiday expresses. The DA class diesels became the standard power in the early 1960s. Since about 1972 DX diesels have been used on this line. Initially they were uncommon, but now they run most freight trains, assisted by the DC and DFT classes.

Like most other lines, freight traffic in the early years was mainly local, but now the line mainly handles long-distance traffic. Wanganui is no longer a port, and New Plymouth mainly handles specialised cargoes. This means that the meat and dairy products from the Taranaki and Wanganui regions are a major traffic south on this line, whilst general freight moves north. The oil and gas developments of Taranaki in the last two decades have contributed some new railway traffic, such as Liquefied Petroleum Gas from Kapuni which travels as far south as Dunedin, and Urea produced from Natural Gas, much of which is railed from Kapuni to New Plymouth harbour for export.

In August 1997 Tranz Rail began running trains of milk from Oringi in Hawke's Bay to the Whareroa dairy factory near Hawera, and in late 1998 milk trains also started from Longburn to Whareroa. These trains with up to 20 wagons, each carrying 52,000 litres of milk, run every day from late August until May, and have so substantially added to the traffic on this line that passing loops had to be reinstated at Kai Iwi and Whangaehu (now renamed Ruatangata).

Mount Egmont Branch

The sole purpose of this short but steep branch up the slopes of Mount Egmont was to obtain ballast, which was in short supply in the Taranaki and Wanganui districts. Construction started in 1905 and the first section

Opposite: Ww 561 heads an excursion train over the Stratford–Okahukura Line in 1969. In the background is Mt Egmont/Taranaki.
Below: A Wellington to New Plymouth express stops at Lepperton in November 1951. NZR

◀*AB 826 and K 926 work the Sunday evening shunt to Eastown out of Wanganui on 21 February 1962. After arrival at Eastown the K will take train 549 onto Palmerston North and the AB will run back to Wanganui depot. In the background is the well known Durie Hill tower.* MARK COLE

▶*J 1226 departs New Plymouth with a train of superphosphate for Kempthorne Prosser's works at Aramoho in October 1961.* MARK COLE

▼*K 912 and K 903 thunder up Westmere Bank from the Taranaki side with a 14 total Taranaki Anniversary Day train on 12 March 1962. This was the last run for K 903.* MARK COLE

Opposite below: K 925 works hard up the 1 in 35 grades of Westmere Bank from the Wanganui side with a Saturday morning goods train to New Plymouth. The boiler had been overfilled hence the whitish smoke and open cylinder cocks. MARK COLE

was opened in April 1908. A short extension, to a point about 11 km from the main line, was nearly complete by 1913, but it was 1920 before the branch and quarry were complete. The crushed rock was used for railway ballast and road metal.

A proposed upper quarry extension would have reached an elevation of 930 metres, which would have been the highest railway in New Zealand by over 100 metres. This was not built however, and it gradually became more economic to bring ballast longer distances, from riverbed shingle plants, rather than quarry it. The easily accessible rock was worked out in 1937, and most of the branch closed in 1938, with the remainder closing in 1951.

Wanganui and Castlecliff Branches

After the 5 km semi-circular branch line from Aramoho to Wanganui had been opened on 21 January 1878, locals saw the need for a further link between Wanganui and the port of Castlecliff. At the time Wanganui had a population of just 4600, but this did not deter those who formed the Wanganui Heads Railway Company in 1885 to operate a private enterprise shortline to the port. The 6 km line was opened on 31 October 1885 for passenger and goods traffic. Small saddle tank steam locomotives were used and named after places in the district.

In April 1889 the company was reorganised as the Castlecliff Railway Company Ltd. Passenger traffic was brisk and at one stage the company ran six trains a day each way with additional services on Saturdays, Sundays and holidays when people flocked from Wanganui to Castlecliff Beach.

Competition from the suburban trams over this route began to bite in 1912 and although a gallant battle was fought over the next 20 years, passenger traffic had become so uneconomic by 1932 that it was discontinued.

Freight traffic, however, continued to grow with the development of new industries and a new overseas port at Castlecliff where steamers from Nauru and the islands discharged phosphate for the chemical works established at Aramoho in 1924. The Castlecliff's greatest triumph, however, came with its part in salvaging materials from the overseas freighter Port Bowen, which stranded as a total loss on Castlecliff Beach in June 1939. A temporary track about 3 km long was built through undulating sand from Castlecliff to the wreck and practically the whole ship was dismantled and removed by rail.

Eventually pressure came from the Wanganui Harbour Board in 1953 for the railway to be taken over by the government. The line was purchased by NZR on 1 February 1956, ending the 71 years of private operation.

The Wanganui Branch lost its passenger traffic on 7 September 1959, with Aramoho on the Marton to New Plymouth line providing the stop for Wanganui passengers on the New Plymouth railcar service, until this ended on 30 July 1977.

Currently freight for Wanganui uses a yard near the old station area, and the private sidings to Castlecliff still have occasional traffic, but Tranz Rail is considering whether it would be cheaper to handle all freight at Aramoho on the main line.

Opunake Branch

The construction of a branch railway across the southern slopes of Mount Egmont to link Opunake with the main New Plymouth–Wanganui railway was authorised in 1912, expenditure on which was to cost no more than £ 400,000. Surveys to determine the best route began in April 1913.

The route from Te Roti along section boundaries north of Skeet Street was chosen in 1914 and work began that year on the 11 km between Te Roti and Kapuni by the Public Works Department.

Work on the railway commenced during 1914 but the rate of progress was seriously affected with the beginning of World War I in August of that year. Due to manpower and materials shortages work on the line was suspended in December 1917 and did not recommence until March 1919. By 1921 the impressive bridge over the Waingongoro River near Te Roti was completed. On completion of the line's second bridge in 1923 the Public Works Department began running goods trains to Kapuni from 1 August 1923.

During the construction of the line two steam shovels were used. One in the Kapuni ballast pit and the other in a big 1.6 km cutting near Waiteika near Opunake. At the peak of construction, 200 men were employed. By December 1924 the Public Works Department was able to carry public goods traffic as far as Mangawhero Road. The new line reached its destination at Opunake on 8 June 1925. The Railways Department took control of the line a month later, on Monday 12 July 1926, and three goods trains each way a week plus passenger services were provided.

A proposed 9 km branch line from Kapuni to Manaia saw 2 1/2 km of track laid between 1920 and 1924, mainly to serve a ballast pit on the Kaupokonui River, but it was decided to abandon this line and the track laid was lifted by 1926.

Passenger services on the Opunake Branch ended on 31 October 1955. The last steam locomotive over the line ran on 1 November 1966 when Ab 707 left Opunake for Stratford. In early years the branch was mainly worked by Ww tank engines, replaced in later years by Ab, Aa, and J classes. From 2 December 1966 DB class diesels were the main power on the line until the advent of the DC class in the 1980s.

As on other rural branch lines, traffic became thinner and thinner and eventually the decision came in April 1976 to close the line to Opunake. With the development of the Kapuni natural gas and petroleum fields, however, traffic to Kapuni had been increasing, and thus it was decided to upgrade this section of the line, so creating the 10.9 km Kapuni Branch from this date.

Waitara Branch

The Waitara branch was originally constructed as part of a New Plymouth to Waitara railway and as such was the first line to be constructed in Taranaki. Originally

*A D*A *hauls two gas towers for Kapuni over the arch bridge near Te Roti on 16 July 1969. Such graceful arch bridges, while standard in the UK, are rare in New Zealand.* NZR

in 1864 a Mr W. Bayley of New Plymouth put forward a proposal for a broad gauge line between Mokau and Patea, estimated to cost £ 2,100,000. Possible extensions later could be made to Wellington and Auckland.

Nothing came of this and it was not until 1872 that surveys were made under Julius Vogel's scheme for a railway between Waitara and New Plymouth by an inland route of 18 km. A contract with Messrs J. Brogden & Sons for construction of the railway was signed on 21 July 1873. Material ordered included 16 km of 40 lb (18.2 Kg) rails, two A class 0-4-0 tank engines (named the Fox and the Ferret), three carriages, three covered goods wagons, six highside and six lowside wagons, two brake vans, two wagon weigh-bridges and twelve tarpaulins. The first sod was turned on Thursday 21 August 1873 and the day was announced as a public holiday.

During 1874 tenders were let for the building of goods shed, passenger stations, and engine sheds at New Plymouth and Waitara. In late 1874 and early 1875 a passenger station at Sentry Hill was built and the building of bridges over the Waiwakahio and Henui rivers commenced.

The need to import all the timber for the sleepers and bridges delayed full completion of the line until 14 October 1875. The first train services consisted of a 9.30 a.m. mixed train from New Plymouth to Waitara, Mondays to Fridays, with another 4.45 p.m. service on Saturdays. A 2.00 p.m. train left Waitara for New Plymouth, Mondays to Fridays with an additional 6.00 p.m. service to this on Saturdays. There were no Sunday trains.

The original purpose of the New Plymouth to Waitara railway was to link New Plymouth with the nearest sheltered port. By 1884 when the New Plymouth breakwater was sufficiently advanced to allow the berthing of coastal vessels, it had fulfilled this purpose. The decline of Waitara as a mail and passenger port dated from this time, and freight traffic would have been similarly affected had not the freezing works opened in 1885.

Work started in 1877 for an extension of the railway southwards from Sentry Hill and was opened as far as Inglewood on 30 November 1877. A railway workshop was located at Sentry Hill, but this was closed on 20 November 1894 when the station was closed there and replaced by a new station of the same name nearer Lepperton. In 1908 a junction was created at Lepperton for traffic to Waitara and thus Waitara became a 7 km branch line.

Passenger services over the branch ended on 29 April 1946. The last steam locomotive to run over the line in regular service was Ab 708 on 8 November 1966. It was to be almost another 23 years before steam next made an appearance with the visit of J 1211 with excursion trains over the line on 3 and 4 June 1989. The freezing works was the main source of traffic on the line, and following its closure at the end of 1998, the line was "mothballed". Currently it is in the process of being sold to a preservation society who hope to run steam trains on the line.

Stratford–Okahukura Line (SOL)

In 1883, as the railway south from New Plymouth to Wanganui was nearing completion, a route from Te Awamutu to Stratford was proposed as part of the Main Trunk railway to link Auckland and Wellington. Mr C. W. Hursthouse, who was sent to conduct a preliminary survey of this route, and his companions, were captured by a group of Maoris and held for 48 hours until rescued by the chiefs Te Kooti and Maniapoto.

A more direct route through the central North Island was chosen for the Main Trunk, but the residents of Taranaki still wanted a railway to Auckland. A survey in 1889 concluded that the best route was from near Stratford to Ongarue, approximately along the route that was eventually followed. Despite further local pressure, it was over 10 years before a railway was

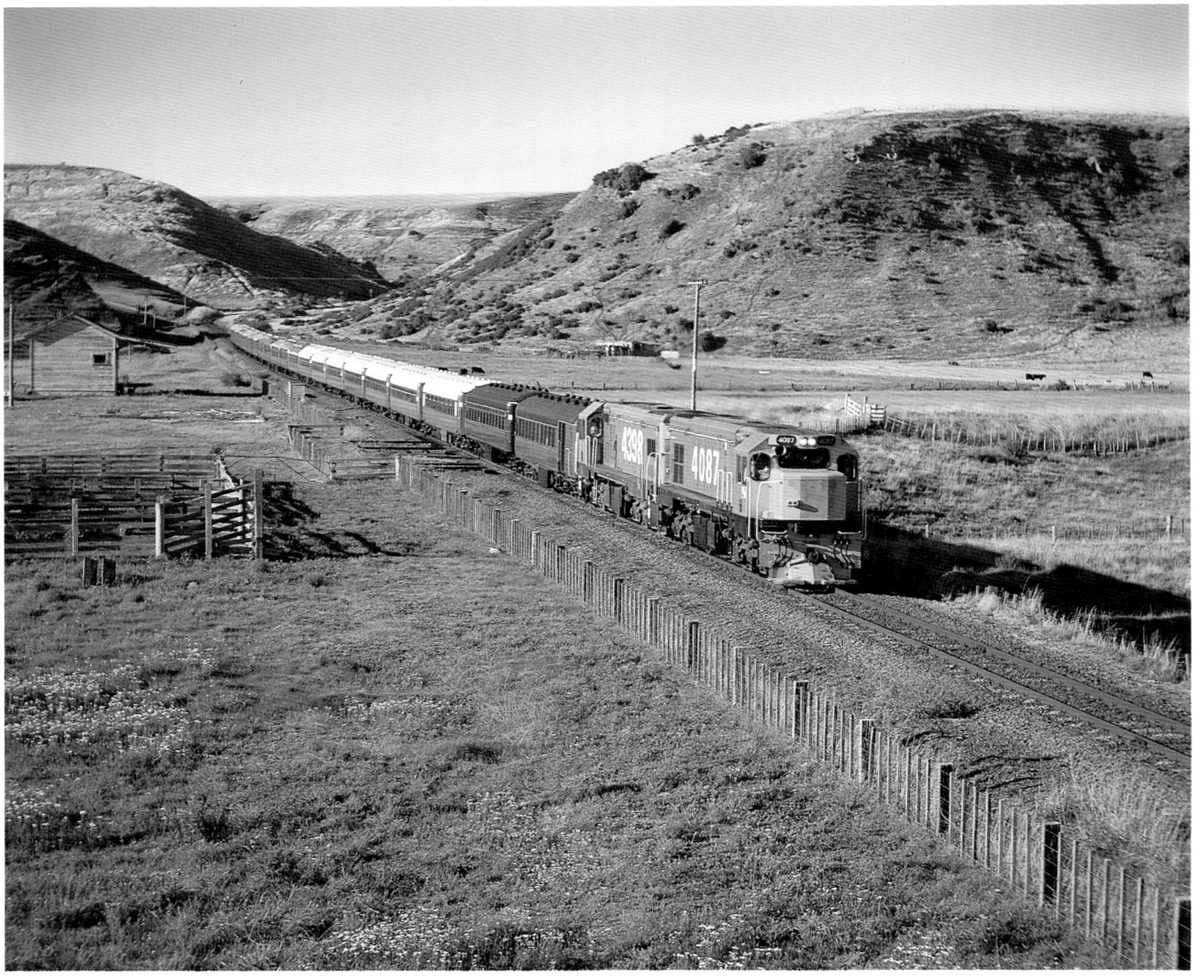

◀*The "Last Great Train Ride" excursion of 25 February 1989 approaches Whangaehu.* MARK COLE

▼*Dx 5477 crosses the Manawapou viaduct on 30 March 1985.* MARK COLE

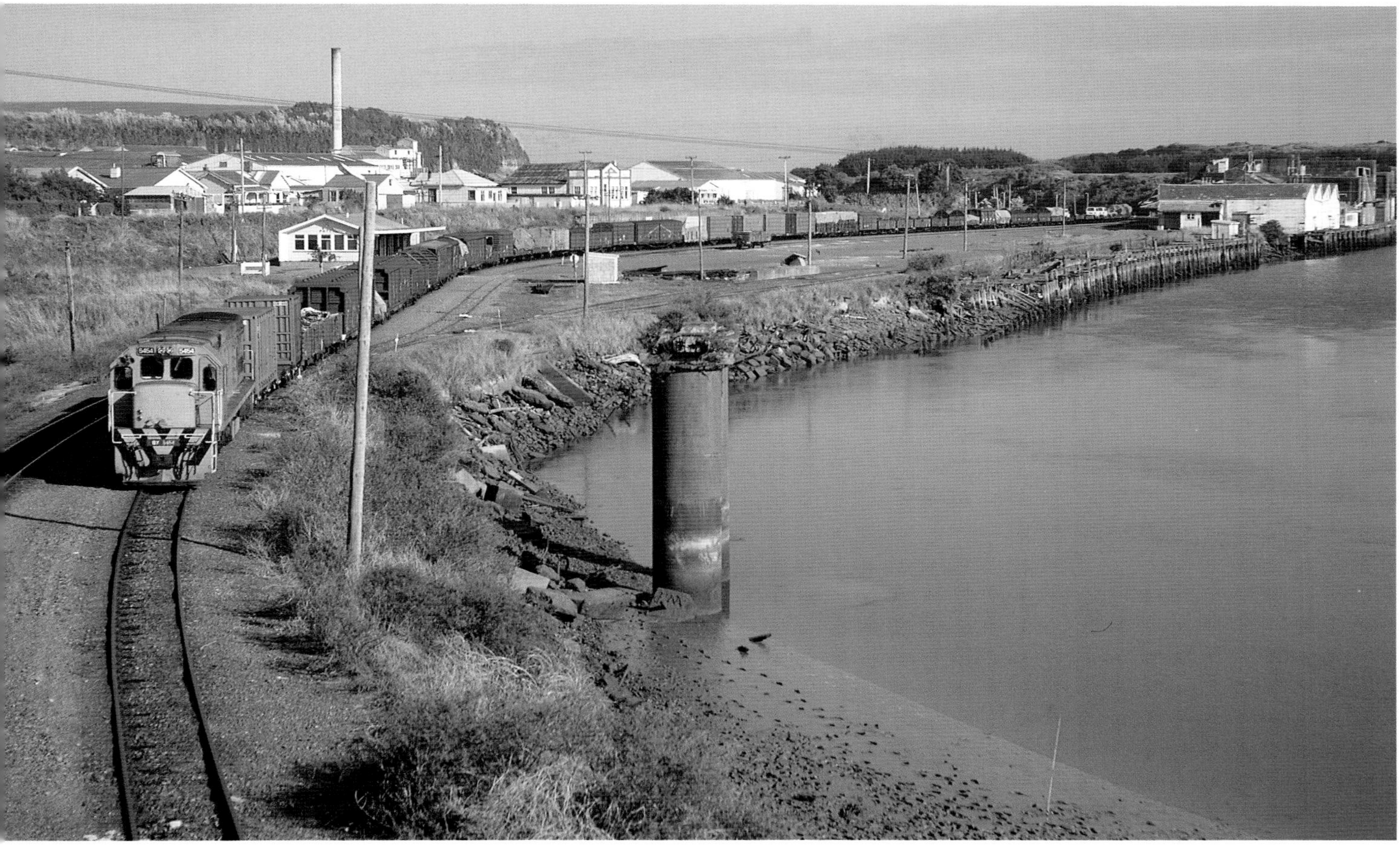

▲ *During electrification works on the North Island Main Trunk in 1985, many freight trains were diverted via Marton–Stratford–Okahukura. This scene shows Dx 5454 with a diverted train at Patea on 23 March 1985.*
MARK COLE

▶ *Two Dc's with a Marton bound freight catch the last rays of the evening sun as they exit the Goat Valley Tunnel between Kai-Iwi and Westmere on 30 May 1985.*
MARK COLE

authorised, and the first sod was turned at Stratford by the Minister for Public Works on 28 March 1901.

The first freight traffic was run to Toko, 10 km from Stratford, in June 1902. Further extensions were opened to Douglas on 1 March 1905, and Huiroa, at 25.5 km, on 1 April 1908, but the locomotive depot was still at Toko. This meant that on Wednesdays and Saturdays, the locomotive and its hardworking crew worked a 6.40am train from Toko to Douglas, and the 7.25 am mixed to Stratford. Then they did a return trip to Huiroa, arriving back at Stratford at 1.50 p.m. The crew probably had a quiet snooze until the mail train from Wellington arrived, and they set off with the 6.50 p.m. from Stratford to Huiroa. They then dropped the cars and van at Douglas, before returning to Toko, with their little D or F class tank engine, about 15 hours after they had first set out. A rather more relaxed schedule applied on other days.

Beyond Huiroa the railway construction moved into more rugged country, with a succession of low but rugged ridges separated by winding rivers. The line eventually required 24 tunnels, cutting through saddles from one narrow river valley to another, or cutting through a ridge to avoid a gorge or a river bend. From 1908 until 1915 work was pushed ahead vigorously, with the longer tunnels being started on a new section before the previous section was opened. The line to Whangamomona, 60 km from Stratford, was handed over to the Railways Department on 1 July 1914, and Whangamomona became the locomotive depot. Larger tank locomotives such as the 2-6-4T Wd and Wf classes, or the 4-6-4T Wg were now allowed to work the line.

Meanwhile, work at the other end of the line started in November 1911, after it was decided that the best route was one leaving the Main Trunk railway about 11 km north of Taumaranui. From the new junction at Okahukura, the line had to cross the Ongarue river with a major bridge, with a lower level used as a road bridge, and a few kilometres later tunnel under the Okahukura saddle with a 1525 metre long tunnel. Because of the effects of World War I, and the difficulties of driving the tunnel, which led two contractors to abandon the job, it was 1922 before the 16 km section from Okahukura to Matiere was opened. The next 15 km section to Ohura, through a developing farming area, was rather easier, and the Public Works Department started a freight and passenger service to Ohura in December 1926. The PWD continued to run trains on the eastern portion of this line until the whole line was complete.

At the western end, work continued slowly during the war, and after the war emphasis was put into completing the line as far as Tahora. Beyond Tahora was the most rugged part of the whole line, in which the railway had to tunnel through a number of ridges in its passage from the Tangarakau valley to the Ohura valley. There was no road access to the route between Tangarakau and Heao, a section in which six tunnels were needed, three of them over a kilometre long. Work on this section started in 1924, and a large camp was set up for the construction workers. By the use of a number of temporary tramways, it was possible to get access to tunnels some distance ahead of the railway, and a number of tunnels were being worked on simultaneously. Comparatively good progress was made, considering the difficult terrain, geology and weather.

By March 1930, the western construction workers had completed the line to Tangarakau, and coal was being railed out from a nearby mine. Of the remaining long tunnels, No 9 was finished, No 10 had been holed through in November 1929 and was being completed, and No 11 was being worked on at the western end by workers from Tangarakau, and at the eastern end by the other construction crew. The earthworks and tunnelling on the section from Ohura to Heao were also close to completion. It was fortunate for this project that it was so close to completion at this time, for the 1930s Depression was developing, and the very pessimistic 1930 Royal Commission on the Railways was looking at all railway construction work, to see what projects could be stopped. Although the Commission expected through freight traffic to be only about 260 tonnes each day, construction continued through the depths of the Depression. On 7 November 1932, the last spike was driven on this railway. Exceptional floods in March 1933 delayed the handing over of the Tahora to Okahukura link to the Railways Department until 4 September 1933. The line is known as "The Branch" to Taumaranui railwayman, who only work one main line and one branch line.

Passenger trains commenced very early on 4 September 1933, with carriages that had come down from Auckland attached to the Auckland to Wellington Limited being taken on by a train leaving Taumaranui at 12.45 am. This service ran Monday, Wednesday and Friday, as did a passenger train leaving New Plymouth at 7.10 p.m., with carriages to be attached to the Wellington Auckland express. Two mixed trains ran each way between Stratford and Taumaranui on five or six days a week, with about 7 hour schedules.

Despite the expectations of the 1930 Royal Commission, this line has carried a substantial amount of through freight traffic. The coal mine near Tangarakau closed in the 1930s, but the Tatu State Mine sent large tonnages via an overhead cableway to loading bins at Mangaparo until its closure in 1971. A number of small mines near Ohura were working until recently. Traffic to and from the farms, and timber until the accessible bush was worked out, were also important, but on-line traffic is now insignificant. The importance of this line is now as a through route for freight to or from Taranaki, and as a diversion when the Main Trunk is closed because of maintenance or accident.

Ab class tender locomotives were used from the opening of the through line, supplemented by Aa and X class locomotives. The X class 4-8-2 were used for many years on the freight and mixed services on this line. In the 1940s, J class locomotives were introduced. Oil-burning Jb locomotives were predominant in the last years before the DA class diesels took over in 1963. Trains on this line are now usually worked by DC, DFT and DX locomotives. A major source of traffic is milk powder and other products from the Dairy Factory at Whareroa near Hawera, much of which is exported through Tauranga. In 2001 work was completed that allows 2.9 metre high "hi-cube" containers to be car-

An excursion train swings onto the Stratford–Okahukura Line at Stratford in 1989. In the background is Mt Egmont/Taranaki.
G.B. CHURCHMAN

ried on this line, indicating that it is seen as a vital part of the Tranz Rail network.

The overnight express schedules between Auckland and New Plymouth were the most practical way of operating the service in its first years, but they established an unfortunate precedent. Perhaps the Railways were more interested in mail and newspaper traffic, or perhaps they didn't consider making a change, but the service remained a night one after the Taranaki carriages were worked separately to and from Auckland, and even when railcars were introduced in 1956. It has been suggested that the railcar service was first intended as a Taumaranui Auckland and return run, that was then extended to New Plymouth. Whatever the reason, the northbound departure times through the 1960s of New Plymouth 2.34 am, Stratford, 3.24 am and Taumaranui 6.45 am did not seem designed to encourage passenger traffic. The southbound timings were not quite so bad, but arrival at New Plymouth was at the rather late time of 11.23 p.m. Thus anyone wanting to travel by rail between New Plymouth and Auckland had to be prepared to arrive at New Plymouth station in the small hours of the night.

It was only in December 1973, some time after the 1971 cancellation of the Auckland–Taumaranui section of these services, that the railcars were retimed to a daylight service, leaving New Plymouth at 8.30 am, and returning from Taumaranui at 3.10 p.m. This service was more useful for local people, and made the carriages attached to freight trains less necessary. The last of these mixed trains, with the cars attached to the 8.55 am Taumaranui-Stratford and the 4.45 p.m. Stratford–Taumaranui freight trains, ran on 30 November 1975.

The last railcars on this route ran on 11 February 1978, but were replaced by locomotive hauled AC converted railcars. Later, ordinary carriages were used on this service. Although the road over this route was still unsealed in 1990, the low population along the line and increasing car ownership meant the service was losing money which was no longer supported by the government. The last regular passenger train on this route ran on 21 January 1983. However, occasional excursion trains are popular, including regular ones for the "Republic Day" celebrations at Whangamomona.

(Top left) A Dc class diesel heads the New Plymouth–Taumarunui passenger train past the "wild-west" town of Whangamomona in the early 1980s. NZR

(Other scenes) Images of the Stratford–Okahukura line from the early 1980s, portraying the typical landscape on this back-blocks railway. NZR

▶*JB 1239 starts to emerge from the hill country on the Stratford–Okahukura line on the approach to Huiroa on 5 June 1966.* MARK COLE

CHAPTER TEN

Hawke's Bay and Gisborne

Palmerston North to Napier

As with nearly every significant area of European settlement, Hawke's Bay had a railway authorised in the 1870s. The line authorised in 1871 was from Napier south through Hastings towards Waipukurau, together with a line to link Napier to its port at Ahuriri. At this date the area between Napier and Hastings was much more low-lying than it is now, presenting a substantial obstacle to the railway. The route chosen was to follow the shingle ridge along the coast south of Napier, and then turn inland near the town of Clive. Construction of the line started in 1872, and on 13 October 1874 the line from Napier to Hastings was opened with considerable festivities. The Hawke's Bay residents certainly seemed to like opening railways, as there had already been a ceremonial opening of the first 19 km section on 1 July 1874.

The route south was through easy country as far as the Takapau Plains, south of Waipukurau, but beyond this was the difficult section through the "Seventy Mile Bush". The main obstacle to the railway was that the upper reaches of the Manawatu River, and the streams flowing into it, had cut down below the general level of the land. This required a succession of viaducts between Kopua and Dannevirke. Surveys were made of more easterly routes, but the country there was even more rugged, and gave no hope of an easier route.

The line to Waipukurau was opened on 1 September 1876, and to Kopua on 25 January 1878. The next section, with three viaducts including the 280 metre long and 39 metre high Ormondville viaduct, was opened on 9 August 1880, but by then the coming of the 1880s depression was slowing progress. There was also a shortage of labour, despite the depression, but work continued and after Dannevirke, reached on 1 December 1884, the terrain was easier. The timber from

A Dc with a Wellington bound "Endeavour" is seen passing the lakes at the top of the Opapa Bank. NZR

A Wellington bound Napier Express heads through the Manawatu Gorge in 1939. ALEXANDER TURNBULL LIBRARY

the Seventy Mile Bush provided useful traffic for the railway, and was also used to build some of the viaducts. These timber trestles were soon replaced by steel viaducts to cope with larger and faster trains.

On 22 March 1887, the line from Hawkes Bay was the first railway to reach Woodville, at the east end of the Manawatu Gorge. Work on the line through the Manawatu Gorge had only commenced in 1886. If the problems encountered on this stretch had been foreseen, work might have started earlier. A major problem was encountered at the second tunnel in the gorge, with a slip covering the northern portal. The tunnel was dug further into the hill, with a new northern portal in a safer place. Another problem was that when the underlying rocks were exposed to air, they lost their strength, so extra retaining walls were required. It was 9 March 1891 before the Palmerston North to Woodville section was opened, completing a through rail route from Napier to Wellington.

Up until this time, all trains on the Napier section were mixed, and were mainly worked by F class 0-6-0T tank locomotives, but with the completion of the line to Palmerston North, a daily "express" train each way was introduced. The southbound express left Napier at 10.45 am., and connected at Palmerston North with a train which was scheduled to arrive at Wellington via the Wellington and Manawatu Company's line at 9.50 pm. J class 2-6-0 locomotives were initially used on these expresses on the Napier line.

In 1897, the line from Masterton arrived at Woodville, and the Napier trains were diverted via this route. Because of the time taken on the Rimutaka Incline, this resulted in the trains to and from Wellington taking over an hour longer, which was naturally unpopular. N class 2-6-2's were introduced in 1899, and the schedules were accelerated. By 1901 the Napier–Wellington schedule was 10 1/2 hours. At this stage, a locomotive and its crew would work Masterton-Cross Creek-Napier one day, and back the next. The N's were sometimes assisted by the rebuilt M 2-4-4T locomotives, known as the "pullets" for their comparative lack of power, and the combination was known as the " 'en and chicken".

In 1908 the government bought the Manawatu Company's railway, and the Napier–Wellington trains were soon altered back to the Manawatu route. In 1914 the authorised speeds on this line, and a number of others, was raised to 73 km/hour, and schedules of just over 9 hours were introduced for haulage by the A class compound Pacifics. In 1925 the Napier–Wellington journey time was reduced to about 7 hours 45 minutes, while the opening of the Tawa Flat Deviation and the introduction of K class 4-8-4's onto the expresses cut the time to 7 hours in 1949. In 1954, the daily expresses were replaced by twice daily "Standard" railcars, which were soon replaced by the new "Fiat" 88-seater articulated railcars. These railcars took only 5 1/2 hours to run between Napier and Wellington. As the railcars wore out in the late 1960s, with no new passenger stock to replace them, two services were replaced by the "Endeavour" express. This train started running on 6 November 1972, on a similar schedule to the railcars. Initially this train comprised five carriages, one buffet car, in blue livery with a matching van, and was hauled by a Da diesel locomotive bearing a headboard. The remaining railcar services all ceased by 1976. The standard of the "Endeavour" deteriorated somewhat in the early 1980s with the loss of the buffet car and late arrivals due to the use of under-powered DBR locomotives. An improved service, again including a buffet car, was introduced in November 1989 in the form of the "Bay Express" on the fastest ever schedule of 5 1/2 hours each way, but with far more competition from buses, planes and cars than existed in the days of steam-hauled expresses, its future was in doubt at the time of writing.

In its early days freight traffic on this line was related to farm activities, especially sheep and cattle to the freezing works and wool. Tranz Rail no longer carries sheep and cattle, and the emphasis is now on longer-distance traffic, such as containers of frozen meat to Wellington. The meat processing plants at Tomoana,

Waipukurau, Takapau and Oringi, together with the fruit and vegetable canneries and processors at Gisborne and Hastings, provide much of the traffic for this line. Fertiliser goes from the works at Awatoto, near Napier, to Aramoho and New Plymouth, but Hatuma lime near Waipukurau stopped using rail transport in early 2001 when Tranz Rail decided to no longer run 4-wheel wagons. Recently Oringi in southern Hawkes Bay has become a major traffic centre, with a modern freezing works, and a loading point for milk trains to the Kiwi Dairy plant near Hawera.

When transport licensing was in force, traffic from Napier or Hastings to the Auckland area had to go by rail, and some consignors were most unhappy over this, especially since the road route via Taupo was considerably shorter. Now Tranz Rail has to maintain its share of the traffic by competing on price and service, and overnight transit is a necessity. For some years, roadrailer wagons went by road to Rotorua and then by rail, but this service was withdrawn in 1999. Now each afternoon there is a 3.30 p.m. close-off for freight from Hastings to be loaded for a train that provides overnight transit to destinations as far north as Auckland.

Ahuriri/Breakwater Branch

The original port for Hawkes Bay was Ahuriri, by the Inner Harbour, just west of the hills on which Napier was sited. A 3 km line from Napier to Ahuriri, then rejoicing in the name of Spit, was opened on 25 November 1874, only a month after the opening of the line to Hastings. Passenger services were run on this line until 1908.

The Hawkes Bay earthquake of 3 February 1931 produced an uplift of about 2.5 metres in this area, which made the port at Ahuriri unusable for large ships. The Napier Harbour Board accordingly built new wharves at Breakwater, to the north-east of Bluff Hill. The Harbour Board also built a 2.4 km line from Ahuriri to Breakwater, which they operated with two small Fowler 0-4-0 tank locomotives. The line to Breakwater was taken over by NZR in 1957, although the Fowler locomotives were still used by the Harbour Board on the actual breakwater until 1965. Both locomotives were sold for preservation, and currently one is regularly steamed at the Tokomaru Steam Museum. The wharves are normally shunted by DSC and DSG diesel shunting locomotives.

Napier–Gisborne Railway (including Ngatapa Branch)

This is a line which was difficult and expensive to construct, and a number of floods, and the occasional earthquakes, have made it a difficult line to keep going. Flooding from Cyclone Bola in March 1988 resulted in the loss of passenger services, and the line is not profitable with the current level of freight traffic. Its future may depend on government intervention, based on future forestry traffic prospects and its value for regional development.

Gisborne city and its surrounding district is separated from any other main centre by a considerable distance of rugged hill country, and so it took some time before thoughts of a railway connection were taken seriously. By about 1900 the residents had formed a Railway League to press for lines to Auckland via Rotorua, and to Wellington via Napier. A line to Napier via an

A JA and AB haul a goods train on the Napier–Gisborne line upgrade just north of the Esk River bridge in 1961. BOB HEPBURN.

Above: A Napier bound "Endeavour" crosses the Ashurst Bridge before entering the Manawatu Gorge in the early 1980s. NZR

Right: Returning to Wellington from an excursion to Gisborne, a train of "Northerner" cars is seen climbing the Opapa Bank in February 1986. MARK COLE

Below: DBR 1267 with an "Endeavour" stops at Dannevirke in 1983. The station building is relatively modern but the awning dates from the 1900s. NZR

inland route to the Wairoa River, and then down this river to Wairoa, was approved in 1911. Construction started on this route from Gisborne in 1912, and by December 1915 the 18 km to Ngatapa was carrying freight traffic under the control of the Public Works Department. By then, work past Ngatapa had been suspended because of World War I. A small amount of work was done in 1919, but about this time the engineers were probably having second thoughts about the route between Gisborne and Wairoa. Between 1920 and 1923 a branch was built between Wairoa and the small port of Waikokopu to ship meat from the Wairoa freezing works. This then enabled the inspecting engineer to report in 1924 that the coastal route, which would incorporate the Waikokopu branch, would be "better in every way than the Ngatapa route". And so the Ngatapa section, which as a branch was virtually useless, was handed over to the Railways Department, who closed it in 1931. Construction on the new coastal route between Gisborne and Wairoa only started in March 1929, and closed down in January 1931 because of the great Depression.

Meanwhile, the first sod at the Napier end of the line was turned on 29 January 1912. It took until 1919 to complete the bridge and embankment over the inner harbour at Napier, but by 1923 the line was open to Eskdale. Beyond Eskdale, the line was in hill country, with large amounts of earthmoving required, for which 12 steam shovels were at work by 1924. There were also eight tunnels, six major viaducts, and a bridge over the Wairoa River to be constructed on this line. Work was pushed ahead, and on 6 October 1930, NZR took over the line as far as Putorino, 62 km from Napier,

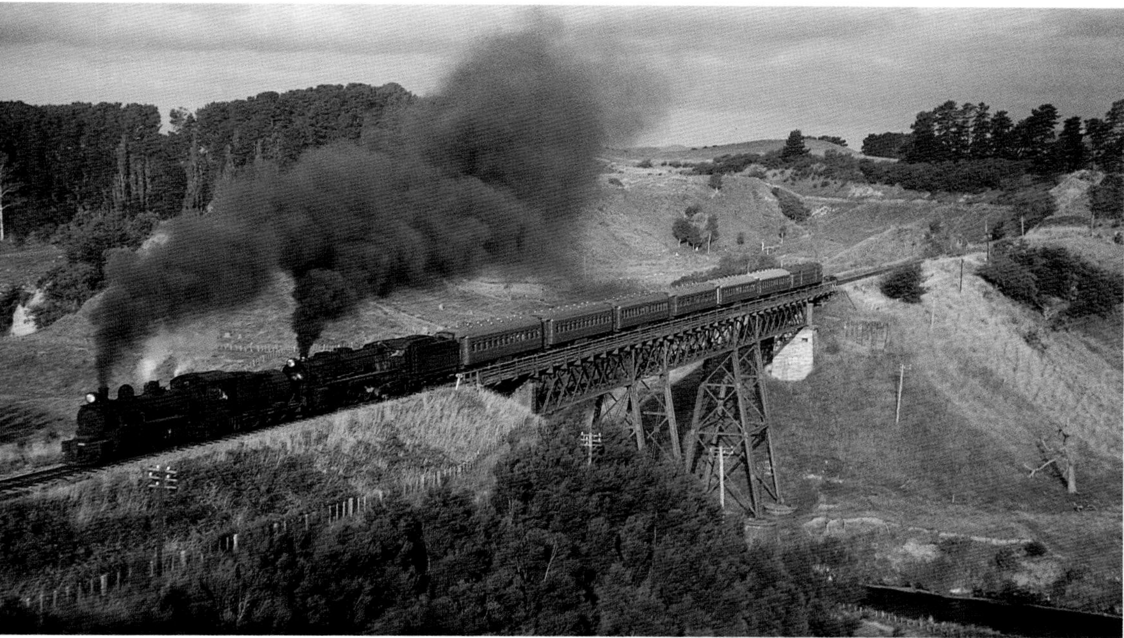

Left: AB 838 and KA 930 haul the last regular steam train in Hawke's Bay across the Matamau Viaduct on 12 February 1966.
MARK COLE

Below: KA 963 with a goods train crosses the Waipukurau Bridge on 8 May 1962.
J.A.T. TERRY

although this section was closed by the effects of the Hawke's Bay earthquake of February 1931.

By the end of 1931 the only work required to have a complete line from Napier to Wairoa was the completion of the Kotemaori Tunnel, the building of the Mohaka viaduct, 275 metres long and the highest in New Zealand at 97 metres, and 13 km of track laying. Incredibly, the Railways Board recommended in September 1931 that work should be stopped, and the whole line abandoned. This was an extreme case of how negative the attitude to public works was in the 1930s Depression.

The policy of the Labour Government elected in 1935 of promoting public works, saw the resumption of work early in 1936 with as many as 1300 men working on the line. The opening of the Mohaka Viaduct on 1 July 1937 completed the line from Napier to Waikokopu. Efforts were by then concentrated on the 13 tunnels required north of Waikokopu and on the Waipaoa River Bridge. Very heavy rain in February 1938 resulted in a flash flood in which 22 persons were drowned at a construction camp in the Kopuawhara valley, and caused major damage to the railway works in this area and in the Esk Valley. The first through train reached Gisborne in August 1942.

A Napier–Wairoa service worked by a "Standard" railcar commenced on 3 July 1939, and passenger trains to Gisborne in September 1942. The heyday of passenger services came when the "Fiat" 88-seater railcars were introduced on 1 August 1955, and two railcars ran each way most days, with one service each way running through to Wellington. Some services were withdrawn in 1968, more in 1971, and the last railcar ran on 30 May 1976. A train service, initially using a "grass-grub" converted railcar, restarted on 20 March 1978, but ceased after major damage closed the line when Cyclone Bola struck Poverty Bay on 8 March 1988.

The damage from Cyclone Bola, which included the washout of the southern approach to the Waipaoa River bridge, was estimated at $3.5 million, and took nearly five months to repair. Major storm damage is a recurrent feature of this line. Since the 1938 floods, there also have been major floods or slips in August 1957, June 1977 and July 1985, in each case closing the line for a number of weeks, and numerous minor problems.

Freight services were generally worked by X, Aa and Ab steam locomotives at first, then by Ja and Jb oil-burning 4-8-2 steam locomotives until 1966, when DA locomotives took over. DX locomotives were brought into service on this line in September 1988 for the reopening to Gisborne.

Much of the traditional freight traffic has disappeared. Even the Wairoa freezing works does not currently use rail. A major traffic for the three freight trains weekly each way is fertiliser, conveyed in CF class high-capacity covered hopper wagons to Matawhero, near Gisborne. For a couple of years tomatoes were transported by rail from the Gisborne area to Hastings for processing, but such long-distance transport proved not to be the best way of handling the crop. There was considerable log traffic in the 1990s, for instance 30,000 tonnes of logs were loaded in Wairoa in 1994-95, but currently none of the forests being cut require rail transport for their logs. The future hope of this line is that major forest harvesting north of Gisborne in a few years will increase traffic. Tranz Rail has said the line is currently uneconomic, but with strong local resistance to closure, an alternative such as local operation and/or a government subsidy may well eventuate.

◀*Two coupled "Fiat" railcars cross the 97 metre high Mohaka viaduct, the highest on NZR, on a Gisborne–Wellington run in 1957.* NZR

▶*A preview of the new "grassgrub" service on the Gisborne line seen here behind a DA at Beach Loop on 18 March 1978.* NZR

Opposite below: An AB headed Gisborne–Napier goods train skirts the shore of Opoutama Bay in the 1950s. NZR

▼*Everything but the kitchen sink seems to be on this train on the Moutuhora Branch in 1908. No doubt it all belongs to construction workers in the process of shifting camp.* NZR

A Bb class locomotive sits in Rakauroa Station yard on the Moutohora Branch. OIL PAINTING, P.J. BAKER

Moutohora Branch

Gisborne's first railway was a 16 km section up the Waipaoa valley to Ormond, opened on 26 June 1902. This line was intended to link Gisborne to its hinterland, but was also seen as the beginning of a railway connection with Auckland. This line was authorised as a Gisborne to Rotorua line and was labelled as such in the official Public Works Statement until 1910. The line reached Te Karaka in 1905, and Waikohu, 37 km from Gisborne in 1908.

The line to this point mainly followed the river flats, with easy grades, but a few kilometres past Waikohu a steep climb began, as the line climbed from a height of 50 metres above sea level to 570 metres in only 30 km. This Otoko Bank, with significant lengths as steep as 1 in 33, was a major obstacle to operating the line. The Wa's used when this line was an isolated section could only haul 110 tonnes up this bank, while of the engines commonly used in later years, a Ww could haul 135 tonnes, and an Ab, 140 tonnes. The construction of this steep section through rugged bush country, including the Otoko viaduct and a short tunnel near the summit, was surprisingly rapid, and the line to Matawai, in the head-waters of the Motu River, was opened in November 1914. The final terminus of Moutohora, (initially spelt Motuhora), 78 km from Gisborne, was reached in November 1917.

Although the railway was now over the main divide, there was no easy way down to the Bay of Plenty. The originally intended route north from Moutohora would have required another tunnel and then some sort of spiral to lose height quickly. An alternative, surveyed in 1925, was to branch off to the south-west near the highest point on the line, to reach the head-waters of the Koranga River. The route then followed this river down to the Waioeka River, to reach Opotiki through the Waioeka gorge. The prospects for completion of any route to the Bay of Plenty were dealt a fatal blow when construction of the line from Taneatua towards Opotiki was abandoned soon after the start of World War II, although a Railway Promotion League was still active in the 1950s seeking to have the line built.

Regular passenger traffic on this branch ceased in January 1945 as one of the results of the wartime coal shortages. Freight traffic declined in the 1950s, and the line was officially closed on 24 March 1959. In its last years, the main traffic was railway ballast and road metal from a quarry at Moutohora. The last freight train actually ran on 14 April 1959, with Ab 826 bringing out a last load of road metal, ironically for highway improvements that would use the former railway formation. The first short section to Makaraka still exists.

CHAPTER ELEVEN

Wellington

Hutt Valley Line

Initial proposals for railway construction in Wellington involved investigation of horse tramway routes by the Provincial Government in 1853 and 1857, but nothing came of them. Around 1858 a member of the Provincial Council, Robert Stokes, became interested and proposed a railway from Wellington over the Rimutakas. Eventually in 1863 the Provincial Council gave its support and an investigating committee was set up. Three years later the venture was approved when the Wellington, Hutt Valley and Wairarapa Railway Ordinance was passed on 2 July 1866 authorising the Superintendent to enter into a contract, the cost of which was not to exceed £ 300,000 for the building of a 4'8" (1425 mm) or 3'6" gauge railway to carry 200 tons at speeds of 15 mph (24 km/h). However the inability to raise funds in England prevented the venture from going further.

Part of Sir Julius Vogel's Public Works policy of 1870 was a Wellington-Wairarapa railway. On his visit to London the next year to arrange a loan of £ 1,200,000 to finance this policy he was approached by several contracting firms which included Brogden & Sons who offered to send out surveyors in advance. This firm duly received a contract which included the Wellington to Lower Hutt section of the Wairarapa Railway. On 20 August 1872 the first sod was turned at a ceremony at Pipitea Point. By the following July, rails had reached Kaiwharawhara (1.6 km). The railway took longer to build than expected because the original intention of pushing down rock cliffs along the harbour shoreline to form an embankment did not prove feasible, and the railway ended up following every contour involving some sharp curves. By New Year 1874 the line had reached Ngauranga followed shortly by the arrival of the first locomotive which enabled progress to be speeded up. On 14 April 1874 the line was opened as far as Lower Hutt without ceremony. Four trains a day (three on Sundays) each way transporting passengers in 6 wheel cars were scheduled between Lower Hutt and Wellington.

The route onwards to Upper Hutt followed the western bank of the Hutt River and there was often little space between the river and the bank. Some 5,000 bags of cement were used in one place to divert the course of the river and in another part a long concrete wall was built. Silverstream was reached in December 1875. Just before Silverstream the Hutt River was crossed with a 272 metre long timber bridge built of totara and reinforced with iron. This remained in use until the new deviation was opened in 1954.

On 1 February 1876 the line was opened as far as Upper Hutt, and the same year two new stations at Belmont and Haywards were opened, mainly for passenger traffic. By 1878 ten locomotives were in use on the Wellington to Hutt line - six L class 2-4-0T's, two D class 2-4-0T's and two C class 0-4-2T's, the latter two being used on reclamation works at Thorndon and were later sent out to work at Waitara in Taranaki.

On 16 January 1878 fire broke out in the Railway Hotel at Pipitea Point Station, and within an hour, the hotel, the station and the workshops were destroyed.

At Wellington Station on 20 August 1976, DA 1451 departs with a Hutt Valley suburban train ("subby") while DA 1447 arrives with a train from Masterton. MARK COLE

Above: A scene from the early 1920s at Lambton Station showing WD 316, built by Baldwin in 1901, a 2-6-4T loco, with a G class horse box, possibly picked up at Trentham, and in front of that a 60ft car van built about 1906, when "motor trains" were deployed with a D class locomotive and one of these car vans between Lower Hutt and Upper Hutt. These were soon discontinued and the car vans were used on ordinary trains.
W.W. STEWART

Right: ED 103 and EW 1802 double head a petrol train across the bridge over the Hutt Road into tunnel No. 1 on the North Island Main Trunk on 12 January 1966.
W.W.G. PRICE

Left: A Wairarapa railcar en route to Woodville via the Rimutaka Incline passes the junction of the old and new Hutt Valley lines, just south of Lower Hutt station on 2 January 1950. TOM McGAVIN

Below: A three car multiple unit set approaches Manor Park on 25 July 1955. In the foreground is a cattle stop. NZR

Thus Wellington's first station had become history. A new station was built on a site in the present day Featherston Street and opened on 1 November 1880, coinciding with the opening of the Wellington to Masterton line. In 1885 this building was shifted on rollers to a new site near the intersection of Thorndon and Lambton Quays, and became known as Lambton Station.

In 1903 the Hutt Railway and Road Improvements Act was passed, providing for reclamation works to straighten out the road-bed between Wellington and Petone and to double the line. Work on this started the next year and by 1911 the whole line between Wellington and Lower Hutt had been duplicated.

A new branch line to Waterloo joining with the main line between Petone and Lower Hutt was opened on 26 May 1927. This was the first 4 km of what would ultimately become the main line. From the start it was built to mainline standards with double track, three position colour light signalling and road overbridges instead of level crossings. The line involved no difficulties but included the 233 km long Ava Bridge over the Hutt River. The next stage was the opening of a 3 km industrial branch line on 1 April 1929. This line also serves the Hutt Workshops which replaced the former workshops at Petone.

In the period following World War II with severe coal shortages plaguing the country, authorisation for extending the electrification of the Wellington suburban system to the Hutt Valley lines was given in 1946. The remarkable growth of the Hutt Valley from market gardens to a residential city in the 1940s brought about the decision to electrify these lines, which even in 1939 had been said to be "out of the question" by a Government spokesman. The route to Upper Hutt and the Wairarapa changed with electrification. In 1946 the double tracked Waterloo branch was extended to Naenae (2.75 km) and in 1947 it was continued another 2.3 km to Taita as single track. On 14 September 1953 the Wellington to Taita section was electrified, the double track to Taita having been completed in February of that year. The Hutt Valley Branch as the section from the junction south of Lower Hutt to Taita was known, only lasted another six months, when upon completion of the line between Taita and Manor Park, the branch now became the main line. Because the old bridge across the Hutt River to Silverstream was unsuitable for electrification, a new bridge was built further north and the line now enters the township on a new alignment some distance to the west. A second bridge was also built at Pomare to take the line across the Hutt River to Manor Park. The original intention here was for a tunnel through the area known as Taita Gorge, but the ground was found to be unsuitable and the two bridges built instead.

By June 1955 the line had been double tracked as far as Trentham and on 24 July 1955 all locomotive hauled trains between Wellington and Upper Hutt were replaced by electric multiple units. The platforms at all stations between Wellington, Woburn and Lower Hutt had to be raised for the electric units and most were lengthened. New station buildings were erected at Waterloo, Epuni, Naenae, Wingate, Taita, Pomare, Manor Park, Silverstream and Heretaunga, all of which were island platforms. New stations were also built at Trentham, Upper Hutt and Melling. The last mentioned station is now the end of a branch line, as the old line between Melling and Haywards was closed as from 1 March 1954.

Overhead catenary masts on the Hutt Valley were spaced at 67 metre intervals and the contact wire was between 4.2 metres and 5.5 metres above the rails. Two classes of electric locomotives were built for use on the Wellington suburban sections. The prototype of what would be known as the Ed class was ordered from the English Electric Company in 1935, and seven more were built at the Hutt workshops. The wheel arrangement was an unusual 1-Do-2 and the long rigid wheelbase made the class very hard on the track. The four traction motors developed 925 kW and the engine was designed to haul 500 tonnes of freight between Wellington and Paekakariki. In 1940 two further Ed's were built at Addington workshops for use on the Otira-Arthur's Pass section, but did not prove suitable for this section and in 1943 were transferred to Wellington.

With the decision to electrify the Hutt Valley line to Upper Hutt being made, a new electric locomotive was developed. The seven members of the Ew class, built by the English Electric Company, had a Bo-Bo-Bo wheel arrangement and with a one hour power output of 1,340 kW on entry into service in 1952 were the most powerful locomotive on NZR for 20 years. At 76 tonnes they were five tonnes lighter than the Ed's yet could haul 20% heavier trains. The last Ed's were withdrawn from service in 1980 and the last Ew's in early 1983. Since then all freight traffic around Wellington, as well as relief passenger trains, has been handled by diesels.

On 26 November 1988 a new rail-bus interchange station was opened at Waterloo and fully integrated by the following March.

ED 103 arrives at Wingate Station with a seven total morning train to Wellington on 4 February 1969. MARK COLE

Left: A two car electric multiple unit from Melling approaches the old Lower Hutt station on 23 December 1988. G.B. CHURCHMAN

Below: Crossing of passenger trains, both headed by Dcs, between Waterloo and Woburn on 3 January 1981. MARK COLE

Melling Branch

This short 3 km branch line formed part of the main Wellington-Masterton line until 1954 when the Hutt Branch was extended across to join up with the main line close to the intersection of the State highway and the Haywards Hill Road. This Hutt line was then turned into the main line and the old main line from Melling to the junction was removed.

Like the Johnsonville Branch, the line today is exclusively used by electric multiple-unit trains for commuter traffic. It runs alongside the State highway and has two stations—the former Hutt station, dating from 1906, now known as Western Hutt, and the terminus at Melling. There are proposals to extend it into the Lower Hutt shopping area, but whether anything will happen remains to be seen.

Hutt Park Railway

This former line existed to provide transport for patrons of the Hutt Park Racecourse from Petone. The line was first proposed soon after the railway from Wellington to the Hutt Valley was built in 1874. The Royal Commission of 1880 turned the proposal down, but in 1884, with competition looming from the racecourse at Island Bay, the Hutt Park Railway Company was formed with a capital of £4,000, the shares of which were taken up in one day. The line was built in just 38 days and was 3.2 km long, ending alongside a pipe bridge across the Hutt river at a 122 metre long platform. The junction with the main line was the site of a secondary stopping place called "Beach". The Government supplied the trains and collected the fares for the company. A Wa class locomotive was the normal traction on the line, and trains ran through to Wellington.

The line was abandoned some time in the early 1900s, the exact closure date being uncertain. Part of the line continued, however, in the form of the industrial sidings for the Gear Meat works along the Petone foreshore. Two locomotives used by Gear Meat, a ex-NZR D class 2-4-0 tank and a Dubs A class 0-4-0 tank, later sold to Thomas Borthwick, ultimately ended up in the Silver Stream museum, near Upper Hutt.

With the closure of the Gear Meat Company in 1982, the last remnants of this line were removed.

The Rimutaka Incline

The 5 km long section of railway line down the slopes on the Wairarapa side of the Rimutaka ranges earned for itself a firm place in the annals of not only New Zealand railway history, but also world railway history. For it employed the only commercially successful application of the centre rail system designed by English engineer John Barraclough Fell. The Rimutaka Incline formed part of the main Wellington-Masterton rail link and every passenger train between Wellington and the Wairarapa had to transport its passengers over it, providing them with an unforgettable experience in the process.

From its opening in October 1878 to its closure on 29 October 1955 the Rimutaka Incline was the third and only lasting utilisation of the Fell principle. The first was on a temporary line opened in 1866 on Mount Cenis in the European Alps between France and Italy, which closed again in 1871 when made redundant by a

◀*Marshalling operations at Summit on 1 October 1955 with two* DE*'s on the right and two Fell locomotives on the left. The Fell locos were never turned and went up and down the incline facing the same way.* NZR

▼*A classic New Zealand railways image – four of the H class Fell locomotives plod up the Rimutaka Incline at Siberia Curve on 1 October 1955.* NZR

An AB waits to take train away from 'ross Creek into the 'airarapa in 1952. 'he beginning of the cline can be seen in e background. NZR

A turn of the century iew of Cross Creek. LEXANDER URNBULL LIBRARY

An excursion train arrives at Summit in the last days. A greenery bedecked DE *waits to take it to Wellington.*
MAURIE DUSTON

tunnel. The second was on the Cantagallo Railway in Brazil on a steep climb from the coastal plains around Rio de Janeiro to the Inland plateau. The locomotives had been shipped there after the closure of the Mount Cenis line and were used until 1883, when they were replaced by normal locomotives, although the Fell centre rail continued to be used for braking the trains.

The Wellington to Masterton railway had reached Upper Hutt in 1876 and on 1 January 1878 it was opened as far as Kaitoke (269 metres above sea level). From Kaitoke the line was built along the valley of the Pakuratahi river, which it followed to a saddle in the main range and the Summit Station (348 metres above sea level). The gradient from Kaitoke to the Summit Station was a gradual 1 in 40 to 1 in 39. However, once a tunnel had been bored through to the other side of the saddle, the railway constructors were faced with a gradient of between 1 in 16 to 1 in 14 from there to the bottom at Cross Creek (83 metres above sea level).

This was clearly too steep for a standard locomotive to hold without slipping on the track, and the Fell centre rail system was adopted. This involved the laying of a double sided smooth rail raised between the two standard rails with secure fastening.

The Fell locomotives (the class H 0-4-2 tanks), had a special extra set of 60 cm diameter driving wheels which clasped the centre rail from underneath with powerful springs exerting a pressure of 15 tonnes. These wheels were driven through an extra set of cylinders. Because these latter revolved faster than the cylinders for the outside wheels, the locomotives had their own peculiar syncopated exhaust beats. As well as the extra set of horizontal driving wheels, there was also a brake fitted under the engines which likewise gripped the centre rail to provide extra braking power. Guard's vans equipped with their own brakes completed the system.

The wear on these centre rail brakes was enormous and after every round trip new shoes had to be fitted.

Initially the practice was for only one locomotive per train to be used transporting a weight of 50 tonnes, but eventually up to five locomotives per train were deployed. A passenger train arriving at either the Summit or at Cross Creek was split up into groups of three carriages each with its own Fell engine. The train was then reunited, together with a number of Fell brake vans, and proceeded to plod up or down the hill.

Needless to say the whole process was slow and the 106 km from Wellington to Masterton took 3½ hours. The 5 km from Cross Creek to the Summit took 30 minutes at a speed of 10 km/h.

The incline was also expensive. Each Fell engine had a crew of two and each brake van was manned, so that one train needed a total crew of some 15 people. Besides this, personnel were required for shunting the locomotives and maintaining the engine sheds and centre rail. As much coal was consumed by a southbound train on the Incline as on the whole rest of the journey from Masterton to Wellington.

For the 11 km from Kaitoke to Summit the normal speed going up was 26 km/h and 32 km/h going down, involving journey times of 30 minutes and 20 minutes respectively.

Railcars (nicknamed "Tin Hares") were placed on the run in 1936. These resembled buses and had passenger seating of 49 (second class). A total of six named after Maori canoes were deployed. They reduced the overall journey time from Wellington to Masterton by an hour through the elimination of the shunting time.

The weather on the Rimutakas is always changeable and often the wind is treacherous in exposed places - a problem which continues to affect users of the state highway over the ranges, which lies some distance to the west of the former railway road-bed. On 13 September 1880 a strong wind gust on the long Siberia Curve blew the two leading coaches and a brake van of a mixed train off the tracks, killing three children in one of the carriages which fell into the gully and seriously injuring five adults. After this a wind break was built at the curve. This did not prevent two further incidents on the flat near Pigeon Bush, although no fatalities resulted

Above: The last train climbs the Incline on 29 October 1955. The spectacular displays then were consigned to the history books. MAURIE DUSTON
Right: The centre rail in the last days of use. NZR

on either occasion.

Eventually in 1948 the decision was made to build a tunnel under the Rimutakas to replace the costly Fell section. The tunnel was holed through in April 1954 after three years of boring and on 3 November 1955 the new deviation was opened, thus ending the epoch of the unique Rimutaka Incline.

Today the entire 16 km road-bed of the former railway line from Kaitoke to Cross Creek is a walking track and represents a pleasant day's outing. From Kaitoke to the Summit the line is on the territory of the Wellington Regional Council, and from the Summit to Cross Creek it is in the Rimutaka Forest Park controlled by the Department of Conservation. Both authorities have put some effort in recent years into keeping the track well maintained and clearing the historical sites of scrub to reveal what remains. During 1987 mock stations were built at Kaitoke, Summit and Cross Creek, which include pictorial displays of the old railway days. On 1 November 1987 the walkway was officially opened by the Governor General.

The walking track is easy to find. On the Kaitoke side a small group of buildings which includes the former station building signals the beginning of the old line which runs alongside the state highway for a few metres. A roadsign points out the car-park about 1.2 km along the former line. Beyond this, cars, motorbikes and horses are not permitted. On the Cross Creek side, the Western Lake Road turns off the main highway at Featherston and after 10 km the turn-off for the car-park at Cross Creek is indicated by a sign pointing out the Rimutaka Forest Park on the right.

There are four tunnels on the walk, the longest of which is at the Summit (584 metres) for which a good flashlight should be brought.

Those who plan to walk over the line should allow 3½ hours for the line itself inclusive of stops, and an additional 20 minutes for the walk from Cross Creek to the car park nearby. From there a visit should be made to the Fell Museum on the main road at Featherston, which houses the sole surviving example of the original Fell locomotives, H 199, a restored Fell brakevan, a model of the Cross Creek yard and photo displays.

Two ABs head a Wellington–Auckland express, diverted over the Wairarapa Line, on 28 January 1953 near Kaitoke. NZR

Wairarapa Line

The Rimutaka Ranges represented the major difficulty facing the builders of the railway from Wellington to the Wairarapa. Once this major undertaking was finished it was only another two years of road-bed building through relatively easy terrain before the line from Cross Creek through Featherston and Carterton to Masterton, 61 km, was completed. This now gave the settlers in the southern Wairarapa the vital rail link with the port of Wellington. The extension of the line northwards from Masterton however, took a little longer to get underway. This part of the country was known as "Forty Mile Bush" and had been settled mainly by Scandinavians. The first 20 km from Masterton to Mauriceville was opened on 14 June 1886, and a further 6 km from there to Mangamahoe on 10 January 1887. The next 10 km to Eketahuna containing the only tunnel on the line from Masterton to Woodville, the 150 m long Wiwaka tunnel, was opened on 8 April 1889. The tunnel at 286 m altitude is located on what can be regarded as the watershed between the southern and northern Wairarapa. From Eketahuna it was another seven years until the next short 4 km section was built to Newman. The next 24 km section from there to Pahiatua was opened the next year. This section contained the longest bridge on the line, the 162 m long Mangatainoka River Bridge. The settlement of Mangatainoka, some 24 km from the aforementioned bridge was the next railhead three months later, and finally on 11 December 1897 the complete line to Woodville, 186 km from Wellington via the Rimutaka Incline, was opened.

The completion of the line through the Wairarapa gave the Government Railways their connection with the Taranaki and Hawkes Bay regions. Up to then the only through connecting line from Wellington was the Wellington and Manawatu Railway Company's line to Longburn, opened back in 1886. The Napier Mail trains from Wellington to Napier now went through the Wairarapa instead of connecting with the WMR. at Longburn. At this stage two 2-4-2 K class locomotive from the South Island were transferred to the line and were later augmented by two N class 2-6-2 locomotives, also from the South Island. In 1909 following the Government's purchase of the WMR., the Napier Express trains were transferred to the western side of the Tararuas through the Manawatu. A new train known as the Wairarapa Mail, ran through the Wairarapa as far as Woodville. A mixed train left Masterton around 7.00 a.m. and connected with the Napier Express at Woodville. The cars from the

Above: A Fiat railcar on its way to Woodville stops at Featherston in 1965. The station was replaced in 1982. NZR

Right: Greytown station in the 1920s with a 2-4-0T D class in the yard. NZR

Wairarapa Mail were attached to a mixed train which left Dannevirke for Palmerston North. Woodville station had a dining room where passengers could have a meal while waiting for the train.

In 1936 new "Tin Hare" railcars were introduced for the Wairarapa run as far as Woodville. These enabled a significant shortening of the timetable from Wellington to Woodville mainly because of their speed over the Rimutaka Incline. They had not long been in service when one was blown off the rails by a wind gust at Pigeon Bush, north of Cross Creek in October 1936. In 1948 they completely replaced the Wairarapa Mail trains, although some mixed trains continued.

The completion of the Rimutaka Tunnel and deviation in November 1955 spelt major operational changes for the Wairarapa line. The deviation shortened the route length by 14.4 km and journey times for goods trains were reduced by over an hour and a half. With the tunnel came dieselisation with the new diesel-electric DG class locomotives and thus the Wairarapa line was the first to be fully dieselised in New Zealand. Twin-set "Fiat" railcars took over from the "tin hares" within a few months of the new tunnel being opened and continued to provide passenger services over the line until 1977. Until 1963 there was a Friday railcar evening service each way from Masterton to Woodville. By December 1963 the morning commuter railcar service was seeing over 200 passengers, too many for two "Fiat" sets with a combined capacity of just 176 seats, and a carriage train was introduced. Initially this consisted of 5 cars plus a van, hauled by a pair of DEs. Later DAs took over the haulage of this service. In December 1977 the "Fiat" railcars were withdrawn and replaced with AC "grassgrub" carriages. Later in the mid-1980s these were in turn replaced by trains of up to 7 standard carriages.

Although only 137 metres above sea level, an alpine impression is created by this scene of a DBR hauled Masterton–Wellington passenger train crossing the Mangaroa Bridge near Maymorn in the 1980s. MARK COLE

The Wairarapa line was the only means of access for DA locomotives to Wellington until the tunnels on the Main Trunk between Paekakariki and Pukerua Bay were lowered in July 1967. The line north of Masterton runs through some difficult terrain although the ruling gradient is a relatively mild 1 in 80 and curves are no sharper than 200 metre radius, with most being over 300 metre radius. There is one 6 km section of perfectly straight track between Hukanui and Mangamaire known in railcar days as the "racetrack". One feature of interest is the junction at Woodville which features a "balloon loop" opened in July 1966 to enable through trains from the Wairarapa to Hawkes Bay to continue straight through Woodville without the engine having to run around the train. The presence of several streams would have made a conventional "triangle" track a more costly exercise.

Patronage of the through passenger trains north of Masterton to Palmerston North dwindled during the 1980s and the last one ran on 29 July 1988.

For a period about 1990 the Masterton to Woodville section had no regular freight trains either, and was only used as a detour when the Main Trunk between Wellington and Palmerston North was blocked by derailments or for repair work. Then the congestion on the Manawatu line became such that an overnight freight each way between Napier and Wellington was diverted to this route. There are currently proposals to send more traffic this way, due to the increasing use of hi-cube containers, which cannot fit through the Manawatu Gorge tunnels. The section from Masterton to Wellington is now seeing four weekday passenger trains each way, and the Wellington Regional Council is talking to Tranz Rail about more passenger services. Freight on this section is mainly logs, and wood products from the Juken Nissho plant just south of Masterton.

Greytown Branch

As with so many other branch lines, the 5 km branch from Woodside on the Wairarapa line to Greytown was clamoured for by the local townspeople and the Public Works Department obliged. The line was an easy job, the work being completed in two months on 10 January 1880. The rails laid were 24 kg/m and had the distinction of still being in use when the line was closed 73 years later. After platelaying and ballasting the opening day came on 14 May 1880. The timetable after opening was virtually an extension of the timetable between Wellington and Featherston until the Wairarapa line was extended beyond Woodside junction in November 1880, with an extra 35 minutes being allowed for the new additional 12 km. The usual locomotive was a L class 2-4-0 stabled at Greytown.

As from 1880 most traffic was in the form of pigs and sheep—passenger numbers never quite reached expectations. The branch was always worked by small tank locomotives; in the early days these were L's or D's or the occasional C. In the 1930s they were replaced by two Wf's, 398 and 400. Wf 398 was adapted in 1931 for one man operation, something that was to become widespread over 50 years later.

The branch had no stations other than the termini and the only signal was a home signal guarding Woodside station. As late as 1952 there were five trains a day each with a passenger car attached (often with no passengers). That year the number of trains were cut to two each way a day. The Royal Commission of 1952 identified the Greytown Branch as proportionately the biggest loss making line in the country with revenue less than a tenth of operating costs and not surprisingly it was closed the following year on 24 December 1953.

▲*Picturesque although seldom photographed, the Mangaroa valley lies between the Maoribank and Rimutaka tunnels. Two DA's approach Maymorn Station with a Wellington–Napier goods train via the Wairarapa in 1975.*
MARK COLE

▶*Eight years and a few hundred metres further on, two DC's lead a 32 total Wellington–Napier train into the 8.80 km Rimutaka tunnel.*
MARK COLE

A W&MR train leaves Khandallah Station, a scene from a late 19th century postcard. MUIR & MOODIE

The Wellington and Manawatu Railway

By the 1870s the need to establish a rail link out of Wellington along the West Coast to the Manawatu region had become pressing. Existing traffic was in the form of either coastal shipping from Wellington to the river port at Foxton, or via an arduous overland route involving two substantial hill crossings and several rivers which had to be forded—conditions that were hardly pleasant for those making the journey.

In 1874 the first line out of Wellington to Lower Hutt had been built and in the following years continued over the Rimutaka Ranges to the Wairarapa and then through to Woodville, there branching one way to Palmerston North and the other to Hawkes Bay. This, however, was seen by many Wellington residents as in indirect route to the north, whose people looked to a more direct route up the West Coast. A Wellington grocer, Mr James Wallace, took up the cause, drawing up plans on how to best traverse the hills surrounding Wellington. He convinced the then Minister of Works and in 1879 Parliament allocated £15,000 for the project. Of three alternative routes out of Wellington, the one chosen was the existing stage coach route through Johnsonville. On 1 September 1879 work commenced and within six months the formation for the line had progressed the 10.5 km to Johnsonville. A further £40,000 was voted by Parliament late in 1879, but a few weeks later the government of Sir George Grey was defeated on a motion claiming extravagant expenditure. Work on the Wellington to Manawatu line stopped.

A new Parliament was elected and one of the first steps of the new Premier, Sir John Hall, was to set up a Royal Commission to investigate all railway construction projects. In June 1880 its findings were presented, among them the view that the West Coast Railway project was in competition with the Wairarapa line and was premature because of the land being over rated and still in the hands of Maori landowners. The recommendation was for a cessation of the project and for the labour to be transferred to complete the Wairarapa railway.

Needless to say this was not well received by merchants in Wellington and Porirua who, led by James Wallace and John Plimmer, organised meetings and deputations to press for a resumption. At one meeting the Premier stated that the Government had no money available due to the depression and suggested that the people of Wellington should pursue the line themselves. That was what happened.

On 29 September 1880, a meeting called by the Wellington Chamber of Commerce voted to form a company and a committee was set up. In line with an earlier promise, the Government agreed to hand over all railway works to the company and permission was given to reclaim 2.7 hectares of land at Thorndon. The total concessions, including track, rails, wagons and fencing and three blacksmith's shops, was put at £49,500.

The next stage was for the company to raise capital of £500,000, which was obtained in the form of £5 shares, paid to five shillings on allotment, with periodic calls of a shilling. The initial target total of £50,000 was not quick in coming, however, and was realised only through tireless efforts of men such as John Plimmer, William Levin and George Shannon, who themselves took 2,000 shares each. Later the towns of Plimmerton, Levin and Shannon along the line were named in their honour.

The original government plan for the West Coast Railway was for it to run directly to Wanganui via Foxton and Bulls, thus omitting Palmerston North. The Foxton to Wanganui Railway ran through Palmerston North, however, this would have become a branch line in the event that the main line followed the original plan. The Wellington and Manawatu Railway Company was only interested in the most profitable route and decided on a route across the Makerua Swamp that linked with the Foxton to Wanganui Railway at Longburn. The Railway Construction and Land Act of 1881 effectively empowered the project to proceed, and it was the only line to be completed under this Act. The company was registered on 23 August 1881, the day after the second reading of the Bill. On 22 March 1882 the company entered into a contract with the Government, as required by the Act, which provided that for completion of the railway within five years, the Government would grant 87,295 hectares of Government land (valued at £96,000) to the company plus the works already completed. The contract also required the company to spend £50,000 within the first year and to conform to NZR rolling stock and plant specifications, as well as keeping within fare tariffs that the Government thought reasonable. By the end of 1882, more than £235,000 of capital had been subscribed, almost all of it by Wellington residents, contrary to expectations that most of it would have to be raised in England.

Work commenced in September 1882 and was let to various contractors. Because of the deficiency of roads it was necessary to ship most of the materials along the coast, with special wharves, tracks and inclines being built to carry them to the road-bed. The construction involved overcoming the hills out of Wellington, thick bush along most of the route and swampy areas north of Levin. Thirteen tunnels, five major bridges and a viaduct were required. The latter was north of Johnsonville and known as the Belmont viaduct. It was originally built in wood and was 52 metres high and 113 metres long, utilising in total 6,425 metres of timber and 35 tonnes of iron bolts and braces. At the time it was the largest wooden viaduct in New Zealand. Seven of the tunnels were on what is now the Johnsonville Branch and the other six were on the hillside between Pukerua Bay and Paekakariki. At Wellington, reclamation was necessary at Thorndon for a terminal station and a goods yard.

The first coaches arrived from the United States in February 1885 and drew attention with their high roofs, large windows and wheel bogies which made them look like giants compared with NZR stock. Locomotives from the U.K. arrived shortly afterwards.

On 21 September 1885 the first 25 km section of the line from Wellington to Paremata was opened without ceremony. Traffic was able to reach Plimmerton in October and Pukerua Bay by the end of 1885. By February 1886 the section north of tunnel number thirteen to Paekakariki and the section from Longburn to Otaki were ready for traffic.

The public opening ceremony of the complete line was held on 3 November 1886 at Otaihanga about halfway between Paraparaumu and Waikanae, when the Governor, Sir William Jervois, drove home the last spike. It was a gala occasion for the people of Wellington and Palmerston North, and some 1,200 arrived on two special trains to witness the event. Before handing over a commemorative gold plated spike to the Governor, the company's chairman, Mr Joseph Nathan, described the railway as the "royal road" to development and requested that the last link to unite Wellington with Auckland, New Plymouth and Napier be completed.

Twenty days later the first agreement containing some thirty-four points on the interchange of traffic was signed with NZR. This was necessary if the company was to receive its share of through traffic from the north, although the rival route from Palmerston North through the Manawatu Gorge and the Wairarapa was not connected until 1897. One clause in the agreement which was the cause of much ill feeling was that all fares and charges applying to the NZR also applied to the company. Later, when the Wairarapa line was connected, the Government declared the distance between Palmerston North and Wellington via the Manawatu line (139 km) and the Wairarapa line (213 km) to be the same for the purpose of computing fares and freight rates. The company also claimed that timetables on the line from Napier were altered so that there were no convenient connections for passengers wanting to travel via the Manawatu. Despite this "friendly rivalry", as Premier Dick Seddon put it, the W.M.R. prospered and the initial debt of £100,000 was soon cleared, helped in part from land and sales revenue from flax and sawmills, and in 1891 shareholders received their first dividend of 3 1/2 percent. Eventually the dividend reached 7 percent, the maximum permitted under the Railway Construction and Land Act. Operating ratios increased from 34.7 percent in 1890 to 61.3 percent in 1908, very healthy figures particularly by today's standards.

The company's first eight locomotives came from England - five Manning Wardle 2-6-2 tank engines and three Nasmyth Wilson 2-6-2 tender engines, which arrived between 1884 and 1886. The first two locomotives to actually work on the line were a New Zealand built Davidson P class 0-6-0 saddle tank from 1876 and a Neilson & Co. 'C' class 0-4-0 saddle tank from 1873, both bought second-hand from NZR. Both of these two locomotives had interesting careers after their service on the W.M.R.

With its coaching stock as well as its operating methods and terminology originating from the United States, it was perhaps natural that the W.M.R. would acquire locomotives from the United States as well. From 1888 all the company's locomotives came from the Baldwin Locomotive Works in Philadelphia and by 1900 the company had the largest and most powerful locomotives in the country, among them seven compounds. Its first, No. 13 from 1894, was the first narrow gauge Vauclain compound and the first compound to run in New Zealand. Another interesting locomotive was No. 17, the only Mikado or 2-8-2 to run in New Zealand, and at 71 tonnes, the heaviest in the fleet. Locomotive No. 10, a Baldwin 2-6-2, achieved fame when on 20 July 1892 it broke the speed record for 1,067 mm gauge at 103 km/h.

The W.M.R. pioneered the dining car in New Zealand in the form of a converted brake van, the first true dining car being built two years later. Two further dining cars from America followed in 1894 and 1904. The W.M.R. was progressive, too, in its use of the telephone for communication rather than Morse telegraph, and

in the illumination of its trains by electricity (at first by experimental dynamos, then by storage batteries from 1896) at a time when the kerosene lamp was standard.

During its time the Wellington and Manawatu Railway Co. developed a very efficient railway operation that did much to develop the territories in the Horowhenua and Manawatu. However, there was never any doubt that ultimately the line would form part of the complete North Island Main Trunk under the ownership and control of the state. The private operation was not without its critics, particularly farmers in Taranaki and other regions who felt that it increased freight costs to Wellington. This arose because the NZR tariffs were on a reducing sliding scale, but this computation ended at Longburn. Even the Wellington Chamber of Commerce, which had done so much to support the formation of the company, joined with others in the southern half of the North Island in 1899 in urging the Government to buy the railway, considering that friction and conflicts of interest between the Government railways and the private line was not in the public interest. An obstacle to the Government was the twenty-one year penalty clause in the empowering Act. The Government had to wait until 1907 before it could buy the line without compensation. When that time came, and with the completion of the Main Trunk in sight, the Prime Minister, Sir Joseph Ward, acted by giving the company formal notice of its intention to buy, which the company received on 7 December 1907. The purchase price was finally agreed at £900,000 with an additional £10,000 for stores and another £15,000 on the condition that the company handed over on 7 December 1908, twelve months after the notice of purchase. A total of £933,000 was paid by the Government, considered a bargain by shareholders as the company's book value was £828,376 in 1908, after allowing for £218,000 to be written off.

So ended the Wellington and Manawatu Railway at a luncheon in the Concert Chamber of the Wellington Town Hall when the chairman, John Kirkcaldie, handed the railway over to Sir Joseph after 22 years of successful operation. The 135 km of track, 20 locomotives, 415 pieces of rolling stock and a staff of 324 were transferred to the NZR.

For the staff, the changeover meant having to learn the Morse code and how to operate the gas lighting in place of electric lighting in the coaches. However, with the increased volume of traffic following the shifting of much Hawkes Bay volume onto the line rather than via the Wairarapa and the Rimutaka Incline, plus the new traffic generated from the completion of the Main Trunk, the NZR had to install new signalling and train control in the form of Tyer's electric tablet instruments between Wellington and Longburn plus additions to the interlocking equipment and signals. This had actually been put in place prior to the change-over, so staff were trained in its use. In the first year of Government control, traffic increased from 46 to 110 trains per week with additional suburban and Sunday services.

Today, increasing demand for an alternative to the congested Highway 1 route to Wellington has resulted in the introduction of a new commuter train. Since 1991 the "Capital Connection" has provided an early morning service from Palmerston North to Wellington, taking only 2 hours 1 minute, together with a return service. The success of this service led to the introduction in 1994 of a late morning train from Wellington, and an afternoon return, plus a Sunday afternoon train pair.

▶A nine car English Electric multiple-unit set on its way to Paraparaumu, seen at South Junction north of Muri on 26 January 1983. MARK COLE

◀The spirit of the Wellington and Manawatu Railway Company is recalled by the regular steam hauled excursions over the line. Here KA *945 rolls out of Shannon after a trip to Taumarunui on 5 June 1989.* MARK COLE

▲A four car Hungarian built multiple-unit set descends the Paekakariki bank to Paekakariki in the evening of 30 December 1982. This corner has been the site of a few derailments over the years. MARK COLE

▶The tranquillity of the Paremata Inlet north of Wellington is temporarily disturbed by a southbound express freight headed by a DX/DC *combination on 4 December 1988.* MARK COLE

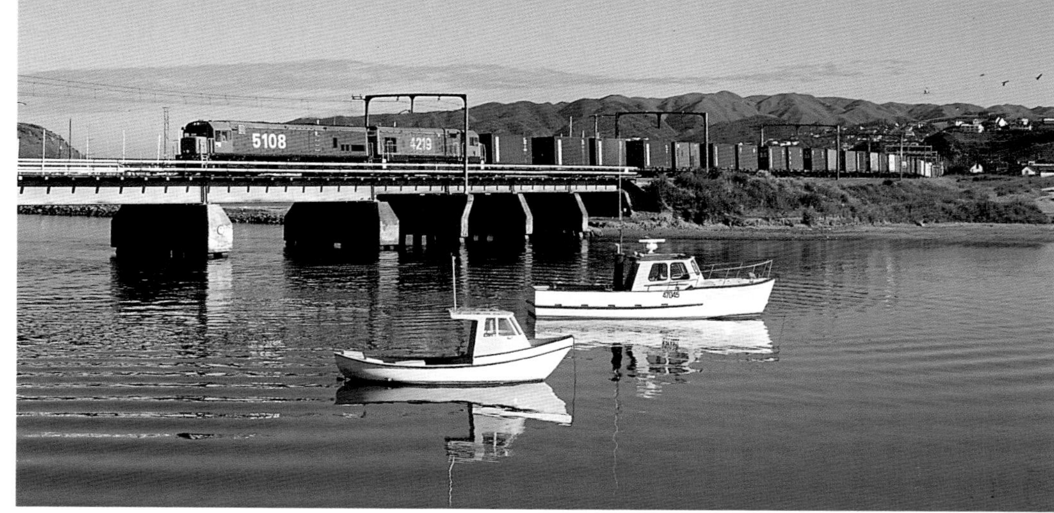

These did not get many patrons, and lasted less than a year. The original service became even more popular when a set of second-hard carriages from Britain, which had been re-gauged and refurbished in the Hutt Workshops, took over this service on 1 November 1999. These carriages provide a superior standard of commuter train, with such facilities as power points for laptops. Fast trains with better carriages thus provide something of an echo of the old "Manawatu". The only likely future problem is that if the long-promised extension of electrification to Waikanae or Otaki takes place, the customers will want electric trains of the same high standard.

Te Aro extension

In 1893 the Government line ending at Thorndon was extended along the present day Customhouse and Jervois Quays through to Te Aro, a distance of 1.8 km. The Te Aro Station was located at approximately where the intersection of Tory and Wakefield streets now is. The line never achieved popularity or success. It was intended for passenger transport and the matter of building freight handling facilities at Te Aro station was a subject of debate. It is doubtful if freight was ever carried on the line.

At its peak, 212 passenger trains a week were run but by 1916 this number had dwindled to 62. Businesses had long complained about the smoke and noise that trains produced, and eventually, in March 1917, with the country involved in World War I and coal saving measures in force, the line was closed. The tracks were removed soon after.

The Te Aro Extension should not be confused with the Te Aro Tramway, a 3 metre high trestle causeway built in 1883. This was part of reclamation activities at Te Aro and ran in a line from the Town Hall across the water to Clyde Quay and along the beach to the far end of Oriental Bay below Roseneath.

The Wellington Cable Car

For Wellington City, the cable car is just as much a civic symbol as are those of San Francisco in the USA. The line with a 1 in 5 gradient line was built from Cable Car Lane, just off Lambton Quay, in the city area to Kelburn between 1899 and 1902 to develop the housing settlements of Kelburn and Karori. Opened on 22 February 1902, the system utilised steam-driven winding machinery in a power-house at the top until 1933, when an electric motor was installed.

The operation was owned for its first 44 years by the Kelburne and Karori Tramway Company Ltd. In 1946 the cable car was bought by the Wellington City Council.

A few years after opening the original cars had been augmented by trailers, but transport safety regulations forced the removal of the trailers as from 22 July 1974. By this stage the whole system was well worn, and in 1976 the City Council decided to replace the whole system rather than face the costs of a major upgrading. The last journey of the old cars took place on 22 September 1978.

The new cable car system was built by the firm of Habegger AG in Switzerland and was officially opened on 6 October 1979. The present line is metre gauge and is 0.61 km in length. The system is a standing funicular with the two cars at the opposite ends of a single cable driven by an electric motor in the top station. The cars run on a single track (as opposed to the original double track) and pass each other at a passing loop in the middle. The top station offers good views of the harbour and is adjacent to the Botanic Gardens. Some 800,000 passengers a year make the 6 minute journey on this cableway, which combines part of the old Edwardian ambience with modern comfort and safety.

On 5 December 2000 a museum of the Cable Car was opened adjacent to the Kelburn Terminus.

The Wellington Cable Car seen in the 1900s. In 1979 when the system was reopened, it was converted to single track with a passing loop in the centre. ALEXANDER TURNBULL LIBRARY

Above: A 4-car electric multiple unit arrives at Crofton Downs station on the Johnsonville Branch to take schoolboys and office workers into the city in 1972. NZR

Right: An ED *electric hauls a livestock train between NIMT tunnels 1 and 2 in 1949 with a deserted Ngauranga Gorge in the background.* NZR

The Tawa deviation

Not long after the Wellington and Manawatu Railway Company had been absorbed into the NZR system, traffic over the steep twisting Wellington to Johnsonville section reached the limit of its capacity, and as early as 1912 plans were drawn up to find a better alternative egress.

In 1928 work began on a deviation from Kaiwharawhara to Tawa Flat via two tunnels of 1.2 km and 4.3 km respectively. This double tracked deviation completed in 1937, significantly reduced the distance and journey time between Wellington and Tawa. The steepest grade on the deviation is 1 in 100, compared with 1 in 36 on the Johnsonville line. The highest point on the deviation is 59 metres at the north portal of the second tunnel, compared with the highest point of 152 metres on the Johnsonville line. With the opening of the deviation, the line between Johnsonville and Tawa was lifted. This included the Belmont viaduct (rebuilt as a steel structure in 1904) north of Johnsonville, although the viaduct itself was not demolished until December 1951.

Johnsonville Branch

After the Tawa deviation was completed in 1937, the section of the until-then main trunk line as far as Johnsonville was retained as a branch line to provide suburban commuter transport from Wellington's northern suburbs to the city.

This move had not been an automatic one, however. In 1931 the Government had announced that the line would be closed and offered it to the Wellington City Corporation as an extension to their urban tramways system. This proposal was hotly opposed by local citizens' groups who wanted the railway line to remain. Eventually the decision was made following recommendations of the Government Railways Board to Parliament in 1935, to not only retain the line but to electrify it with the use of multiple unit trains. The first passenger service was inaugurated by the then Minister of Railways, D.G. Sullivan, on 2 July 1938, beginning the era of electrified commuter trains in Wellington.

When the new Hungarian units were introduced in 1982 to Wellington's suburban network no allowance had been made for the tight clearances inside the tunnels on the line and thus they could not be used. Thus the old units continued in use, with upgrading in the form of new interior linings and lighting, reconditioned motors, new twin sealed beam lighting and the new external livery of olive green and ivory paintwork.

The line's continuation has been under scrutiny in recent years but reports indicating a distinct commuter preference for the railway over buses suggest that the line's future is secure, at least for a few more years. In 1992 trials were undertaken, to see how easy it would be to enlarge the tunnels for Ganz-Mavag units. Greater patronage on other lines makes this not such a promising idea, and another refurbishment of the old units is underway, with blue being the new external colour. Increased services, including Sunday trains, were introduced in September 1997, reflecting partly social changes with far more inner-city activity in Wellington at the weekend.

The line rises from Wellington Station (2.4 metres above sea level) to a maximum height of 152 metres above sea level at Mt. Misery, them dropping slightly, reaching the terminus at Johnsonville at 142 metres above sea level. Over its 10.5 km length, it contains no fewer than seven tunnels and many curves, because of which the maximum authorised speed is 64 km/h in the open and 40 km/h inside the tunnels. There are eight stations on the line, the first being Crofton Downs and the last Johnsonville. Until 1984 Johnsonville had its own small yard, but then the station was rebuilt and shortened, eliminating the yard in the process. At Johnsonville one can look across the traffic islands and see where the main trunk line used to continue, following closely the route of the present Wellington-Porirua motorway. The journey takes 21 minutes each way, passing through interesting terrain and is a recommended excursion.

Foxton Branch

The 31 km Longburn to Foxton branch originally began life as a wooden tramway built between Foxton and Palmerston North. In the 1860s Foxton was a small settlement near the mouth of the Manawatu River and was a potential part for the Manawatu region. Accordingly the need arose for rail transport between it and the hinterland. The terrain of the Manawatu was swampy and in wet weather roads became a quagmire. With finances not being healthy, wooden construction was seen as the only way of getting the tramway built. Even so, the provincial government could not afford the expense and it was not until the Vogel era began in 1870 that the project got underway the following year with the signing of contracts. The tramway, built to the 3'6" (1067 mm) gauge, had its rails and sleepers made of matai and totara. The road-bed work was mainly done by immigrant Scandinavian labour.

In 1872 a 10 horsepower (6 kW) steam locomotive was built for the tramway by the Dunedin firm of Messrs R. S. Sparrow and Co., thus making it technically the

Junction of the Foxton Branch (left) and the NIMT (right) in 1959. In the centre is the (uncompleted) Milson Deviation. NZR

first steam locomotive to be built in New Zealand (a replica of it is now displayed in Foxton). The following year the wharf at Foxton was built. On 25 July 1873 the last rail of the tramway between Foxton and Palmerston (North) Terrace End, 40 km, was laid.

It was not long before continuation of the route to Wanganui was being mooted, initially as a straight extension of the wooden tramway, but it was soon realised that such an idea was impracticable. Complaints about the wooden tramway between Foxton and Palmerston began appearing towards the end of 1874, as the 40 km journey often took as long as 5 hours. The following year conversion work to turn the tramway into a railway started with the arrival of iron rails at Foxton wharf. On 27 April 1876 the reopening as a railway took place and F class locomotives began operation. The line was generally flat and the only real natural obstacle was the Oroua River, which required a 56 metre long bridge.

In 1881 a new station was built at Foxton and port facilities were significantly improved. The most significant development during the 1880s was, however, the approaching completion of the Wellington and Manawatu Railway Company's line. Originally the Government's proposal had been to link with the Manawatu at Foxton, but with private enterprise in charge, the decision was made for the shortest route between Palmerston and Wellington, and accordingly the junction point of Longburn was chosen. Foxton residents, as might have been expected, reacted unfavourably at being by-passed. Nevertheless the W.M.R. stuck to its plans and on 1 December 1886 the W.M.R. was opened. Foxton thus became the end of a branch line.

The opening of the Wellington and Manawatu Railway Company's line all but eliminated seaborne passenger trade to and from Foxton. Freight traffic also suffered, although the Government continued to ship railway coal through Foxton rather than use the W.M.R., and the flax trade, which channelled its products through the port was experiencing an upturn. Against this the port itself was deteriorating with the fall in the spring tides causing increasing strandings in both the river and at the bar. Shippers were turning elsewhere. Following the take-over of the W.M.R. by the Government in 1908, the Railways had no further interest in shipping through Foxton. By 1916 all shipping trade through Foxton was in the hands of the shipping company Levin and Company and was handled by two steamers, the 121 tonne Queen of the South which carried general cargo, and the 151 tonne Awahou which carried mainly coal. The latter could only use Foxton at spring tides. The company had their own wharf at Foxton served by a large shed. When the shed was destroyed by fire in 1922 the company did not rebuild and withdrew from the shipping business. With a general economic downturn occurring at the same time coupled with competition from motor traffic, the Foxton Branch was now a loss-maker. A limited amount of shipping via the port continued, organised by local interests.

On 22 August 1932 passenger services on the Foxton Branch in the form of mixed trains were axed and the locomotive depot at Foxton was closed. This move was not unexpected as daily passenger counts on the two trains each was had fallen from 127 in 1925 to 25 in 1932, most of these being school children. The following day all stations between Longburn and Foxton became flag stations.

During World War II troop trains were carried on the Foxton Branch after the Manawatu Mounted Rifles set up a camp on the Foxton racecourse and in early 1942 a special train carrying the Palmerston North Home Guard, consisting of a Bb class locomotive and 18 cars was probably the longest ever seen on the line. Shipping ceased at Foxton in 1942.

By the beginning of the 1950s outwards goods traffic over the branch of some 5,500 tonnes per annum was mainly woolpacks and root crops while inwards traffic of some 13,000 tonnes per annum was mainly timber, lime manure and coal. As Foxton was within 50 km of Palmerston North, and well served by NZR road traffic, the closure of the Foxton Branch was recommended by the 1952 Royal Commission. The line was not closed immediately, but was allowed to run down over the next seven years and closure came on 18 July 1959. That day there was a farewell excursion train organised by the New Zealand Railway and Locomotive Society. It consisted of A 601 and a seven total train. It left Palmerston North at 11.50 a.m. and had returned there by 2.40 p.m. The last goods train ran over the Foxton branch on Tuesday 21 July 1959.

The Sanson Tramway

As early as 1877 settlers north of Foxton were pressing for a rail link with the port and consequently the following year the Foxton and Sanson Railway Company was formed, its object being to form a railway along the roadway between Carnarvon (later Himitangi), a station on the Foxton-Palmerston railway, and Sanson. Before building began, however, changes in legislation made it more appropriate for the County Council of the Manawatu to build the line as a tramway and accordingly qualify for a three-to-one government subsidy. The company was thus dissolved.

Work started from the Carnarvon end in 1882 and after many stops and starts the line reached Sanson in 1885.

The former Wellington steam tram *Hibernia* was the first source of motive power over the line, but proved inadequate. By the time the line reached Sanson, the old Foxton engine *Wallaby* had joined it, which coped a little better with the unorthodox undulations of the road-bed. After the initial very light traffic had become a little more substantial, an ex-NZR 0-4-0T A class followed in 1889, and in 1897 came an ex-NZR 0-6-0T P class ex the Wellington and Manawatu Railway Company. Through running to Foxton ceased in 1932 when passenger services over the Foxton Branch ended. Just before World War II the needs of contractors at the Ohakea Air Force base gave the Sanson Tramway some revitalisation as did petrol restrictions during World War II. With the coming of peace in 1945, the Manawatu County Council's tramway no longer had any raison d'être and it was closed on 29 November 1945.

CHAPTER TWELVE

Nelson and Marlborough

Nelson Section

This 100 km or so of line which finally closed in September 1955 was one of the most unlucky railway construction projects in New Zealand.

A rail link between Nelson and the West Coast had been a very early proposal and in 1867-68, a 352 km preliminary survey had been carried out by a Mr Henry Wigg between Nelson and the town of Cobden across the Grey River from Greymouth.

Consequently the Nelson Provincial Council passed the Nelson & Cobden Railway Act in 1868 empowering the construction of the line. It was to have been built on the land grant system with as much as 4200 hectares to be provided for each 1.6 km of line. But that was as far as the venture went.

In 1871 the project was put on the list of national trunk lines by the first Minister of Public Works, Mr W. Gisborne. The first annual report of the Public Works Department of the same year made mention of an amended survey for the section between Nelson and Foxhill which ultimately would form part of the entire Nelson to Cobden line. Work on this section commenced in 1873 by the firm of Scott and Robertson of Nelson, the successful tenderers for the contract.

In January 1873 locomotives were ordered for this section in the form of two small 2-4-0 tank locomotives, later named as *Trout* and *Kingfisher* and classified as D steam locomotives. At the same time six 2-axle carriages, two 2-axle brake vans and 24 goods wagons were ordered.

The first 34 km section from Nelson to Foxhill was opened on 31 January 1876 and in the first financial year to 30 June 1877, a total of 49,797 passenger journeys were made.

In 1880 a 1.6 km extension from Nelson to Port Nelson was opened and the next year a further 1.5 km was built from Foxhill to Belgrove. About this time another 2-4-0 Tank locomotive was obtained, followed by a 'F' class 0-6-0 tank locomotive in 1885.

The completion of the Belgrove section represented the start of a series of delays and abandonments that continued to the end. In 1886 concessions were granted to the New Zealand Midland Railway Company for the construction of a line from Springfield in Canterbury to Brunner in Westland (then the end of the line from Greymouth), and northwards at Stillwater to Reefton and on through the Buller Gorge to connect up with Belgrove in the Nelson province. This work was carried out very slowly, and by 1894 the Midland Railway Company had completed only part of the Midland line and just an 11 km section south of Belgrove. The Government took over the works in January 1895, alleging breach of contract on the part of the Midland Railway Company.

The section of railway from Belgrove to Motupiko (then called Kohatu) that the Public Works Department took over in January 1895 comprised a 1 in 40 gradient and a 308 metre tunnel through to the Summit of Spooner's Range (279 metres above sea level) followed by a similarly steep descent to Motupiko (189 metres above sea level). The whole of this 14.7 km

WF 404, a 2-6-4T locomotive, shunts at Glenhope on 19 May 1954. NZR

A general view of Nelson Station and yard on 19 May 1954. NZR

section was handed over to the Railways on 1 March 1899 although it was not finally vested in the Government until 23 July 1901, along with the rest of the Midland Railway Company's works.

The line then extended from Motupiko along the valley of the Motueka River to Tapawera where it crossed the river by way of a combined road-rail wooden upper truss bridge (which survived until 1977 when it was replaced by a concrete road-only bridge). At Tapawera the line turned south into the Tadmor Valley to reach Tadmor 16.7 km from Motupiko. Work on this section commenced in 1901 and was completed and opened for traffic in August 1906. The next 8.2 km section south to Kiwi was opened on 18 December 1908. From Kiwi the gradient steepened through Tui and Kaka (site of a limeworks) to a summit 453 metres above sea level in a cutting which was the saddle between the head-waters of the Hope and Tadmor rivers. From this summit the line descended alongside the Hope River to a clearing and the terminus of the line at Glenhope. This 20.3 km section from Kiwi to Glenhope was opened on 2 September 1912 providing a total Nelson to Glenhope route length of 96 km.

On the Westland side the rail link from Greymouth to Westport had reached Inangahua Junction (105 km from Greymouth) by July 1914 (although the railway through the lower Buller Gorge to connect Greymouth and Westport was not completed until July 1942) leaving a 94 km gap between Glenhope and Inangahua.

Next work commenced on the extension from Glenhope to Kawatiri, which was resumed in 1920 after being suspended in 1917 due to manpower shortages resulting from World War I. The 7 km Glenhope to Kawatiri section, inclusive of a tunnel at the Hope River Spur was opened on 21 June 1926. By 1930, the 6 km Gowanbridge section was virtually complete and the Public Works Department ran trains to Gowanbridge station.

In December 1930 the formation was almost ready for 24 km beyond Gowanbridge to Mangles River, some 6 km from Murchison. However, just before Christmas 1930 the Government ordered the suspension of all construction works on the line in view of the approaching depression. In effect this decision meant that the track would never find its way down the Buller River and that the heavy rails waiting for the platelayers would rust in their stacks by the small platform at Kawatiri. The embankments crumbled, the rails rusted and the works buildings were transferred to other construction projects or sold, and gradually undergrowth covered over the foundations and demolitions.

The section from Glenhope to Kawatiri was closed as from 12 July 1931, having only been opened five years earlier. In 1942 the tracks and the bridge girders were lifted as a war expedient and transferred to other railway construction projects.

No further moves towards completing the Nelson-West Coast link were ever made apart from a trial line survey along the Buller River in 1939. In 1949 the then Labour Government announced that it had decided to extend the Nelson-Glenhope line to Gowanbridge again and then on to Murchison as soon as resources permitted - but in November of that year the general election saw a change of government.

The 1952 Royal Commission recommended that the Nelson-Glenhope line be closed but that this should not happen until the roads in the area were brought up to standard. This announcement saw the quantities of timber and other goods handled by the railway in 1953 reduced to nearly one half of that carried in 1952.

In May 1954 the National Government's Minister of Railways announced the suspension of the Nelson-Glenhope line as from 13 June. As could be expected, this met strong local opposition headed by the Nelson Provincial Progress League. This was to be the second transport loss for the region - on 17 April 1953 the overnight Nelson to Wellington passenger/freight ferry had been abolished.

The league accused the Railways Department of allowing the line to die from purposeful neglect. Also

A passenger train from Glenhope to Nelson passes Tui Station in the 1940s. OIL PAINTING, P.J. BAKER

targeted as villains were Transport Nelson Ltd (TNL) which had an exemption from the then prevailing 50 km limit on road transport operators, designed to protect the railways against direct competition from road transport.

A major demonstration was organised by the league and approximately 5,000 people marched from the railway station to the church steps to hear speeches against the closure. This impressive demonstration of local solidarity won a temporary reprieve for the railway. The then Prime Minister, Sidney Holland, said that the Nelson people could have their railway if they would use it. The railway reopened for goods only on the understanding that the league received freight guarantees equal to at least that carried in 1952, i.e. an annual tonnage of least 25,000.

In a report dated 19 July 1954 the league told the Prime Minister that 239 guarantees of freight totalling 29,276 tonnes had been obtained. Nine months later, however, a report on progress with estimates for the remaining quarter had bad news. Of the 9,533 "guaranteed" tonnes of coal, only about 2,500 would be seen; the expected 4,500 tonnes of timber would be more like 1,700; the target for general freight would fall short by some 3,400 tonnes. Only about half of the required 25,000 tonnes was forthcoming.

The Progress League thus recognised its failure to obtain freight traffic for the line and again blamed TNL for this. At one public meeting the stationmaster at Nelson pointed out that in spite of its competition, TNL was Railways' biggest customer at Nelson, Glenhope and at Blenheim. It had a legal right to carry freight right through the Nelson to Inangahua region, but was transporting cement only between Glenhope and Inangahua, and coal and timber back the other way.

Despite rising tonnage figures and additional rolling stock (17 wagons transferred from Christchurch) and handling appliances in the later stages of the reprieve, the Prime Minister announced on 15 August 1955 that because the Government was faced with virtually rebuilding the whole line, including nine bridges and nearly all the buildings, and because the required volume of traffic had not been achieved by a wide margin, it had been decided to close the Nelson - Glenhope line as from Saturday 3 September 1955.

Thus the line was closed amidst protest meetings and "sit-ins" on the line to stop demolition gangs, and a 12,000-strong petition calling for the reopening of the line and an investigation into an alternative route, with the idea of a link up to the South Island rail network at Blenheim.

In regard to the latter part of the petition, Prime Minister Holland wrote to the Mayor of Nelson (published in the Nelson Evening Mail of 28 May 1957) promising completion of a survey of possible northern routes to Blenheim and a report on a possible West Coast route. After completion of the surveys a decision on the rail link which could cost upwards of œ8 million and take 10 years, would be made. In the meantime, in recognition of the transport problems Nelson had, and during the period in which deliberations were being made on the rail link decision, the Government would subsidise the cost of transporting goods and passengers between Nelson and Blenheim so that the charges would be the same as if a railway was in existence. Thus was born the "Nelson Notional Railway".

Proposed Nelson—Blenheim Line

In 1957 the Labour Party was elected to the Government benches with a one seat majority. The Labour Party had promised action on the line and on 19 March 1958 the Minister of Railways released the results of an examination of possible routes from Nelson to Blenheim. These had been narrowed to two, namely:

(a) Nelson–Wakapuaka–Havelock (via Tinline and Pelorus Valleys) Grovetown/Blenheim. This 91.5 km route would involve a 6.5 km tunnel through the Bryant Range as well as a further 3 km of tunnels and 2.6 km of bridging.

(b) Nelson–Brightwater–Wairoa River valley to Richmond Range divide which would be tunnelled for about 5.6 km prior to following Goulter River valley to the Wairau about 64 km upstream from Blenheim. This route was 120 km.

Later, on 8 April 1959, the Minister of Works mentioned another favoured route which went via Whangamoa and the Rai Valley, and although 10.2 km longer, involved only 4.8 km of tunnelling and 2.3 km of bridging. Press reports in April 1960 suggested that this 101.8 km route was the most likely and the Acting Prime Minister, Mr Skinner, told the National Opposition that the Government had approved the cheapest route at a cost of £10,300,000—the most expensive route would have cost £16,500,000.

On March 1 1960 the construction work for the proposed railway was opened at Nelson by Prime Minister Walter Nash before a crowd of 3,000. A plaque commemorating the beginning of the work remains today in an open field in front of the town. The Government ran into constitutional problems as it had not first obtained Parliamentary sanction for the project as required by the Public Works Act 1928. The Auditor General declared the construction work illegal until a special authorising Bill was passed, so on Friday 29 July 1960, after a stormy 25 1/2 hour sitting, the Nelson Railway Authorisation Bill was passed, the Government winning each vote 38-37.

In the meantime, reclamation work on the new Nelson railway station and yards site had progressed and a raised embankment across the mudflats towards the main road was being built.

Railways Department costings suggested that the line would not be economic to begin with, but within 10 years heavy timber traffic would completely cover operating costs without considering other traffic from industries in the region that would follow. This estimate was supported by Mr L.H.H. Baigent & Sons, but was disputed by the managing director of TNL, Mr P.S. Boyes.

On the eve of the 1960 General Election the Prime Minister, Walter Nash, said a shorter route had been selected for the proposed line. The National Party, however, had a policy of stopping the line and it won the election. On 14 December 1960 the new Prime Minister, Keith Holyoake, announced that all work on the Nelson—Blenheim line was to stop immediately and the authorising legislation would be repealed in the first session of the new parliament.

Thus ended the saga of the Nelson region's railway lines, the last word coming on 1 October 1979 with the abolition of the "Notional Railway" subsidy, at that stage costing some $10,000,000 a year.

The Dun Mountain Railway

As the first length of railway line to be opened in New Zealand, the Dun Mountain Railway assumes a significance out of proportion to its intrinsic importance. The distinction between a tramway and a railway is sometimes a point of contention and some would say that because the Dun Mountain Railway was only ever worked by horses, it was only a tramway like that constructed the previous year near Kaitangata. However, the line had been authorised as a railway and was designed and constructed by qualified railway engineers. As the Dun Mountain Railway Act 1861 also required the company operating the line to provide a passenger service, it also represents the first public passenger tramway service in New Zealand.

In 1852 copper ore had been identified in the rocks of the Dun Mountain (1,129 m), so named after the colour of its dunite rock - yellow green in the normal state, turning to rusty brown after exposure to weather. Exploration suggested promising commercial qualities of copper ore and an association was formed for mining the copper deposits in the mountain. Investor support was obtained in England and in 1857 the Dun Mountain Copper Mining Company Ltd. was formed with a capital of £75,000 in £1 shares.

Part of the project involved the building of a railway between the mountain and the Port of Nelson where the ore could be shipped abroad. The alternative was to use pack animals, the cost of which was found to be excessive. On 12 January 1858 the barge Acasta arrived at Nelson from London carrying the first consignment of railway materials to be landed in New Zealand. Further batches arrived in February and June. Four wagons had been included in the shipments, but the majority did not arrive until 1861. By early 1860 surveys had been completed and involved a proposal for a wooden chute between an upper and lower level of the railway so as to avoid otherwise steep descent.

In July 1860 the company's new engineer, W.T. Doyne, arrived with his associate, G. C. Fitzgibbon. They set about surveying a new route which avoided the proposed mountain side chute. Parliament's approval to build the line was sought, but, the Dun Mountain Railway Bill 1860 was thrown out because of the "incomplete nature of the plans". Preliminary work started regardless in March 1861. Contracts for forming the roadbed and laying the permanent way were secured in August. By this time some 3,000 tonnes of chrome ore (to which attention had shifted because copper deposits had not proved to be as plentiful as first thought), and urgency was attached to the work. By December 14.5 km of narrow gauge track had been laid.

On 17 August 1861 Parliament passed the Dun Mountain Railway Act 1861 which empowered the company to construct a railway along a route starting at Albion Wharf and running via Haven Road, Waimea, Hardy,

Alton, Manuka and Brook Streets, across Manuaka Road and through "other lands"—to section 35 on the company's property.

The Act allowed the company to employ "locomotive engines or other motive power" but then went on to prohibit their use within Nelson city! The speed limit within the city was set at 4 miles per hour (6.4 km/h) and fares were 2 shillings per ton per 1.6 km for goods and 4 pence for 1.6 km for passengers. The Company was further required to run at least one train a day between the station at Nelson and the harbour terminus. A return train was also to be run, if at the time of departure, 10 shillings of fares were available.

The railway had a length of 21.4 km with a gauge of 915 mm. The sleepers were of black birch and were placed 915 mm apart. The formation was 1.83 metres wide and ballasted with broken stone to a depth of 20 cm. The cost of the line inclusive of rolling stock was £2,000 per 1.6 km.

Gradients varied from almost level along Brook St to 1 in 20 on the first ascent into the hills and later at the 17 km stage until it emerged from the forest at the 20 km stage before a final 0.8 km climb up the slopes of the Dun Mountain at a gradient of 1 in 36 to reach the terminus at a height of 853 m above sea level. Speed up the slopes was a slow 3.2 km/h with 2 horses pulling a load of 1 1/4 tonnes. The downward trips were controlled by the wagon brakes and the speed varied between 6 and 10 km/h.

The line was festively opened on 3 February 1862, the 20th anniversary of the founding of Nelson Province. In its first year the railway carried 3,950 tonnes of chrome ore and the maximum capacity of the company was put at over 10,000 tonnes annually. Very soon after, however, the hand of fate moved against the company. The American Civil War had resulted in the South's cotton ports being blockaded, cutting off supply to the English cotton mills in Lancashire which were the main customers of the Dun Mountain Company. By early 1863 the company decided to cease mining operations, wood and lime transport and sale providing alternative revenue, albeit limited. In 1864 the company lost most of its employees to a gold rush near Nelson and the company ceased completely in 1866.

The company was wound up in 1872 and its assets auctioned off. The rails ultimately ended up being used on the Picton to Blenheim line. The 1.6 km of the line between Nelson and the Port continued to be used by the horse tram for another 29 years, however, owned by different individuals. The first 4 wheeled vehicle for the service had been ordered from Sydney and arrived at Nelson on 24 March 1862 on the steamer Prince Alfred. Passenger services commenced on 7 May 1862 after some legal wrangles had been settled.

Eventually, in 1901 the Nelson City Council decided to upgrade and widen Haven Road, in the process dismantling the port tramway, which by that time had a competitor in the form of a horse drawn bus service, and the iron rails were in bad condition. Some consideration had been given to electrification of the line and extending it another 3.2 km to Tahunanui Sands, but the cost of this was beyond the resources of the city. On 26 June 1901 removal work on the rails began.

Today about 8 km of the former Dun Mountain line is a walking track and is easily found at the end of Brook Street.

Main North Line (Christchurch–Picton)

The proposal for a railway linking Blenheim with Christchurch, a distance of some 320 km, first came from the Marlborough Provincial Council in April 1861. It was not until 84 years later on 15 December 1945 that the line was fully completed, making it the longest railway construction project of New Zealand history.

A line had been completed between the port at Picton and the Opawa river at Blenheim in 1875, while in Canterbury the provincial government had built a network of broad and narrow gauge lines that in 1876 had reached as far north as Amberley and also included branches to Oxford and Eyreton. In between lay the Kaikoura mountain range and the rugged coast, the traversing of which involved an expense which would not be justified for many years. Apart from the fact that coastal shipping was at its height, there was also the provincial rivalry which saw Canterbury, along with Westland and Nelson preferring a trans-alpine line over the Southern Alps to the West Coast and through to Nelson. Marlborough residents on the other hand, naturally wanted a direct route along the east coast and not a long involved route via Nelson and Buller.

The Royal Commission of 1880 considered the East Coast line to be premature although recognised it as a possible main line in the future. In 1882 a special commission known as the Middle Island Railway Extension Commission was established to study three alternatives: First, a line from Culverden through to Hamner and Tophouse with branches from there to Nelson and Blenheim down the valley of the Wairau river, a proposal that remained on the drawing board until the 1930s. Second, a line from Culverden up the Waiau River to Reefton and through the Buller gorge. Third, and the one finally recommended, was the coastal line. Needless to say, this proposal was not met without opposition but work started on extending the Marlborough portion slowly southwards. No further work was done at the Canterbury end, however, until the turn of the century. World War I brought a halt to development and some track was actually removed and sent to more urgent projects in the North Island. Nevertheless in 1915 track laying had reached Ward in the north and Parnassus in the south.

The Royal Commission of 1925 was of the opinion that railways in New Zealand would never pay their way until the Wharanui–Parnassus gap in the South Island Main Trunk between Christchurch and Picton was filled. The Government of the day had a contrary opinion. Fortunately the change of Government in 1928 brought about a resumption of progress on the line along the Kaikoura coast. The onset of the Depression in 1931, however, stopped work for a third time. Things were not helped by a recommendation of the 1930 Royal Commission that passenger trains on both sections of the line be replaced by mixed trains. The Marlborough Progress League was not giving up hope, pointing out

With the photographer's motorcycle in the foreground, an AB crosses the Awatere double decker bridge northbound on 29 August 1952. One notes the 20 mph speed restriction for "A, AB and Q locomotives." HUGH BENNETT

that the proposed rail ferry service between the two Islands would require the completion of the railway first. Some 500 people joined a protest visitation to the Prime Minister in Wellington, involving a charter of the SS *Tamahine*. In 1936 with a new Government and the economy improving orders for a resumption of work on the Main Trunk were given, with a completion target of four years. By this stage the gap between railheads was 105 km with half of it to be finally surveyed. World War II intervened again with further delays, but with the tide of the war turning and an end to hostilities in sight, the last spike was driven and a ceremony at Kaikoura marked the completion of the South Island Main Trunk along the whole length of the island.

The Picton to Christchurch railway line is 350 km long, a lengthy part of which from Wharanui to Claverley (98 km) runs along the Kaikoura coast where the railway line and the state highway often share the only available space between the cliffs and the beach. In parts the railway line is virtually on the beach. Altogether some 21 tunnels are located on this section. A tunnel was at the northern ascent to the Dashwood Pass between Vernon and Seddon, now daylighted, like the former tunnel at the pass summit. Another tunnel is north of Tuamarina. The steepest grade is 1 in 37 on a 3 km portion between Picton and Elevation. This is followed by the gradients at Dashwood where on the north side it is 1 in 50 and on the south side 1 in 53. The highest point on the line is 180 metres above sea level at Spye summit in North Canterbury.

The longest of the tunnels is at the Amuri Bluff which is 975 metres long, and was one of the hardest to build with a tendency for rock falls and the excavated earth to swell on contact with air, requiring much excavation and innovative construction techniques. Overall the 23 tunnels total 5.8 km in length, 10 of them being located in the 8 km between Goose Bay and Puketa. There are 47 bridges on the line, the best known of which is the Waitohi Viaduct just outside of Picton, for many years the largest timber trestle in New Zealand. Other interesting bridges are the double decker across the Awatere River where the railway runs on the top and the former combined rail/road bridge across the Waima and Clarence Rivers, now rail-only bridges. The longest bridge is the 706 metre crossing of the Waiau river just south of Parnassus. Single line automatic signalling was installed between Waipara and Picton in 1946 after the complete line was opened while between Waipara and Addington electric train tablet continued to be used until recently when the route was converted to Track Warrant control.

Nearly all the traffic on this line travels to or from the rail ferries, with Spring Creek, for Marlborough and Nelson traffic, and Lake Grassmere salt works the only significant traffic generators along the line. Northbound traffic tonnages are only about 60% of southbound, indicating the tendency for a southward flow of imports and manufactured goods.

With its magnificent coastal scenery, the line was chosen as the second of the routes for the new-look luxury passenger trains, with the introduction of the "Coastal Pacific Express" as from 25 September 1988 with a 5 hr 20 min journey time each way. In May 2000 this train was renamed the "TranzCoastal" to link it more closely to the popular "TranzAlpine" service.

CHAPTER THIRTEEN

Canterbury

For the first hundred years, the main role of the railways in Canterbury was to link the city of Christchurch and its port of Lyttelton to the rest of Canterbury. A network of branches took goods out to the farms and towns, and brought back livestock, wool and grain. As road transport took over this short distance traffic, the branches withered, and the railway concentrated on long-distance traffic, with containers of manufacture commodities and processed farm products, and coal from the Buller coalfields being exported via Lyttelton.

As with the passenger traffic, the commuter trains and the country passenger or mixed trains have gone, and Christchurch is now the hub for three long-distance trains, which aim as much for the tourist market as for the local traveller. In 1991 the comparatively modern Christchurch station was sold and replaced by a new station on the old Addington Workshops site, opened on 5 April 1993.

Lyttelton Line

The crater rim representing the Port Hills made Lyttelton a natural sheltered harbour for shipping, but also presented a major obstacle for traffic between the Port and the Canterbury Plains. A railway line including a tunnel was the obvious solution for overcoming this obstacle. On 9 November 1867, four years after the opening of the 7 km line from Christchurch to Ferrymead Wharf on 1 December 1863, the 9.8 km line to Lyttelton was opened. This included the 2.6 km long Lyttelton tunnel, the first railway tunnel to be built in New Zealand, at the time an impressive engineering feat, and even today it still ranks as the sixth longest railway tunnel in New Zealand. As with the other Canterbury provincial railways, the line was built to a 1600 mm (5'3") broad gauge. Later in 1877 it was converted to the New Zealand 1067 mm (3'6") gauge, and the year later the line was double-tracked as far as Heathcote.

To overcome the smoke nuisance created by steam locomotives inside the tunnel, trials were conducted with a Wf class steam locomotive No. 433 converted to burn oil in August 1909 hauling 450 tonne goods trains, however this was abandoned after it was found that while technically satisfactory, the cost over the use of the same class of locomotive burning coal was out of all proportion to the benefits obtained. Following the success of the Arthur's Pass-Otira electrification in 1923, it was decided in 1925 to similarly electrify the Lyttelton line. The electrified line was opened on 14 February 1929, and at the time was seen as being part of a wider scheme for the Christchurch suburban services. Like the Otira section the current system chosen was 1.5 kV D.C. with a sub-station at Woolston, and six new Bo-Bo electric locomotives—the Ec class—were built by the English Electric Company.

The first train comprising 18 passenger cars, two of them reserved for early settlers who had travelled on the first train through the tunnel in 1867, and headed by locomotive Ec 12, completed the 10 km journey in just 10 min 30 sec, with the tunnel being negotiated in 3 minutes.

Although the electric locomotives ran the distance to Lyttelton station, 0-6-0 F class steam tank locomotives took over from the Ec's for wharfside embarkation of boat trains to the overnight ferries, due to the sharp curvature and complex track of the Lyttelton wharf. These locomotives continued to be used right into the diesel days of the South Island Limited in the

AB 778, now one of the two "Kingston Flyer" engines, moves away from the inter-island ferry wharf at Lyttelton, its job of heating the carriages for the "South Island Limited" done.
B.J. McKENZIE

The JA hauled "South Island Limited" crosses the Canterbury Plains south of Ashburton at Winslow in 1970.
B.J. McKENZIE

At school holiday times the number of cars on the "South Island Limited" often required double heading of JAs.
B.J. McKENZIE

late 1960s. In 1969 six of the TR shunters built by Hitachi were specifically assigned to the line before the present day profusion of bogie shunters.

Eventually in 1970 when the Ec electrics had reached the end of their working lives, the decision was made to dieselise the line, rather than build new electric locomotives for it. The operational cost of maintaining the electric sub-station and attaching locomotives onto through trains just for this 10 km section was another factor in this decision. On 19 September 1970 the last electric train service ran over the line.

With the completion of the Lyttelton road tunnel, passenger trains over the line ended on 28 February 1972. The main traffic on the line now is the export coal trains, usually hauled by a pair of DQ class locomotives from Middleton Yard to Lyttelton and back, so enabling the main-line locomotives to be fuelled and serviced. Regular shunts convey other freight between Christchurch and the Port.

South Island Main Trunk (Christchurch–Dunedin)

William Moorhouse, a strong proponent of railways who was the Superintendent of Canterbury Province for eight years in all, told those gathered to open the Christchurch to Ferrymead railway on 1 December 1863, that he expected to live to see a railway that would make it possible to travel from Lyttelton to Timaru, and return the same day. This produced some incredulity in his audience, yet his vision of the future was realised within fifteen years.

The first sod of the Canterbury Great Southern Railway was turned on 24 May 1865, and the section to Rolleston was opened on 13 October 1866. This line was built to the 1,600 mm broad gauge used by the Canterbury Provincial Railways.

There was considerable discussion as to the route to be followed. A route that went well inland was suggested, to cross the major rivers where they were confined to narrow channels. Others suggested a line nearer the coast, passing through more fertile country. The route finally chosen passes through long stretches of barren gravels, unsuitable for intensive agriculture, but it is the most direct route that gives a reasonable crossing of the Rakaia River, albeit on a 1740 metre long bridge. The line gradually climbs from Christchurch to an elevation of 116 metres at Chertsey, south of Rakaia. In the northbound direction, this was the most famous racing section of New Zealand Railways. On the straight track with a gently falling gradient, the Ja hauled South Island Limited Expresses would treat the 50 miles per hour (80 km/h) speed limit with contempt,

G 98 and G 100 seen at the Colombo Street crossing in Christchurch on 22 February 1950. The crossing keeper's huts were then a feature of the scene. HUGH BENNETT

especially when running late for the connection with the Inter-Island Steamer Express at Lyttelton Wharf. Drivers trying to make up time would regularly run their train for long distances at over a "mile a minute" (96 km/h), with reliable timings of at least 72 miles per hour, (115 km/h) and rather less reliable stories of the speedometers, which read to 75 miles per hour, being firmly off the scale.

This was still a long way in the future as the line was laid south towards Rakaia. In October 1867, when construction had reached Selwyn, the Canterbury Provincial Council was so short of money that it had to stop construction on the south line, while it concentrated on completing the Lyttelton Tunnel. Construction did not restart until the central government took a hand.

The "Great Public Works Policy" of Julius Vogel, announced in 1870, gave a high priority to the line between Christchurch and Dunedin, and as well as working south from Selwyn and north from Dunedin, work was undertaken in both directions from the intermediate port towns of Timaru and Oamaru, so the rails were being advanced at six working places. The Act of Parliament establishing the uniform gauge contained an exemption allowing the broad gauge to be extended as far south as Rakaia, which was reached in June 1873. By the time the narrow gauge extension to Ashburton opened in the following year, the Canterbury Provincial Council had bowed to the inevitable, and was laying rails to the 1067 mm gauge between the broad gauge rails, from Rakaia back towards Christchurch.

The first narrow gauge locomotives in Canterbury were the 11 tonne A class 0-4-0T well tanks, which seemed a backward step compared to the broad gauge locomotives, which weighed up to 31 tonnes. In 1874 the J class 2-6-0 tender locomotives were introduced. These were 27 tonne locomotives, with 17 tonne tenders, and they hauled trains on the narrow gauge which were as heavy as the heaviest trains that had been used on the broad gauge.

Meanwhile, the section from Timaru north to Temuka was opened on 26 October 1875, and on 4 February 1876, the opening of the Ealing–Temuka section, which included the difficult Rangitata River crossing, completed a railway between Christchurch and Timaru. Through trains became possible a month later when narrow gauge rails reached Christchurch. The Waitaki river bridge was opened on 17 April 1876, bringing the line from Oamaru into Canterbury, and on 1 February 1877, Christchurch was linked to Oamaru.

The first section south of Oamaru, the 40 km to Hillgrove had already been opened in November 1876. A 2.5 km branch from Hillgrove to Port Moeraki was opened in January 1877, but closed after only two years. Port Moeraki could not compete with Oamaru as a port, and there were problems in protecting the railway as it ran between a steep hillside and the sea. Another short branch, at Shag Point, was opened in 1879, and served local coal mines for nearly thirty years. At the Dunedin end, the Dunedin and Port Chalmers Railway had been opened on 1 January 1873, as the first line of 1,067 mm gauge in New Zealand. The route north from Dunedin used by the main line to Christchurch included a difficult climb, traversing along a steep hillside, from the junction at Sawyers Bay, just short of Port Chalmers. After the 1,400 metre Mihiwaka tunnel, there was another winding descent to Waitati. This section of line required considerable engineering works, and it was

A 2-6-0 J class locomotive heads a Lyttelton–Christchurch passenger train through semi-rural landscape in 1923. W.W. STEWART/NZR

December 1877 when the section from Sawyers Bay to Waitati was opened, by which time the rails were well advanced south from Oamaru. As a result, it was at Goodwood, 310 km from Christchurch but only 57 km from Dunedin, that the rails from Christchurch and Dunedin met. The line was opened on 7 September 1878, and with through expresses between Christchurch and Dunedin, reality had exceeded the vision of Moorhouse in only 15 years.

The J class 2-6-0 locomotives were designed for freight trains, but they also proved to be suitable for expresses, which were initially limited to 60 km/hour, and took 11 hours between Christchurch and Dunedin. The K class 2-4-2's were specially designed for passenger service, and were noted to reach speeds of nearly 90 km/hour. Over the hilly section south of Oamaru, T class 2-8-0 locomotives were used. The expresses between Christchurch and Dunedin were the prestige service of New Zealand Railways in those days, and always had the newest and fastest locomotives available. The 2-6-2 N class took over in 1885, then came the 4-6-0 U and Ub classes. The first of the locally built A class Pacific (4-6-2) compounds arrived in 1906 and ran on an eight hour schedule between Christchurch and Dunedin. The superheated Ab class of 1915 handled these expresses for many years, and were capable of such feats as hauling a 390 tonne train at 107 km/h.

The final development of steam was the 4-8-2 J and Ja classes, introduced in 1939 and 1946 respectively. They ran the "South Island Limited" expresses on a schedule of 7 hour 9 minutes until the DJ-hauled Southerner replaced them on 1 December 1970. As well as the fast running mentioned earlier, they were also noted for their ability to haul up to half a dozen bogie vans of mail and parcels behind a similar number of carriages. The long station stops to handle this roadsider traffic were often the reason why high speeds were necessary to regain time. The "Southerner", with passenger cars only, and no stops for water or changing engines ran initially on a 6 hour 14 minute schedule northbound, and a few minutes longer southbound. By using more powerful DX locomotives, Christchurch–Dunedin schedules of 5 1/2 hours were introduced in 1992, and fairly similar schedules apply today.

Other passenger services included evening railcars which ran on a 6 hour 10 minute schedule until they were withdrawn in April 1976, and the Friday and Sunday night expresses. These were the last ordinary NZR service to be steam-hauled, the final steam services terminating on 26 October 1971. This train was usually lightly loaded, but co-author Tony Hurst remembers the impressive night departure of a single Ja setting out from Christchurch with a 14-total train on this service during Easter 1971.

From the Ub class onward, the locomotives used on expresses have also been suitable for freight trains, especially on the flatter sections. Up until the 1950s, much of the freight traffic on this line was between the country districts and the major centres and ports. Manufactured imports were distributed mainly from Christchurch and Dunedin, and farm products were exported from Lyttelton, Timaru, Oamaru and Port Chalmers. The South Island Main Trunk (SIMT) was feeding the branches and small towns, rather than carrying through traffic. As the branch traffic declined after 1950, it was replaced by more long-distance traffic. Two factors which have further increased long-distance traffic are the concentration of overseas traffic at fewer ports with containerisation, and the Picton rail ferries.

The freight train of today on the SIMT is typified by the service which reaches Dunedin early each morning, carrying wagons that left Auckland only 36 hours earlier, or the container trains run at short notice to meet ships which have had their port calls altered.

Little River Branch

The 36.4 km Little River Branch along the flat terrain near Lake Ellesmere was originally seen as part of a complete line to Akaroa, but Little River was as far as it got. The line left the Southbridge Branch at Lincoln and was opened as far as Birdlings Flat on 16 May 1882. The next 11 km to Little River were opened on 11 March 1886.

One of the interesting aspects of this line's history was the use over it of the Edison battery electric railcar built in 1926, originally for the Christchurch–Lyttelton line before it was electrified. The Bo-Bo type 90 kW railcar lasted until 1934 when it was burnt out. The end of passenger services on the line came on 12 April 1951 and complete closure came on 30 June 1962.

Southbridge Branch

In a resolution made on 2 November 1870 the Canterbury Provincial Council proposed to the Colonial Government that a line be built from Rolleston to Southbridge. Later in April 1872 the Provincial Government recommended a different route so that the line would pass through the Lincoln and Prebbleton districts and join the main line near the station of Hornby. The Province was willing to subsidise the deviation and thus it was accorded in an amendment to the schedule of the Railways Act 1875.

Above: The Edison battery-electric railcar built in 1926 passes Lake Forsyth on the Little River Branch. The formations for the road-bed seen here are still substantially intact. NZR
Below: A DSG *twin bogie diesel shunter on what is now the Hornby industrial line, all that is left of the branches to Little River, Lincoln and Southbridge.* TONY HURST

The final stage of the 42 km line was opened for traffic on 18 July 1875.

Passenger traffic over the line lasted 76 years until 12 April 1951. The 29 km section of the line past Lincoln to Southbridge was closed completely on 30 June 1962. The line from Hornby to Lincoln closed on 1 December 1967, except for the first 2.9 km from Hornby which served five local industries with private sidings. This remnant was known as the Hornby Industrial Line and survives today.

Methven Branch

One of the companies formed under the District Railways Act of 1877 was the Rakaia and Ashburton Forks Railway Company Ltd. This company built the 35.6 km Rakaia to Methven branch line, the first sod being turned at Rakaia in November 1878. This ceremony was somewhat delayed when the guests that had arrived from Christchurch by special train went to lunch and it was discovered that the cups had been inadvertently left in Christchurch, so the festivities were held up until the mail train arrived with the cups at 2.30 p.m.

The construction of the branch, however, did not incur any delays and it was completed in February 1880. As from 13 December 1880 the line was operated by the government, but the locomotives and rolling stock were supplied by the company. The first two locomotives were built by Rogers Locomotive Works in New Jersey. They were 2-4-4 tank locomotives, later classified Q, and proved useful for light fast trains, being capable of speeds up to 80 km/h, although the maximum permitted speed was only half this.

On 1 April 1885 the state exercised its right of purchase and the line became part of the government railways. Most of the inwards traffic on the line was fertiliser and outwards traffic livestock, the latter increasing from 8806 head in 1890 to 150,000 by 1920. The busiest period of the line for goods traffic was during the 1940s when 37,000 tonnes of general goods were transported annually. The peak of passenger numbers was during the 1920s, however, and by 1949 the annual passenger count had declined to just 749. Mixed trains on the branch ended on 7 September 1958. As with other branch lines, traffic declined steadily during the 1950s and 1960s and in 1969 only 1000 head of livestock were transported. In this year trains were reduced to just three shunts a week. Complete closure came on 31 July 1976. The Ab steam locomotives were the dominant power of the line for many years until September 1967 when diesels took over.

Although there were nine stations on the line, there were no other towns apart from Methven and the only buildings of note on the line were those at the terminus.

Mount Somers Branch

Originally known as the Springburn Branch, this 43.2 km line was built from Tinwald, just south of Ashburton, to Springburn, a farming settlement near the foothills of the Southern Alps. The first section to Mount Somers, 37.6 km, was opened on 4 October 1886, and the second section to Springburn on 9 September 1889. A narrow gauge tramway was built in 1886 from Mount Somers station into the hills to serve coal mines and a lime works. Another important commodity from the district was silica sand which was railed to the glassworks at Hornby in Christchurch. Passenger services on the line ended on 9 January 1933. The section

A goods train headed by an AB locomotive arrives at Lincoln Junction en route to Southbridge in the late 1950s. The line curving to the right went to Little River. NZR

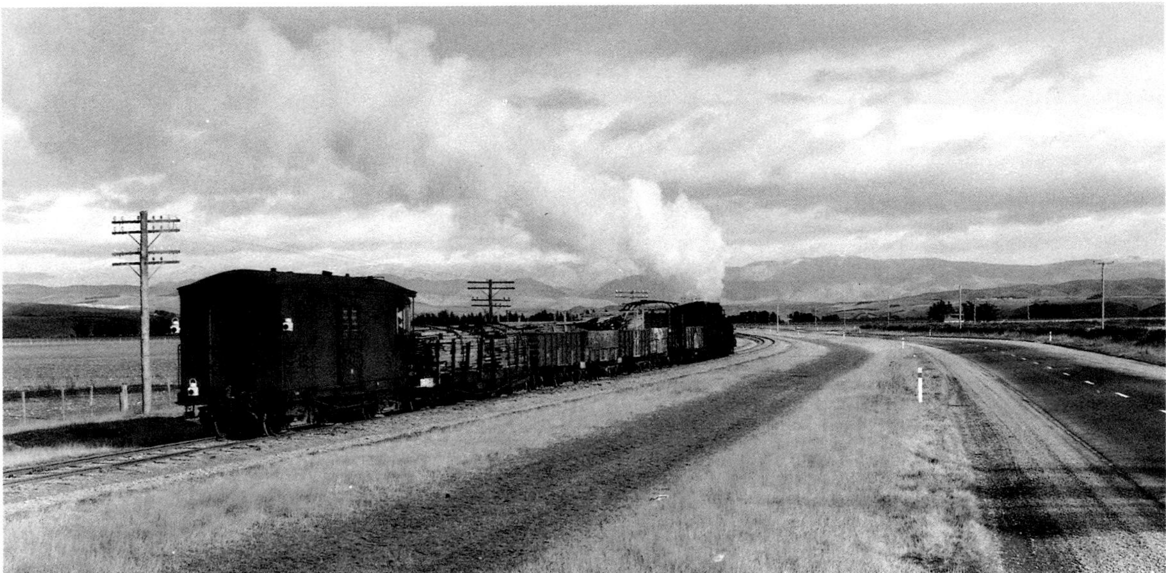

Left: An AB with a goods train for Fairlie is seen near Pleasant Point in May 1967. NZR

Opposite: An AB climbs through Weka Pass on the Waiau Branch in 1968. In the background is the landmark known as Frog Rock. D.L.A. TURNER

from Mount Somers to Springburn was closed on 20 March 1957, and the complete closure of the line came on I January 1968, although wheat was railed from Valetta, a station mid-way up the line, until April 1968. A 2 km section of the line from Tinwald to Fraser's Road was reopened as a railway preservation project by the Plains Railway on 25 November 1973.

Waimate Branch

When the citizens of Waimate found that their township was to be by-passed by the Main South Railway in the mid 1870s, they clamoured for a branch railway from the town to the main line. The branch line was approved and a 7.4 km line was built by the government from Studholme to Waimate, opening on 19 March 1877. In 1883 a further 13.3 km that had been built by the Waimate Railway Company was opened to Waihao Downs. This line, known as the Waimate Gorge Branch, was worked from opening by the government, and purchased by the state on 1 April 1885. There was local pressure for an extension to this line and some kilometres of formation was constructed, but by 1924 further development of rural branch lines was seen as no longer economic and work was stopped. The line was one of the first to lose its passenger traffic, this being taken over by buses as from 9 February 1931. The line beyond Waimate was closed on 11 December 1953 and the Waimate to Studholme section was closed on 1 April 1966. At the time it was the first large town to lose its rail link, as branch line closures up until then had been only those serving small townships and villages.

Fairlie Branch

Like most other South Island branch lines the Fairlie branch was constructed to open up and develop the rural hinterland behind Timaru in the 1870s. On 24 December 1875 the first 14.4 km from the junction with the main line at Washdyke to Pleasant Point was opened. On 1 January 1877 the line as far as Albury was opened and on 28 January 1884 the full 58.2 km to Eversley, just past Fairlie, was ready for traffic. A special excursion train to mark the opening was run from Timaru to Fairlie Creek and back two days later on 30 January 1884. So began 84 years of passenger service on the line.

On 1 April 1934 the short portion from Eversley to Fairlie was closed. The closure of the whole line came on 1 March 1968 and the next day a special excursion of the "Fairlie Flyer" was run, observed by crowds of locals and those who had personal experience of the train whether as passengers or as staff.

A short 2.4 km of the former branch at Pleasant Point has been preserved as part of the Pleasant Point Railway and Historical Museum.

White Cliffs Branch

The 18 km White Cliffs Branch was originally built as an extension of a branch line to Darfield, deviating from a planned straight line to Sheffield and Springfield. The kink in the Midland Line today between Kirwee, Darfield and Sheffield is a legacy of this plan. The extension past Darfield to the Malvern Hills was incited by the discovery of coal in the hills and although it was only lignite or brown coal it was nevertheless a convenient coal supply for Canterbury, unlike the supplies from the West Coast which, before the completion of the trans-alpine route, had to come a long way by ship. At the time of its building in 1874/75 the Malvern Hills line was seen as the possible first stage in a trans-alpine route via the Wilberforce River and Brownings Pass, but this proposal did not proceed very far. The White Cliffs branch opened as such on 3 November 1875, with stations at Hawkins, Homebush, Coalgate, Glentunnel, South Malvern and the terminus. The section between Hawkins and Homebush involved a sharp 1 in 43 ascent before a descent and then another ascent to Whitecliffs (The modern spelling).

The line had two accompanying private lines, one at Homebush owned by the Homebush brick and tile company, and another owned by the Homebush Coal Company at Coalgate.

Passenger traffic over the line ended on 13 March 1949 and complete closure of the line came on 31 March 1962, once the coal field was exhausted.

Waiau Branch

At one time proposed as part of the main route to Blenheim, the Waiau branch was opened as far as Waikari in 1882, and extended to Medbury in 1884, Culverden in 1886 and to Waiau, 66.5 km from Waipara in 1919.

The first 13 km from Waipara (75 metres above sea level) involved an ascent through the Weka Pass through distinctive limestone outcrops to Waikari (225 metres above sea level).

Passenger traffic on the branch ended on 29 January 1939, but logging traffic on the line was sufficient to keep it open for goods operations until 15 January 1978, when the line was closed. In fact the period just prior to its closure was marked by unusually brisk business as the pine forests that the line ran through were ravaged by gales in August 1975, the clearance of which took over two years. The line in this period saw several trains a day, some double headed.

The first section of the line, 13km through the Weka Pass from Waipara to Waikari, has been preserved as the Weka Pass Railway rail museum project.

Oxford and Eyreton Branches

These two basically parallel branches were built inland from Rangiora and Kaiapoi in 1874 and 1875 respectively to 1067 mm gauge at the time when the main line was still being built to 1600 mm gauge. That the two branches were only 10 km apart is a reflection of the parochialism of the day when rival groups of settlers each wanted a railway line to serve and develop their own areas. In 1878 the Eyreton branch was extended to connect with the Oxford branch at Bennetts Junction, and in 1884 the line at Oxford was extended across the Waimakariri river to connect with the Midland line at Sheffield. This latter section only ever saw local traffic and picnic trains and closed on 14 July 1930.

The distance from Rangiora to Sheffield was 55 km. After the closure of the section to Sheffield the line was 35.5 km long. A few months later, on 9 February 1931, passenger traffic on both the Oxford and Eyreton branches was terminated and the connection from Bennetts Junction to Horrelville on the Eyreton Branch, a distance of 4.5 km, was closed. The Eyreton Branch was thus reduced to 28 km in length. The Oxford Branch was closed completely on 19 April 1959 and the Eyreton Branch 5 years earlier on 26 May 1954, except for a 5 km spur serving a flour mill at Wetheral which survived into the 1970s.

CHAPTER FOURTEEN

Across the alps – the Midland Line

Probably the most scenically spectacular railway in New Zealand is the 212 km line between Rolleston on the South Island Main Trunk and Greymouth on the West Coast.

The discovery of gold on the West Coast in the early 1860s led to a stage coach road being pushed through the Southern Alps in 1866 via Arthur's Pass, one of several passes through the mountains. About the same time ideas were being promulgated in both Canterbury and Nelson to build a railway line through the mountains to connect the two regions respectively with Westland, and thereby also with each other. The people of Nelson Province advanced such plans the most and by the 1870s the province was ready to finance such a line from its own resources. Sir Julius Vogel, however, pre-empted the carrying out of the Nelsonians' plan in his 1873 Financial Statement in which he promised to carry out surveys to establish a suitable line from Nelson to the West Coast and from there across the Southern Alps to Canterbury.

The first survey looked at the possibility of a line from Hokitika to the Malvern Hills to connect with the White Cliffs coal railway. However, a report on the Browning Pass section by its namesake J.S. Browning to the engineer-in-chief ended contemplation of this as a suitable route. Further surveys considered northern routes via Ada's Pass, Amuri Pass, the Hope Saddle and other alternatives, but the Arthur's Pass route was conclusively recommended by a 1883 Royal Commission set up by the Government of the time. Notwith-

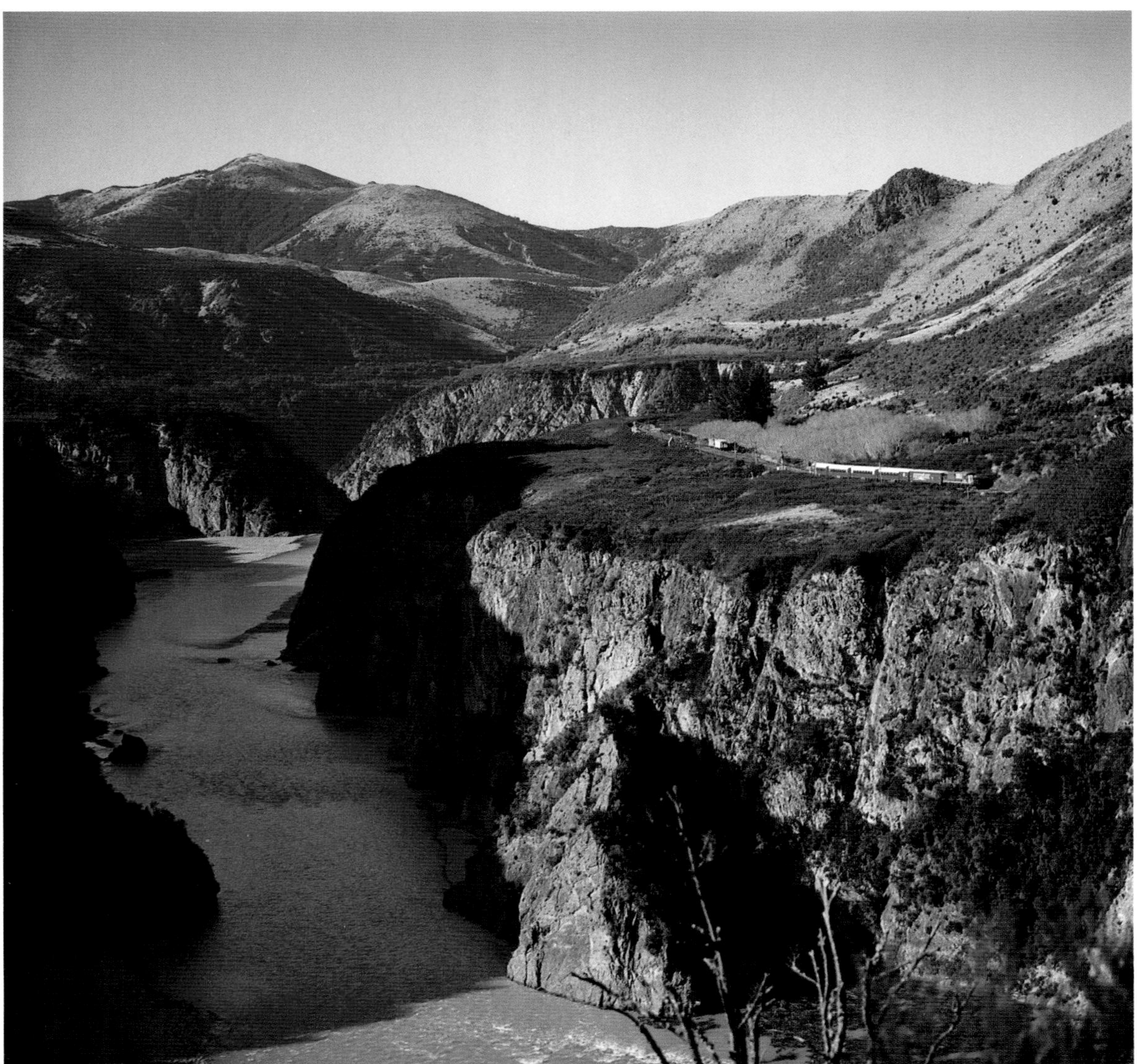

Left: Staircase on the south bank of the Waimakariri River is without doubt the most spectacular railway setting in New Zealand. A Greymouth-bound pre-"TranzAlpine" passenger train leaves the station yard in 1984. NZR

Opposite: Three DJ locomotives drift down the south bank of the Taramakau River towards Jackson with empty coal wagons on 1 July 1989. G.B. CHURCHMAN

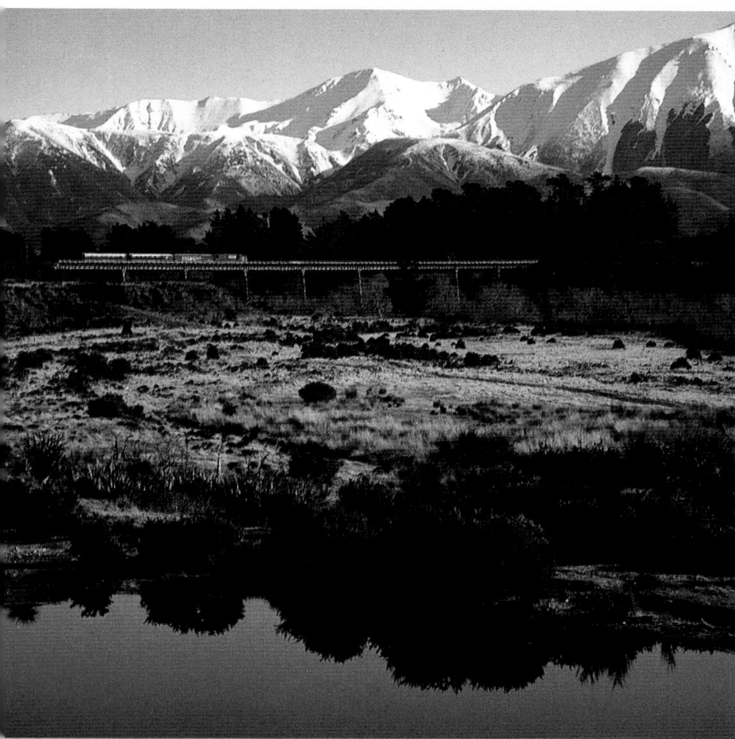

Above: Providing passengers with their first close-up views of the alps since leaving Christchurch, here the Torlesse Range, a pre-"TranzAlpine" crosses the 205 metre long, 20 metre high big Kowai Viaduct not far out of Springfield in 1984. NZR

standing the significant coal and timber resources of Westland and the urgings of the local peoples, this Commission was of a view that the cost of building the line would not be justified by the benefits and recommended accordingly. This view reflected that of parliamentarians of the day who were perhaps daunted by the prospect of forging a line through the Alps and saw other public works projects as being more deserving of attention. Sir Julius Vogel did manage the following year, however, to have a Bill passed that enabled the government to enter into contract with private enterprise to build such a line. A syndicate of Canterbury and Nelson businessmen was established and sent a three-man mission to London in January 1885. Eventually in March 1886 terms were arranged that suited everybody and the New Zealand Midland Railway Company was floated in London in April 1886.

The contract that the local syndicate had signed on 17 January 1885 requiring them to build the 378 km of railway lines between Springfield and Brunnerton (later Brunner) and between Brunnerton and Belgrove on the line south of Nelson within 10 years of that date, was assigned to the Midland Railway Company. The line south of Nelson to Belgrove had been opened in July 1881, and the line from Greymouth to the coal mines at Brunnerton had been opened in April 1876. The branch line from Rolleston had reached Springfield in January 1880. The contract provided for 50% of the costs of construction incurred by the company to be compensated by grants of land at the valuation applying before the contract. This total was put at £2.5 mil-

JA 1269 seen at Springfield on 19 December 1967 with a mixed train for Christchurch. R.J.McGAVIN

lion, of which £1 million represented the section from Brunner to Belgrove and £1.5 million the trans-alpine line from Springfield to Brunner.

The first sod was ceremoniously turned on 24 January 1887 but thereafter progress was very slow. The N.Z. Midland Railway Company performed most of its construction work in the relatively gentle terrain between Brunner and Reefton and between Brunner and Jackson. A total of 120 km was built and opened for traffic in the contract period. Basically the company had not raised enough money in London, and it was continually short of funds. Throughout the period it requested relief from various provisions of the contract, in particular the abandonment of the Reefton to Belgrove (south of Nelson) section of the line, sought (and obtained) permission to build around the eastern rather than the western side of Lake Brunner, and to substitute an incline railway over the alps rather than build a long tunnel. The company also sought, unsuccessfully, an extension of the contract time. Eventually it was unable to raise further funds—leaving about four fifths of the work, on a cost basis, uncompleted. The government exercised its power to take possession of the line on 25 May 1895. The company continued to battle through the courts for another four years, but eventually in July 1900, full control of the company's works was vested in the Government.

In the period to 1900 the government had completed the Jackson to Otira section of the line.

The task then remained for the Public Works Department to complete the line from the West Coast to Nelson, and the Midland Line from Otira to Otarama in Canterbury, including a decision on how to traverse from Otira to Arthur's Pass. The Midland Railway Company's proposal of an incline and switchback over the mountains was rejected in favour of a tunnel. While the switchback would have saved on construction costs, it would have been more than made up for by operating costs and inconvenience. A long tunnel could have a gentler gradient but would cost more, and the compromise was a tunnel 8.55 km in length on a gradient of 1 in 33. The first shot was fired by the Prime Minister, Sir Joseph Ward, on 25 May 1908. Like the Midland Railway Company before them, the contractors, J. McLean & Sons, did not find the going easy and eventually gave up in 1912 with only about half the tunnelling completed. Sandstone, shale and copious water proved their undoing, and in 1913 the Public Works Department took over.

In the meantime the rails from Canterbury were approaching Arthur's Pass. Broken River was reached in 1906, Cass in 1910, and on 1 July 1914 the eastern railhead was Arthur's Pass, leaving Cobb & Co. stage-coaches the task of transporting passengers and goods over just the pass road. "Holethrough" on the tunnel boring came in July 1918 and the official ceremony took place on 21 August 1918. The discrepancy was found to be only 29 mm in level and only 19 mm in alignment.

Lining work on the tunnel took another three years and this was followed by the installation of catenary for the electric locomotives that were to use the line. The use of electric locomotives on the Otira to Arthur's Pass section was a first for New Zealand Railways. Steam locomotives could not operate successfully in the long Otira tunnel because of the steep 1 in 33 gradient and the smoke generated that would have made working conditions in the cabs of steam locomotives very unpleasant. Five new Bo-Bo class "E" class (later Eo class) electric locomotives were ordered from the English Electric Company and these arrived in April 1923. These were designed for the 1,500 Volt DC system adopted for the section from Otira to Arthur's Pass (14 km). At the same time a battery-powered shunting and inspection locomotive E 1 arrived.

The opening of the Otira tunnel and hence the complete line took place on 4 August 1923. The Prime Minister, William Massey, and the Minister of Public Works, Gordon Coates, plus other invited guests were there to witness the opening of the longest tunnel in the Southern Hemisphere (since exceeded by the Rimutaka and Kaimai tunnels). The trans-alpine railway linking east and west coasts was now complete after more than 60 years of battling for it by Canterbury and Westland interests.

1939 saw the introduction of the 4-8-4 "Kb" class, which became the most powerful steam locomotives running on NZR. Similar to the North Island "Ka", but with extra power from a "booster" engine driving one axle of the cab bogie, the six members of the class hauled freight trains from Arthur's Pass to Springfield until 1968, making this part of the line "Kb Country" for most railway enthusiasts. The same year as the withdrawal of the Kb's, the original Eo class electrics were withdrawn and replaced with five new Ea class locomotives (later the EO class) from Toshiba in Japan.

These electric locomotives served until 1997, as there were considerable difficulties in hauling the coal trains entirely by diesel traction. Eventually the problem of overheating locomotives was solved by fitting a sliding door to the Otira portal, that shut once an uphill train entered the tunnel. This forced air past the locomotives so the back locomotives got more fresh air, whereas normally a train in a tunnel acts as a piston, pushing the air before it. As soon as this system was introduced in July 1997, the electric locomotives were taken out of regular use, and their last working was a special excursion on 1 November 1997. The current standard coal train is 20 CB wagons, with a full train weighing 1440 tonnes, hauled by two DX locomotives. At Otira, two more DX or DFT locomotives are added as bankers through the tunnel to Arthur's Pass.

Today the Midland Line has four coal trains from Ngakawau, and one from Rapahoe each day, plus timber from Ngakawau and Stillwater, dairy products from Hokitika and some cement from Westport.

The passenger services were upgraded in November 1987 with the introduction of the "Tranz-Alpine" Express in recognition of the tourist potential of the line. With a 60% jump in patronage the following year it was an outstanding success, winning the Tourist Industry Federation award for 1988. In 1991 an observation car was added, also a guards van converted so passengers could stand out in the open for better photography. Initially the TranzAlpine was only as long as the two-car trains that preceded it, but with its growing popularity the number of cars grew and it is now so popular that there are sometimes 10 or 11 cars and vans on the daily return service.

Once upon a time there was thunder in the mountains of a different kind. A Kb lifts a coal train into Cass on 28 July 1967.
MARK COLE

CHAPTER FIFTEEN

Westland

The railways of the West Coast of the South Island were isolated for a long time, and the railways and those who ran them have always had a special character. Even in the early 1960s, when old-fashioned features such as steam engines and mixed trains had nearly disappeared from most of the North Island and some parts of the South Island, the West Coast Railways were still operating with little change. The main traffic was still coal, to the river ports of Westport and Greymouth, and through the Otira tunnel to Christchurch. Timber, usually stacked on an angle, overhanging one end of an La wagon, also went through the tunnel. In one week in 1960, eastbound gross tonnage was 28000 tonnes. The Christchurch railcars were well patronised, with holiday expresses at public and school holiday times. More modern powerful steam locomotives, the 4-8-2 J class, only arrived on the "Coast" in 1963.

On a typical day in early 1967 (Monday the 10th of April), in the 19-stall roundhouse at Elmer Lane, Greymouth, the following locomotives were in steam: A 424 and A598, Ab's 610,723,743,808 and 823, B304, J's1201,1208,1209,1210,1232,1235, and 1237,Wf 383 and 403, Ww 672 and 684. At Ross Ab755 had the day off for a boiler washout, but at the other outlying sheds, J1216 at Otira and A 423 and 598 at Reefton were all ready for work. At Westport, Ab715 was used on the morning train to Greymouth, and about 5 of the 6 Ww locomotives there would have worked around and north of Westport. Elmer Lane alone had more steam locomotives at this time than the whole of the North Island, more variety than any other part of the South Island, and most of the locomotives were working hard.

However, this did not last long. In September 1967, the local railcars and mixed trains were cancelled and less freight trains were run. DSB and DSC shunters arrived at about this time, and started replacing steam, especially in the Westport area. DJ locomotives were used on the Greymouth - Westport line to restore services after the 1968 Inangahua earthquake, but it was early 1969 before enough were available to replace the remaining steam locomotives. The last steam workings were probably on Tuesday the 17th of June 1969, although Ab 782, J 1212 and Ww 644 were steamed up until the 19th or 20th, vainly hoping that they would be needed. Some locomotives steamed away from the Coast in 1969 and 1970 to preservation societies in the North Island, and a couple of those towed away have been preserved, as have some that were dug out of the rivers where they had been dumped.

Greymouth–Westport line

On 7 April 1876 an 11 km line was opened from Greymouth to Brunner to bring coal from the mines at Brunner to the Greymouth wharf. Further progress to the north and east was halted by the arguments over the possible rail routes to link Westland with Canterbury and Nelson, and by the depression of the 1880s. The New Zealand Midland Railway, already mentioned

A 428 draws its goods train into Landing, south of Inangahua, on 14 June 1967. MARK COLE

Left: Ww 571 nears Sergeants Hill about 5 km north of Westport with a goods train on 13 June 1967. MARK COLE

Below: Shunting at Westport Depot on 12 June 1976. Ww 678 is on the left with an A on the right. MARK COLE

in connection with its activity in Nelson and on the Midland Line from Canterbury, was formed in 1886, to link Nelson and Canterbury via the West Coast. The company's construction activity concentrated on the line to Reefton, because of its importance as a gold mining centre at this time, and because construction in the Grey Valley was comparatively easy. The first section, from Brunner to Ngahere, was opened in 1889, and on 29 February 1892 the line was opened to a station on the south bank of the Inangahua River, across the river from Reefton, and 74 km from Greymouth.

With Reefton reached, the Midland Railway Company concentrated on the route to Canterbury, and the line north was not extended further before the Government took over the Midland Railway Company in 1895. The section to Cronadun, including the bridge over the Inangahua River, and the present Reefton station, was opened in 1908, and that to Inangahua Junction, in 1914. Inangahua Junction was not named in expectation of the line from Nelson which never reached there—it was already the name of the locality, derived from the junction of the Buller and Inangahua rivers. The first section from Westport, 9 km to Te Kuha, had been opened in 1912.

Construction stopped with the First World War, and little work was done on the difficult lower Buller Gorge section until the Labour Government came to power in 1935 and restarted many public works. The Second World War delayed progress, but by July 1942 the Public Works Department was able to transport freight traffic over the line, and it was handed over to NZR on 5 December 1943.

Coal, timber and cement were the main traffic on this line. Both Westport and Greymouth normally shipped coal from their local mines, but if either river bar became shallow, the coal boats could not use that port, and coal had to be taken by rail to the other port. This occurred on several occasions in the 1950s, and every locomotive on "The Coast" that could steam was put into service. Uc locomotives worked on this route until 1957 and B and Ba locomotives performed their last mainline duties here, because weak bridges prevented more modern locomotives being used. Improved bridges then allowed A and Ab locomotives to work this line, until they were replaced by diesels in 1969.

The steepest grades are on either side of the Reefton saddle, and with southbound traffic generally heavier, the most difficult stretch was the climb south out of Reefton. Banking engines were used regularly, either a Reefton-based loco, or a locomotive borrowed from a northbound train. Bankers were still used sometimes with diesels, with two DJ locos at each end of a heavy train. More recently a triangle has been built at Stillwater so the unit coal trains on the Ngakawau–Lyttelton run do not have to reverse. These trains are now loaded so the train locomotives, usually two DXs, can handle the Reefton Saddle and the climb from Jackson to Otira without assistance.

Vulcan railcars ran passenger services over the line once it was opened throughout, connecting at Stillwater with the passenger services to Christchurch. They also ran local services between Greymouth and Reefton until all passenger services on this line were withdrawn in 1967.

This scene at Greymouth wharves in 1967 leaves no doubt as to what the West Coast's main commodity was (and still is). Today all these tracks and most of the wagons have disappeared. NZR

Seddonville Branch

This branch was built primarily for the transport of coal, and unlike most branches, the surviving portion is now carrying a record traffic. Sir Julius von Haast and James Burnett discovered a major coal seam at an elevation of about 900 metres near Mt Rochfort, in the Papahaua range north-east of Westport, in July of 1860. In 1862 Burnett proposed that the coal could be brought down from the plateau by self-acting inclines, in which full descending wagons pulled the empty wagons up. Once the coal wagons reached the narrow coastal plain north of Westport, they would be taken by a conventional railway to Westport, where the coal could be loaded into ships in the Buller River anchorage.

Government approval for the survey of a railway route north from Westport was given in 1872, and construction was approved in the following year. By December 1875, when the first of the three C class locomotives imported from England was set up in running order, the Mt Rochfort railway, as it was initially called, was complete for the first twelve kilometres to Fairdown, and this section was opened on 31 December 1875. Further sections were opened to Waimangaroa on 5 August 1876, and to Ngakawau, 30 Km from Westport, on 26 September 1877.

The line was extended to Mokihinui in 1893, where it met the private line of the Mokihinui Coal Company. This line was bought by the government in 1895, and incorporated into the railway system. The cost of the extension to Mokihinui, and the purchase of the Coal Company's line, was funded by the Westport Harbour Board.

Coal traffic built up rapidly, and the isolated Westport Section became noted for its profitability. In 1898 four of the Baldwin-built Wb class 2-6-2T locomotives were shipped to Westport, with the first three of the larger Ww class following in 1929. Passenger services ceased in 1946, but the coal traffic continued, mainly to the Westport Wharves. Until early 1967, the usual weekday timetable had two Ww locomotives working Ngakawau trains, one working to Seddonville and the Mokihinui Mine, one shuttling up and down the Conns Creek branch, and a fifth Ww working the Westport wharf.

The loss of markets for Buller coal, and the decline of coastal shipping, meant that the tonnage of coal slowly decreased until 1980. The 3 km section from Seddonville to Mokihinui Mine was closed in 1974, and the Ngakawau–Seddonville section in 1981. However, by then there was interest in exporting the high quality coking coal from the mines above Ngakawau. In 1981, 117,000 tonnes of West Coast coal was railed to Lyttelton for export, and by 1989 this had increased to about 500,000 tonnes per year. This traffic was initially hauled in 850 of the traditional LC highsider wagons. The potential competition from a slurry pipeline to load coal into ships offshore from Ngakawau meant that NZR had to find a more economical way of handling the coal traffic. This they did by building 56 new aluminium-bodied hopper wagons, each capable of holding 50 tonnes of coal. These wagons are run in unit trains which can do a Ngakawau–Lyttelton round trip in 30 hours including loading and unloading. These trains were initially hauled by DJ class locomotives, then DCs, but now DXs work to Ngakawau, replacing the DSC shunters which operated this line after the end of steam in 1968.

The Ngakawau Branch now sees three or four 1400-tonne coal trains a day, and continues to transport coal from mine to ship, the purpose for which it was built.

Hokitika–Ross Branch

Transport was a continuing problem during the West Coast gold rushes, but in most cases the rush was over before anything better than a rough bush track was produced. However, on the main route south from Greymouth a horse tramway, mainly using wooden rails, and the a gauge of 1219 mm (4 feet) was opened to Paroa in 1867. It was extended to Kumara by 1877, although the Taramakau had to be crossed in a cage hanging from a wire. This tramway was not replaced by a railway until 1893, at least partly because of local politics.

Work on a railway between Hokitika and Greymouth began at both ends in 1879, and there was soon indignation from Kumara, where Richard "King Dick" Seddon was commencing his political career as mayor, that the proposed coastal route would bypass Kumara. Poor economic times led to work ceasing in 1880, with only 5 km of track laid, and the route still not settled. In 1886 work on the line recommenced, but there were further arguments over the route, with Seddon now the M.P. for Kumara, and still trying to route the railway through that town. A third attempt to divert the line in 1887 was also unsuccessful, and the railway was finally opened between Greymouth and Hokitika in December 1893.

Further extensions to the south were opened to Ruatapu in 1906, and Ross, 61 km from Greymouth, in 1909. Ross remained the terminus, although there were proposals to extend the railway, they never came to anything. A timber tram belonging to Stuart and Chapman Ltd extended south for a considerable distance to the Lake Ianthe area, and operated until the 1950s. Timber was the main traffic on this line, with a succession of sawmills, each with their own bush tram. As farming developed in South Westland, lime and fertiliser traffic went south, and cattle were driven north

B 304 arrives at Stillwater from Blackball & Ngahere in February 1965. The Midland Line can be seen curving to the right. D.L.A. TURNER

▲*Ww 679 pulls away from Dunollie at the beginning of a 1 in 25 ascent to Rewanui on 15 June 1967.* MARK COLE

A general view of Rewanui on Thursday 20 September 1984. In the bottom left are the Rewanui Station, a bath house in which the miners washed, a private coal bin, and a coaling platform. Out of sight to the bottom left was an uphill walking track to the Rewanui mines settlement. A runaway track can be seen mid left and towards the distance the railway to Greymouth can be seen snaking away with a DJ hauling the 2.15 pm afternoon miners' train. Towards the right the track crosses the bridge over the Seven Mile Creek (largely demolished in a landslip in September 1988) to the yard where the coal loading bins can be seen. The Liverpool No. 3 mine entrance is in shadow, while in sunlight on the other side of the track are the workshops. To the bottom on the same side of the creek are sidings with a smithy and a private mine and hopper coal bins. A covered bridge gave access to the bath house. B.J. MCKENZIE

◀ *A view from the passenger car of a mixed train headed by Ww 679 ascending the 1 in 25 grades of the Rewanui Incline in the morning of 15 June 1969.* MARK COLE

▶*A famous view of Ww 679 working hard up the Rewanui Incline on 25 May 1960.* NZR

Above: A classic West Coast scene of yesteryear—in pouring rain W*w* *480 (now preserved at Glenbrook, Auckland) pulls away from Greymouth Riverside with a mixed train in 1967.* R.J. McGAVIN

Below: W*e* *375 shunts at Dunollie on 16 December 1967 preparing for the climb to Rewanui, otherwise known as "The Hill".* NZR&LS COLLECTION

and loaded into rail wagons at Ross. At least up till 1958, during the whitebait season, a box wagon was attached to the afternoon train at Ross, to carry whitebait to Hokitika and Christchurch.

When the Otira Tunnel opened in 1923, some carriages of the Christchurch express were taken on to Ross by mixed train, and vice versa. The introduction of railcars resulted in improved timetables, with two railcars running each way between Ross and Christchurch six days a week. Mixed trains continued, particularly between Ross and Hokitika, until 11 September 1967, when all mixed trains and local railcars on the lines from Greymouth to Hokitika, Otira and Westport were withdrawn. The railcar services from Christchurch ceased to run past Greymouth in October 1972.

Ross had a locomotive shed, used in its latter years by an A or Ab locomotive. From May 1969, this line was operated by Greymouth-based DJ diesels. For a few years in the 1970s, the condition of the Taramakau bridge was such that DSC shunters had to work all trains. The Hokitika river road-rail bridge, known locally as "the longest xylophone in the world" because of the noise and vibration experienced when crossing it, also needed major repairs, and this led to the closure of the line south of Hokitika on 24 November 1980. One daily shunt now suffices for this line, with the Westland Dairy Factory at Hokitika and the remaining timber and wood products traffic the main sources of income. The Hokitika shunt was virtually the last NZR duty of the DJ class, the DBR class finally taking over in August 1991.

Rewanui Branch

A private company with rights to mine coal in the Runanga area originally undertook to build a railway there, but in 1901 the Government took over the coal lease and railway works because of unsatisfactory progress. The line was opened on 1 December 1904 to the new State Mine at what is now Dunollie. The only major engineering on this line, known initially as the Point Elizabeth branch, was the bridge across the Grey River right by Greymouth station.

Good coal deposits were also found high up in the Paparoa range. To gain access to this coal it was necessary to build a steeply-graded railway up the valley of Seven Mile creek, and work on this extension started in July 1908. The maximum grade on this 5.4 km section from Dunollie up to the terminus of Rewanui was 1 in 26. To provide extra braking power for descending trains a Fell centre rail was installed, like that on the Rimutaka Incline, and each train included a Fell brake van.

There was no road access to Rewanui, so as well as the coal traffic from the Liverpool State Mine and a number of private mines, there was a considerable pas-

B 304 with a Dunollie–Greymouth mixed train captured on film in the Runanga yard, August 1964. D.L.A. TURNER

senger traffic. The mixed train which arrived at Rewanui about 11.30 p.m. Sunday to Thursday was known as the "Paddy Webb" or "Bob Semple" after the miners who became Cabinet Ministers in the first Labour Government, and who first arranged this train to make it easier for the miners changing shift at midnight. The 6.35 am from Greymouth was the "Miners Train", while the return working, the 7.35 am from Rewanui was the "Fanny Train", as the women from Dunollie and Rewanui used it to go to work in Greymouth. The early afternoon train back to Greymouth was known as the "wet-timer", as miners working in wet parts of the mine worked a shorter shift. Another feature of the incline was a bike-path beside the tracks, so those working non-standard hours could take up their bikes in the van, and bike down. A Land-Rover converted to run on rails arrived in May 1960, to serve as an ambulance, and was kept in a shed by Rewanui station. Before then, injured miners were taken down the incline in a "gravity-powered" box wagon with no springs.

Only specially authorised engines were allowed to work on the incline. Tank locomotives of the 4-6-4T We class were used for many years. Two of these had been produced by conversion of B 4-8-0 tender locomotives in 1902, to work on the Rimutaka incline. We 377 was sent to Greymouth in 1914, when the line to Rewanui was opened, and We 198 (later numbered 376) followed in 1927. In 1943 another B was converted to We 375. W and Wa class 2-6-2T locomotives were also used on light trains, and during the 1960s three Ww class 4-6-4T locomotives were adapted for the incline.

The Fell centre rail was taken out of use on 20 November 1966, and removed at the end of the year. Only locomotives with two Westinghouse brake pumps were then allowed to work the incline. In practice this meant We 375, the only We still in use, and Ww locomotives fitted with an extra pump. In June 1969, DJ diesels took over, with DSC shunters occasionally working the "Paddy Webbs". Both classes had modified high pressure brake valves to work the incline.

In its last few years, the line became a tourist attraction, and special tourist trains were run during the mine summer holidays. At other times tourists caught the regular afternoon train to Rewanui. The Liverpool mine was reaching the end of its life in the 1980s, and by October 1984 the Rewanui line was ruled to be unfit for passenger service. The last coal was loaded from a private mine on the incline on 28 May 1985, and the line officially closed on 19 August 1985.

A preservation society endeavoured to restore the mine area as a tourist attraction, despite a massive landslide in September 1988, which destroyed bridges and some buildings, and killed the caretaker. The incline was turned into a road, and in 1995 Solid Energy (the successor of the old State Coal Mines) started to develop the new Mount Davy mine near the Rewanui station site. This mine was closed only four years later, after three miners were killed, because mining had proved to be hazardous. Currently, the top end of the incline is inaccessible behind a locked tunnel-mouth, and during the mining period the old Rewanui station was demolished, so there is little chance of a viable tourist attraction being developed.

Rapahoe Branch

This short branch left the Rewanui Branch at Runanga, and went 4 km to the Strongman State Mine coal bins at Rapahoe. The line was opened in 1923. Before 1969 the line was generally operated by tender engines, such as the B and Ba 4-8-0's, or the A class 4-6-2's. DC diesel locomotives now work the line. With a new Strongman coal mine, and a new underground mine at Spring Creek near Dunollie, this line is kept busy. There were proposals for a new bridge over the Grey River, to avoid all trains having to go through the centre of Greymouth to the Elmer Lane freight yard, but these seem now to be on hold.

Blackball–Roa Branch

The Blackball Coal Company mine was on the far side of the Grey River from the Greymouth to Reefton railway, and an aerial cableway was used to bring the coal to Ngahere. In 1901 a railway to Blackball was authorised, but there were considerable problems with its construction. There were problems building the bridge over the Grey River, the contractor for a trestle bridge further on went bankrupt, and it "rained continuously for three months". The 5.5 km section to Blackball was carrying coal in 1909, but was not officially opened until August 1910. A further section of line, built by the Paparoa Coal Company, and later taken over by the State Coal Mines, climbed on a 1 in 25 gradient to the Roa mine bins. This section had a Fell centre rail for braking like the Rewanui line.

The Roa line was worked by New Zealand Railways, using W and Wa locomotives, with Fell vans for braking the descent of the loaded trains, until it closed in 1960. Wf and B locomotives worked to Blackball until a flood on 21 February 1966 badly damaged the bridge over the Grey and it was decided to abandon the line.

Passenger services on this line were replaced by buses in 1940. For many years thereafter, services were worked by special buses with cut down roofs, so they could pass under the support wires of the Taylorville bridge on the way to Blackball.

Conns Creek Branch & Denniston Incline

The short Conns creek branch followed the Waimangaroa River to give access to the coal mines on either side of the river. The first 1.5 km of the branch was built by the Wellington Coal Company in 1877. Their mine was unsuccessful, and the railway was then used to transport coal from the Koranui mine. This mine was at an altitude of about 750 metres on the north side of the river, and coal was brought down by a series of four self-acting inclines, as suggested by Burnett.

Prospecting on the plateau south of the river had discovered better quality coal deposits, and the Westport Colliery Company was formed to exploit these deposits. The railway was extended by a kilometre to the Conns Creek yard in 1878. From this point, the dou-

Ww 571 with wagons of coal and timber from the northern end of the Mokihinui Branch rounds the curve off the Waimangaroa River Bridge in the evening of 13 June 1967. MARK COLE

Ww 575 crosses the river bridge at Ngakawau on 12 June 1967. MARK COLE

ble self-acting incline known as the Denniston Incline was built. This incline was as steep as 1 in 1.25 at one point, and climbed 520 metres in a length of 1.7 km. Descending railway wagons full of coal lifted empty wagons on the other end of a wire rope under the control of a brakeman at the top of each section of the incline. At Middle Brake, half way up, wagons were removed from the rope for one section, and then attached to the other rope to continue their journey. The wagon commonly used for carrying coal to Westport was the Q class, introduced in 1897, with a removable hopper that could be lifted off the wagon body by a wharf crane, and emptied into a ship's hold.

At the turn of the century, four mixed trains a day ran from Westport to Conns Creek. Passenger services ceased in 1931, and in its latter years the Conns Creek branch was worked by a shunting locomotive which shuttled between Conns Creek and Waimangaroa.

A number of mines around Denniston sent coal down the incline, and the peak tonnage on the incline

Above: The lower part of the Denniston Incline above the NZR railhead seen in December 1967, four months after closure. On the left some wagons can be discerned resting where they came to grief after one or more runaways down the incline. R.J. McGAVIN

was 348,000 tonnes in 1910. However, by 1967 there was no longer enough traffic to justify the operation of the labour-intensive incline and the Conns Creek branch, and they both closed on 16 August 1967. A walkway now links the top and bottom of the incline, with access to Middle Brake.

Cape Foulwind Railway

This railway was constructed by the Westport Harbour Board in 1886 to bring rocks from their quarries near Cape Foulwind to strengthen the breakwaters on either side of the Buller River. In 1888 it was linked to Westport by a bridge over the river which also carried the main highway, and was used for this purpose long after the railway was closed. Passenger services were run for a number of years, starting about 1890.

A new section of line including a tunnel, was opened in 1914 to a new quarry south of Cape Foulwind. In 1921 this line, and the three F class locomotives which worked it, was transferred to NZR ownership. It was closed by NZR in 1930, and reverted to the Marine Department, who ran occasional trains for some years. The large cement works at Cape Foulwind, built since the branch closed, trucked cement to a private siding just south of Westport for loading onto railway wagons.

A distant view of the Denniston Incline seen reaching into the clouds in June 1967. MARK COLE

Above: Ww 571, now preserved at Silverstream (Wellington) seen Westport-bound with a train of coal and timber between Seddonville and Summerlea on the Seddonville Branch in the 1960s. E.J. McCLARE

Below: The profile of B 304 crossing the Stillwater Bridge with a Blackball–Greymouth goods train in February 1965. D.L.A. TURNER

CHAPTER SIXTEEN

Otago

A century ago Dunedin was one of the busiest stations in New Zealand and fully justified the impressive stone station building which was completed in 1906 and which has been fully restored, most recently by the Dunedin City Council which acquired the building in 1994. Unfortunately, the effects of changing times on the railways throughout New Zealand have been compounded here by the decline in the relative importance of Dunedin and Otago. The "Southerner" is the only regular Tranz Scenic train to use Dunedin station, and its future is in doubt. The only railway function of the station now is the "Taieri Gorge Limited" booking office, which also sells "Southerner" tickets. The sole survivor of the dozen country branches there were at the start of the 20th century is the portion of the Otago Central line used for the "Taieri Gorge Limited". The emphasis is now on bulk freight, and the Port Chalmers Container Terminal has replaced the now-closed heavy industries of Burnside and Green Island as the main traffic generators around Dunedin.

Otago Central Line

In the early 1870s the Main Trunk line was being built both north and south from Dunedin, and construction of a railway to the Tuapeka diggings, eventually to become the Roxburgh Branch, was also under way. When the residents of Central Otago, particularly those along the Clutha from Alexandra to Cromwell, asked for a

The "Taieri Gorge Limited", operated as a daily round trip from Dunedin, enables thousands of people annually to enjoy the scenery of the most spectacular part of the former Otago Central Railway. Here the setting is the Flat Stream Viaduct.
MARK COLE

railway to come to their district, they initially did not get much support from Dunedin, even though the rapid development of Dunedin had been based upon the wealth from the Otago Goldfields.

Suggested railway routes to the interior included the routes later followed by the Tapanui and Roxburgh branches, the "Pigroot" from Palmerston to Naseby, and a route from Oamaru via Danseys Pass to Naseby. There was also a proposal to extend the Kingston Branch to Queenstown and Cromwell.

All these routes had their difficulties, and with no strong backing from Dunedin for any route, the Otago Provincial Council was unable to decide on the best route for a Central Otago railway before it was abolished in 1876. It was 1877 before the Taieri route eventually followed was suggested by the Taieri County Council, and taken up by Dunedin interests, belatedly concerned that a line from Oamaru or Invercargill might be built and deprive Dunedin of trade.

Mr W.N. Blair, the District Engineer, reported on seven possible routes in July 1877, and recommended the Taieri route. It was one of the most direct routes from Dunedin, and was said to have no major constructional difficulties, steep grades or high summits. It also was a more politically acceptable line, as it opened up the largest area of Crown Land of any route, and had the combined support of the local bodies in the area from Ranfurly through to Clyde, as well as a supporting petition headed by the Mayor of Dunedin.

Construction of the line was authorised in 1877, despite objections to the bill from members from the Oamaru district, and from South Otago and Southland. The first sod was turned at Wingatui, the junction with the South Island Main Trunk, on 7 June 1879, with "the confident hope of all present that the line would be completed to Lake Wanaka by the year 1884". In fact, it was to take 42 years for the line to reach its final terminus of Cromwell.

Unfortunately, because of the time it had taken to decide on the route, the depression of the 1880s drastically slowed down construction before much progress had been made. The central government was prepared to spend some money for labourers, more as unemployment relief than from a desire for rapid progress, but was very reluctant to spend vital overseas funds on rails or iron for bridges. The first difficult section up from the Taieri Plain, through two tunnels to the Taioma stream was completed by August 1884, but it was January 1885 before the contract was let for the viaduct across the Taioma stream, now known as the Wingatui viaduct. A temporary tramway from North Taieri, on the Outram branch, had been needed to get materials to the construction sites on this section.

Most of the formation for the track on the section through the Taieri Gorge to Hindon was ready in 1884, although the five short tunnels still had to be done. The main cause of delay, as happened again and again on this line, was the bridges. Tracklaying was halted until the Taioma Viaduct was completed in 1887. Once this viaduct was completed, the tracklaying and bridge construction work could continue, with the iron components for each bridge railed up from a temporary workshop at Wingatui. Altogether, there were 18 major bridges and viaducts, and 10 tunnels, which had to be completed before the railway climbed out of the Taieri Gorge into the Strath Taieri plain. This is the spectacular gorge section through which the "Taieri Gorge Limited", operated by the Otago Excursion Train Trust, runs regular excursions.

The line to Middlemarch, the centre of the Strath Taieri district, was opened in 1891. The Otago politicians were not pleased with the lines progress, only 64 km in 12 years, and they agitated for a better rate of construction. Vincent Pyke, the M.P. for Dunstan, compared the Taieri Gorge to a garden wall, which had to be climbed before the fruit could be picked. It took another three years to construct the next 25 km through easy country to Hyde, and the increasingly impatient residents formed a railway league to pressure the government into speeding up progress.

Finally, on 1 December 1898, the line was opened to Ranfurly. This town immediately grew at the expense of the gold town of Naseby, and in the process the commercial centre of Ranfurly shifted south some hundreds of metres to the station, producing a curious dogleg in the main road through the town. A permanent locomotive depot was established here, in contrast to the temporary depots which followed the advancing railhead. This depot lasted until the end of steam. Right through until the 1970s this was an important station, with staff of the locomotive, traffic and way and works branches, but deregulation and rationalisation had a drastic effect on this line, and by the end of 1988, there were no railway staff living between Middlemarch and Alexandra.

From Ranfurly progress was significantly faster, with the line open to Ida Valley in 1901, and through the Poolburn Gorge to Omakau in 1904. By the end of 1906 the line had reached Alexandra, and a few months later, on 2 April 1907, the line was opened to Clyde.

Although the residents of Cromwell and Hawea were keen to see the railway continued, the government was concerned at the cost of putting a railway through the Cromwell Gorge. A two foot gauge light railway was considered, but eventually a line was approved using the normal 1067 mm gauge, but with sharper curves and steeper grades than normal, and work started in July 1914. Despite the First World War the Public Works Department were able to run a passenger service to Cromwell from January 1918. It took three more years before the section to Cromwell was handed over to the Railways Department, and the line never passed the big rock at the west end of Cromwell station.

From the time the railway penetrated the Taieri Gorge, wool was an important traffic. Sheep and cattle were taken to coastal farms for fattening, or to freezing works, and stock specials from Omakau, north of Alexandra, were still running in 1968. Once the line reached Alexandra, the "garden wall" metaphor was fully appropriate, with heavy loadings of apricots and other fruits in season. The initial gold rush was well over by the time the railway reached the middle reaches of the Clutha River, but dredging was still important, and there was significant traffic for this industry.

R class Single Fairlie locomotives were used on the first sections of this line taken over by the Railways De-

An AB *hauled passenger train makes its way along the Cromwell Gorge section on 27 December 1954. This section was closed in 1980 and today this area is submerged under the waters of the artificial Lake Dunstan.* DEREK CROSS

partment, replacing the F class used by the Public Works Department. Once a turntable was installed at Hyde, tender locomotives were used, such as the 2-8-0's of the T, O and P classes, and the 2-6-2 V class. When a batch of American Ub locomotives from the Baldwin Locomotive Works arrived in Dunedin in 1901, they were soon sent up the Otago Central. As the heavier Pacific locomotives replaced them on the main line, they worked until the 1930s on the Otago Central. The A and Ab class Pacifics then became the usual locomotives, and from the 1940s until the end of steam, the Ab's were dominant. Dh class diesels were introduced in 1956, but were only allowed as far as Alexandra, and normally worked only to Ranfurly or Omakau. The introduction of DJ locomotives resulted in the end of regular steam working in February 1968.

Until 1900, passengers were only able to travel in mixed trains, but in August 1900, shortly after the line reached Wedderburn, passenger trains were introduced. By the time the terminus was Clyde, the daily passenger trains took over eight hours to do the run, including lunch at Ranfurly and two other refreshment stops. Mixed trains replaced these services during the First World War, and daily passenger services were only fully reinstated in 1936, on about a seven and a half schedule to or from Cromwell. The daily service was reduced to thrice-weekly by coal shortages in 1945, and from 1951 reverted to mixed trains, with passenger trains during the holiday periods.

Vulcan railcars replaced the mixed trains on 1 October 1956, on a schedule of 5 hrs 12 mins, six days a week. They connected at Dunedin with the South Island Limited Express to and from Christchurch. The higher speed of these railcars showed up deterioration in the tracks and sleepers, and the railcar service was suspended for six months in 1957 while repairs were done. In the following year, the railcar run was cut back to Alexandra. For nearly twenty more years these railcars provided a reliable but not very rapid service, until the general decline of the railcar fleet saw the last railcar run on 25 April 1976. A replacement bus service was provided, but the last Railways bus services through Ranfurly were withdrawn in January 1989.

The section of the railway past Clyde was closed on 13 April 1980 to allow the construction of the Clyde high dam. This dam created Lake Dunstan, whose later filling drowned the railway route through the Cromwell Gorge, as well as inundating apricot orchards and the commercial area of Cromwell. From this date the line terminated at a new Clyde station, which had facilities for handling the traffic for the dam construction work. Although the line had been threatened with closure since the early 1970s, the traffic associated with the construction of the Clyde dam kept it open until 30 April 1990.

The first 4 km from Wingatui is used by Tranz Rail for access to private sidings, while the next 60 km sec-

With the Hillside Workshops in the background, a Vulcan railcar arrives at Dunedin after its 248 km run from Cromwell in December 1956. The railcar service was inaugurated on 1 October that year. NZR

tion to Middlemarch is owned by the Taieri Gorge Railway, which is a partnership between the Dunedin City Council and the Otago Excursion Train Trust. This railway operates the "Taieri Gorge Limited", a daily sightseeing train from Dunedin to Pukerangi, with occasional trains running to Middlemarch. Five DJ class diesel locomotives power these trains, and the railway also has a DE class locomotive, usually used on work trains. An interesting possibility is that this railway may be used for log transport when nearby forests are felled.

The remainder of the route, from Middlemarch to Clyde, is a public walkway, with the trackbed and bridges maintained for walking, cycling or horse-riding.

South Island Main Trunk (Dunedin–Invercargill Section)

The Dunedin and Clutha railway was authorised in 1871, one of the first railways authorised under the Vogel Public Works scheme of the 1870s, and it was the first major line built to the new uniform gauge of 1067 mm. The construction of 56 km of the line from Dunedin to Balclutha, and the construction of the line from Invercargill to Mataura, were two of the six contracts which were awarded in August 1872 to the English railway contracting firm of Brogdens. The first section to Abbotsford was opened on 1 July 1874, and on 1 September of the following year it was opened right through to Balclutha, 84 km from Dunedin. This was rapid progress, considering that this line included the 890 metre Chain Hills Tunnel between Abbotsford and Wingatui, and major bridges over the Taieri and Clutha rivers. One reason may have been that the government was keen to use this line as a demonstration of the advantages of the new policy of building railways rapidly, by using a narrower gauge, lighter rails and other lesser standards than previous provincial railways.

Two 0-6-0 saddle tank locomotives were ordered for this line. They were the first of the F class, a very successful type, which eventually numbered 88 locomotives. The last members of this class in regular service were only retired from shunting the Lyttelton wharves in 1964, and a number have been preserved, including F 163 which runs main-line excursions from a base at Palmerston North.

Progress was also rapid on the other end of this line, and the line from Invercargill was opened to Gore in August 1875. The section between Gore and Balclutha was over more undulating countryside, requiring heavier earthworks, but on 22 January 1879 the opening of the Clinton—Balclutha section completed the South Island Main Trunk from Christchurch to Invercargill.

For passenger traffic, this line was most important for long-distance travel, especially after November 1904, when trains began to run between Invercargill and Christchurch in a day. From this date the main passenger services on this line were basically an extension of those between Christchurch and Dunedin.

The situation for freight was rather different until quite recently. There was effectively a watershed for freight traffic near Clinton. Traffic north of this was basically to and from Dunedin, while south of the watershed most traffic was with Invercargill or Bluff. Five branches on the Dunedin side of Clinton, and four on the Invercargill side, added significant short-distance freight traffic until the 1960s. As this traffic disappeared, long-distance traffic increased. The first express freight

▲ *The southbound "South Island Limited" crossed the northbound train at Katiki, north of Palmerston.* B.J. MCKENZIE
▼ *JA 1261 cruises up the Otago Harbour with a "South Island Limited" in tow. The locomotive will be relieved at Dunedin.* B.J. MCKENZIE

Left: Two JAs head a southbound "South Island Limited" towards Waitati in August 1969. MARK COLE

Below: DJ 3257 in one of the less common liveries that the class appeared in, heads the "Southerner" between Purakanui and the coast north of Dunedin in the early 1980s. NZR

train from Christchurch to Invercargill was only introduced in December 1970, on a 16 hour schedule, but increasingly this line is seen as the southern extremity of a single trunk line from Auckland to Invercargill.

A suburban passenger service was operated between Dunedin and Mosgiel until December 1982. For many years until 1968 these services were operated by Ab class tender locomotives, and before that B and Ba locomotives were often used. Railcars were also used on some off-peak services until 1967. DJ locomotives took over in 1968, assisted by DI diesels and DSC diesel shunters, but these services were in decline by then. By the time of final closure only five trains were run each weekday, compared to twelve trains on weekdays, and a lesser weekend service, in early years. A feature of this service was the "Flyers", non-stop services between Dunedin and Mosgiel. The line between Dunedin and Mosgiel was double-tracked in stages from 1908 until 1914, but following the withdrawal of the suburban trains, it has now been converted back to single track.

Dunedin Peninsula and Ocean Beach Railway

The Dunedin Peninsula and Ocean Beach Railway Company was incorporated in 1874, to build local lines from Dunedin City. The 3.5 km line to Ocean Beach was opened in 1876, and a 1.5 km branch to Andersons Bay at the end of 1877. From 1880, this line was normally operated as a steam tramway, although trains ran to Ocean Beach for race meetings at Forbury Park racecourse. The company was wound up in 1883, largely as a result of competition from a horse tram service. A new company ran trains to race and agricultural shows until 1904, and the line was used for taking livestock to and from shows until 1938. The Otago Branch of the New Zealand Railway and Locomotive Society now operates the Ocean Beach Railway in Kettle Park near the former Ocean Beach Terminus.

Roxburgh Branch

The construction of the 94.7 km branch line from Milton to Roxburgh took more than half a century, making it one of the longest railway construction projects in New Zealand history. The section from Clarksville to Waitahuna was opened on 22 January 1877. This was followed in three months by the next section from Waitahuna to Lawrence on 2 April, but it was not until 4 October 1910 that the next section from Lawrence to Big Hill was opened.

The Big Hill to Beaumont section followed on 15 December 1914, the Beaumont to Millers Flat section on 16 December 1925 and finally the Millers Flat to Roxburgh section on 18 April 1928.

Passenger services on the Roxburgh branch ended on 4 September 1936. The line was very steeply graded and sharply curved. On the way to Beaumont, trains encountered grades of 1 in 38 which together with 100 metre and 120 metre radius curves limited speeds to 32 km/h. There were 3 tunnels and 15 stations, six with goods sheds and eight with cattle and sheep yards.

The construction of the Roxburgh Dam in the early 1950s boosted traffic, but by the end of the decade there was only one train each way a day except during the fruit season. Figures for 1959-60 showed that the line carried 9900 tonnes outwards, 24,400 tonnes inwards. In addition trains carried 16,000 cattle and 51,800 sheep.

Following a review of freight operations in the early 1960s, the line's future looked decidedly shaky, however in 1965 the decision was made to continue operating the line because of a significant increase in tonnage. By 1967 the line was losing $100,000 a year and it was announced that it would close on 1 April 1968. This was deferred for two months but in May it was announced that as the Forest Service did not wish to rail export log traffic from the Beaumont state forest to the Port of Otago or Bluff, and as fruit traffic from the Roxburgh area would be sent by road, the line would close. This came on 1 June 1968.

Kurow Branch

The 58.6 km branch from Pukeuri, 9 km north of Oamaru, inland to Kurow was laid at various stages, beginning in 1874 with the commencement of the Awamoko Tramway. The line as far as Duntroon, 35.5 km, was opened on 1 December 1875. Later the Duntroon and Hakataramea Railway Company Ltd. built a track from Duntroon to Kurow and then across the Waitaki River to Hakataramea, 1.8 km from Kurow. The line was complete from Pukeuri Junction to Hakataramea Junction in July 1881. From completion the line was operated by NZR and was fully taken over on 1 April 1885.

Like most similar branch lines, engines used over it were F and T classes, Wf and Ww, then from the late 1940s, the A and Ab classes. From the late 1960s the DJ class diesels were used. Loads that these locomotives could haul were as follows; F- 120 tonnes up, 220 tonnes down, T class - 180 and 260, Wf - 410 and 500, Ww - 460 and 560, A and Ab - 530 and 630, DJ - 560 and 870 tonnes.

During the late 1920s, the experimental Clayton steam railcars were used on the branch. These were replaced in 1929 by an ordinary train service as increased passenger traffic was created by the commencement of the Waitaki hydro construction.

The connection from Kurow to Hakataramea was closed on 14 July 1930. A 6.4 km light railway built by the PWD ran from Kurow to the Waitaki Dam (Awakino) opening on 20 December 1928, which also carried construction workers and lasted over eight years before being dismantled in April 1937.

The branch was closed to passengers on 25 March 1947. Traditional goods traffic in the form of stock and fertiliser gradually declined and traffic was reduced eventually to Ministry of Works material for the building of the Upper Waitaki Hydro Scheme. Two trains a week were scheduled, but usually only one was required to run. With the completion of the dam the end of the branch line was in sight. This came on 5 June 1983. There were originally 13 stations on the line but on closing there were only four still in use - Papakaio, Duntroon, Otekaieke and Kurow. The last train was a special that ran on Tuesday 7 June 1983 to remove all rolling stock on the line.

Kaitangata Line

In 1876 the Kaitangata Railway & Coal Co. built this short line to link their coal mine at Kaitangata with the South Island Main Trunk at Stirling. A short extension down a Kaitangata street served the Castle Hill Mine until 1963. The railway was taken over by the Mines Department in 1956, and closed in December 1970. There was a station of normal NZR appearance and an engine shed at Kaitangata, but by the time the line closed they were in an advanced stage of dereliction. For many years the line was operated by an 0-6-0 side tank locomotive, known as an "Improved F", which was built by Sharp Stewart in Scotland in 1896. This locomotive was replaced by a diesel shunter in August or September 1968, but was kept as a spare engine. When the line closed the 0-6-0 was donated to Shantytown, near Greymouth, where it is in regular operation, wearing the name *Kaitangata* in honour of its former home.

Opposite: An AB heads a goods train aronud Rocky Point on the Roxburgh Branch in August 1964. D.L.A. TURNER

Right: An AB shunts at Kurow before departure for Oamaru on 23 June 1966. NZR

Ngapara & Tokarahi Branches

The residents of the districts inland from Oamaru started asking for a tramway or railway to give them better access to Oamaru in 1870. The Otago Provincial Council decided to construct a line in 1872, and the line was soon under construction. There were no major engineering works needed, but construction took longer than expected, after troubles which included a boiler explosion in a contractors locomotive. Regular services on the 24 km section from Waiareka Junction, on the main line south from Oamaru, to Ngapara, began in April 1877. Ten years later a side branch of 19 km from Windsor Junction to Tokarahi was opened. Plans to extend one or the other branch to a junction with the Kurow branch, or to extend the Tokarahi branch to Livingstone, were abandoned at an early date.

For a number of years until 1926, mixed trains left both branch termini in the morning, and met at Windsor Junction. They shunted to produce a passenger train, which went directly to Oamaru, and a freight train which followed at a slower pace. This working was reversed in the afternoon. Despite this imaginative working, the branch was one of the first to lose passenger services, when NZR began operating a bus service in December 1926. The Tokarahi line was closed to all traffic in 1930.

F and Fa locomotives were used in the early years of these branches, with T class 2-8-0s around the turn of the century. After 1926, an Oamaru locomotive, usually an Ab in later years, worked out and back to Ngapara two or three times a week. By 1959 there was little traffic other than lime from Taylor's siding, 4.5 km from Waiareka. The line from Taylors siding to Ngapara was accordingly closed, with the last freight train leaving Ngapara on 31 July behind Ab 783.

The stub of the line to Taylor's Limeworks continued in operation until the 1990s, finally closing in 1997.

Dunback & Makareao Branches

As with the preceding pair of branches, this was also a Y arrangement of branches with a junction in the middle of nowhere. In this case, however, it was the branch built later which survived the longest. The Dunback branch, known initially as the Waihemo branch, followed the Shag River inland from Palmerston for 15 km, and opened in 1885. Despite local hopes, it soon became apparent that the Pigroot, as the cart road from Palmerston to Ranfurly was known, was not going to be the route for a railway to central Otago. Once the Otago Central Railway reached Ranfurly, the Dunback branch only carried local traffic, and the line past Inch Valley eventually closed completely from 1 January 1968.

A 4 km spur from Inch Valley served the Makareao limeworks, operated for many years by the Milburn Lime and Cement Co Ltd. This spur was opened in 1900, and originally belonged to the Lands Department. Limestone from the limeworks was taken to the Milburn Cement Works at Burnside, just south-west of Dunedin, on the daily "stone train". The Milburn Cement Works closed in December 1988, and the last train ran from the limeworks a few weeks earlier. The branch was officially closed from 1 July 1989.

Tapanui Branch

The branch line to Tapanui was built as far as Edievale 42.3 km from Waipahi, reaching there in February 1905. Before that the section as far as Kelso, 25.1 km, was opened in December 1880, and the next section from Kelso to Heriot, 32.2 km, was opened in April 1884.

The route had been considered in 1877 by district engineer W.N. Blair as a possible route to Central Otago but he could find little favour with such a line beyond Tapanui. Local interests urged the line onward from there, and it was expected that it would join with the Roxburgh Branch at Moa Flat or Raes Junction. The local West Otago newspaper, the Tapanui Courier, maintained that a short tunnel and a few heavy clay cuttings in the Dunrobin Hills were the only engineering difficulties in getting the railway to the Clutha River. By the end of 1900 the Government decided to continue the line 10 km from Heriot to Edievale, pending a final decision on which direction the railway connection would be made with Roxburgh. All hope that the line would be extended was dashed by 1928 when Roxburgh was made the terminus of the railway from Milton via Lawrence.

From Edievale mixed trains began running on a regular timetable, making their connections at Waipahi with main line expresses and local Invercargill-Clinton trains. Passengers declined during the 1930s Depression and on 1 January 1934 buses took over remaining passenger traffic.

The Heriot to Edievale section was closed completely on 1 January 1968, traffic on which was only 4000 tonnes a year. From March 1969 goods services were reorganised to operate from Gore. The ageing A class steam locomotives on the branch were replaced with DJ diesels which were rated to haul 600 tonnes up and 1000 tonnes down.

Traffic on the line in the 1970s varied between 30,000 and 60,000 tonnes and came mostly from the State Forest's Conical Hill sawmill, which had its own private siding 9 km up the branch. There was also a steady traffic of phosphate railed from the Southland Co-op Phosphate Co. works at Awarua to West Otago Transport at Heriot.

Complete closure of the line came in October 1978, two years short of the line's centennial, as a result of flood damage. In the early 1990s proposals for re-opening the line to Conical Hill got as far as Resource Management Act approval, and surplus track from the Otago Central was allegedly stockpiled at Mosgiel for this purpose, but the log traffic was won by road transport.

Port Chalmers Branch

Although constructed by the Dunedin and Port Chalmers Railway Company under the auspices of the Otago Provincial Council and not by the central government, this was the first line built to the new gauge of 1067 mm. The initial motive power used was two Double Fairlie locomotives, in which flexibility for going around sharp corners was obtained by carrying the locomotive on two bogies, each with its own cylinders and coupling rods. Each set of cylinders had its own boiler, so the poor fireman had to feed two fireboxes from his central position. One of these locomotives, *Josephine* survived to be preserved at the Early Settlers Museum at Dunedin.

Once the first section of the main line north was opened in 1877 this branch only consisted of the 2 km section between Sawyers Bay and the wharves at Port Chalmers.

Suburban passenger services ceased at the end of 1979. This branch remains busy, mainly with traffic to and from the Container Terminal at Port Chalmers and export logs from Otago forests.

Catlins River Branch

Today the Catlins River Branch would not be liked by environmentalists. Its main purpose was to assist in the logging of the beech forests of the Catlins district, and once the accessible forest was cleared, it no longer had enough traffic to sustain it. However, now that they have ceased operation, the surviving traces of the railway, the sawmills and the bush tramways are advertised as attractions for those who come to see the bush and the other natural and historic features of this district.

The first contract for a railway to develop the area south of Balclutha was let in 1879, but it was 1885 before the 13 km to Romahapa was opened. It took another ten years before the 19 km section to Owaka was opened in 1896, as the route required crossing the saddle between Glenomaru creek and the Owaka river, including the digging of the 220 metre Hunts Road

Left: Vulcan railcar RM 55 sits at Port Chalmers station in 1961. G.W. EMERSON

Opposite: DJ 1247 heads a train of lime away from Makareao in the early 1970s, with the limeworks in the background. NZR

Tunnel. Increasingly rugged country saw more slow progress, and it was nearly 20 years later when the line was finally opened to Tahakopa on 4 February 1915. The last section included a climb at 1 in 40 for northbound trains between Maclennan and Puketiro, which limited the load for an A or Ab on a mixed train to 190 tonnes. During the 35 years of construction, there had been no less than 8 terminal points as the rails crept onward.

As each section of line was opened, sawmills sprung up alongside it, especially in the inland areas, as the bush areas that were easily accessible from the sea had already been logged. There were over 30 sawmills working in the district in the 1930s, but as the bush became cut out they progressively closed. There was then less need for the passenger services, and the last mixed train ran in 1958. By the late 1960s, timber traffic had declined considerably, as had the inward transport of lime and fertiliser for the farms of the Owaka district, and the line was finally closed in 1971, having just made it into the diesel era.

Tahakopa was one of the most isolated termini on NZR, and the residents had a strong attachment to the railway. When the last Tahakopa-based locomotive departed in 1956, A 476 carried a laurel wreath and was covered in greenery, and the residents sang "Now is the Hour" as it departed over exploding detonators. By the time of final closure in 1971, Tahakopa was a shadow of its former self, but the difficulties of working the line were to be emphasised on a final occasion. On 27 February, Ab 795, one of the locomotives later used on the "Kingston Flyer", ran an excursion from Dunedin, whilst DJ 1243 brought another train from Balclutha for local traffic. While running a trip for enthusiasts and local children from Owaka to Tahakopa, Ab 795 stalled on the climb from Owaka to the summit at Puketiro, because a sand pipe had come adrift, and the locomotive could not get a grip on the rails without sand. The train had to be split in two to get it up to the 157 metre summit at Puketiro. After Ab 795 was serviced at Tahakopa, the train again had to be split to climb the 1 in 40 out of Maclennan. By the time Ab 795 reached Owaka, the continual slipping had collapsed its firebox arch, and it had to hand over its train to the DJ. The excursion finally got back to Dunedin after 1.00 am the next day. The rugged hills of the Catlins had had the last laugh.

Walton Park Industrial Branch

This line was built from Burnside in the southern suburbs of Dunedin to Walton Park, 3.3 km away, which opened on 1 July 1874 and extended to Saddle Hill, 4.21 km from the Junction Points on 24 September 1879. It served freight traffic only and there was never a passenger service. Walton Park to Saddle Hill was closed on 24 July 1944 and Geddes to Walton Park on 1 May 1957. The remaining 0.58 km was closed in 1980.

Outram Branch

In 1875 a company was formed to build a railway from Allanton (near the present day Dunedin Airport) to the settlement of Outram. The Provincial Council agreed to lend the company £12,000 and contracts were quickly let for sleepers, bridges and fences.

Local pressures saw this scheme dropped in favour of a route from Mosgiel and the provincial council voted £27,962 for it. The battle between the two routes was settled when landowners along the route from Mosgiel agreed to make land available for the line free of charge on the condition that trains always ran six days a week.

Construction began in September 1875, but struck engineering difficulties once the line reached the Gladfield–Riverside swamp, where the engineers could not find a solid bottom, even at 12 metres. The problem was solved by using layer upon layer of flax with ditches 2.5 metres wide running parallel to the track.

The 14 km line was completed and opened in October 1877 at a cost of £30,000. It was practically flat and had only three curves. The Silver Stream was crossed by a three span 42 metre wooden bridge, and the Taieri River near Outram was crossed by a similar three span 67 metre timber bridge. Outram had the only manned station and goods shed.

In its early days the line carried goods for the construction of the Otago Central line. Outram sprang to life with the completion of the railway and the goods shed and yards were full of materials for the Taieri Gorge construction.

For many years the line was worked by the ubiquitous F tank locomotives, the Wf being the heaviest class allowed over the Taieri bridge. As the junction at Mosgiel faced south, through trains from Dunedin had to reverse from Mosgiel to Outram.

Passenger trains ended on 13 January 1950, and in 1951 the line lost £5,056—twice its revenue. The major freight into Outram was 107 tons of lime and top dressing fertiliser a week. Seven tons went out a week. Re-sleepering work costing £16,000 was faced. On 5 December 1953 the line closed for all traffic.

Little remains today—a few mounds of earth at the site of the North Taieri station and the engine shed and station at Outram. Trees planted through the swamp by engineers remain, making an impressive tree lined avenue along which the road follows the former route.

CHAPTER SEVENTEEN

Southland

Kingston Branch (Invercargill–Lumsden–Kingston)

One of the reasons for the separation of Southland province from Invercargill in 1861, and the main priority of the new provincial government, was the desire to improve communications from Invercargill to the surrounding areas. The swampy ground swallowed up the early efforts to make roads, and most routes became nearly impassable in winter. The discovery of gold in the Queenstown area in November 1862 made the Southland province more determined than ever to have a better route north. The Provincial Council was already fully committed financially by the construction of the Bluff Harbour & Invercargill Railway (see Bluff Branch), so when the railway contractor J.R. Davies claimed that a railway using wooden rails would be much cheaper and quicker to build than one with iron rails, they accepted this idea. The first 12 km to Makarewa were opened on 18 October 1864, but the problems of the wooden railway were apparent on the first day of public service, on 25 October, when the last excursion train was stalled on slippery rails. Further problems soon followed and it was obvious that the white pine rails could not carry any substantial traffic.

By June 1866, the Provincial Council had decided that iron rails were needed, and the line was converted and extended to Winton, using the same gauge, 1435 mm (4 feet 8 1/2 inches) as the Bluff line. The opening on 22 February 1871 was the furthest extent of this gauge in Southland, as further extensions were built to the 1067 mm gauge, and the Bluff and Winton sections were converted to 1067 mm in December 1875.

The next section to Caroline, 65 km from Invercargill, was opened on 20 October 1875, and Lumsden was reached four months later. Progress was rapid through the gently undulating open terrain, and the railway, known locally as the Great Northern Railway, was opened to Kingston at the south end of Lake Wakatipu, on 10 July 1878. The final link in the route to the goldfields was the assembly at Kingston of the lake steamer *Mountaineer* in February 1879. Her successor, the *Earnslaw*, was assembled at Kingston in 1912 and operated by NZR until 1969. It still steams on Lake Wakatipu, providing tourist trips from Queenstown.

The combined rail and steamer route was the easiest access to Queenstown and district from the south until the road from Kingston to Queenstown was completed in 1936. Rail passenger services were reduced in 1937 to Christmas and Easter holiday trains, which last ran at Easter 1957. Freight trains continued to run, three times a week for many years, mainly for farm traffic, coal for the *Earnslaw*, and general goods for Queenstown.

In May 1971, with steam locomotives disappearing

U 65, a 4-6-0 type from 1898, heads a Makarewa–Invercargill livestock special at Waikiwi, north of Invercargill, on 24 January 1956. Over half a century old, the locomotive was withdrawn from service in October 1959.
DEREK CROSS

The first 4-6-2 "Pacific" class in the world was the Baldwin-built Q. One member is seen on the Bluff Branch with a passenger train in 1956. NZR

from NZR, the Minister of Railways announced that two steam locomotives of the Ab class would be retained to work a summer tourist service on the Lumsden–Kingston route, chosen because of its location near a popular holiday area. The service was called the "Kingston Flyer", after the popular name for the Gore–Kingston trains of 50 or more years earlier. Two return trips, seven days a week, were run during the December to early April season. The "Kingston Flyer" also carried any freight traffic to and from Kingston on its morning northward, and afternoon southward trips. The "Kingston Flyer" was immediately successful, and patronage built up to over 30,000 passengers per season.

However, after the 1977 increase in the distance over which road transport could compete with rail to 150 km, the freight traffic on the line north of Lumsden had declined drastically, so by 1979 the Kingston line was facing closure. The last "Kingston Flyer" from Lumsden ran on 17 April 1979, and the Kingston branch, north of the junction with the Mossburn branch at Mararoa Junction, was closed on 26 November 1979. For the next three summers, the "Kingston Flyer" locomotives and train were used on services out of Invercargill, but these were not so popular. In 1982 a private compny came to an agreement with NZR to lease the locomotives and carriages, and operate them on the 14 km isolated line between Fairlight and Kingston. The first "Flyer" under this company ran on 18 December 1982. This was just 5 days after the Makarewa to Mararoa Junction section closed, removing most of the remainder of the original route to the north from Invercargill. The "Kingston Flyer" had mixed fortunes for the following decade, with poor ridership in some seasons, and proposals to shift it to a different route. On 1 December 1993, NZ Rail took back ownership, and the train is still providing a popular tourist service between Kingston and Fairlight, although its future ownership is again in doubt as this is written.

Bluff Branch

In its first years, the Southland Provincial Council was concerned to improve communication between Invercargill and its port of Bluff, as well as to improve the route to the north. Contracts were let in 1863, and by May 1864 the three contracts were all close to completion. At this point work was suspended, because the Provincial Council was over-committed on railway and

The profile of a AB headed goods train on the causeway across Riverton Harbour on the Tuatapere Branch in November 1965. NZR

harbour construction. There were even attempts to auction the railway rolling stock and works, by a sheriff acting for creditors of the Provincial Council. It took over a year to overcome this financial crisis, and it was 5 February 1867 before the line was finally opened.

Traffic was fairly light at first, but as the farming areas were developed, Bluff became an important export port, and this branch became busier. The main traffic was frozen meat, in W and V type refrigerated wagons, and wool. Mixed trains continued to provide most passenger services until the 1950s, and were some of the last services worked by the survivors of the Q class, the first class of Pacific (4-6-2) locomotives in the world. The last passenger service was a school train, which ran on school days until 1967.

The Bluff branch continues to carry a substantial traffic, with logs as a major export traffic. The Ocean Beach cold store, which used to be part of a freezing works, now acts as a concentration depot from which containers of meat and dairy products are often hauled to Port Chalmers or other ports. The fertiliser works at Awarua sends CF hoppers of fertiliser to Washdyke, near Timaru.

Ohai Branch and Nightcaps & Ohai Railways

The Ohai Branch is the last survivor of the country branches of Southland, although now practically entirely serving the coal mines at Ohai.

The first section of this line, 19 km from Thornbury to Otautau, was opened in 1879. Initially the junction faced towards Riverton, not Invercargill, so it may have been thought at that time that Riverton would be the port for this area. The line was extended 21 km to Wairio in 1882. A short extension, owned by the Nightcaps Coal Company, but worked by the Railways Department, gave access to the Company's mine at Nightcaps.

Another private railway was built in 1914 from Wairio, to serve mines at Moretown, south of Ohai township. Neither of these lines gave reasonable access to the coal leases in the Ohai area, and in 1916 the residents of Ohai were successful in their petition for their area to become a Railway District under the Local Railways Act 1914. This was the only line built under that act. As a temporary measure the new Ohai Railway Board bought the Moretown line, and extended it to Mossbank. However this line was in very poor condition, and it followed a route in a valley below Ohai and could not provide access to many mines. Accordingly, the Board decided to build a third line from Wairio, and after withstanding objections from the Nightcaps Coal Company work on the new line was started in 1919. Trains were running to Ohai in 1924, and the line was opened to its final terminus at Birchwood, 19 km from Wairio in 1934. By this time, both the other lines had closed, as the mines they served were worked out. The Ohai Railway Board bought a number of locomotives second-hand from New Zealand Railways, including X 442 and Wab 794, which were donated to the New Zealand Railway & Locomotive Society in 1968, and are now being restored. After using a number of diesel shunters, the Board final locomotive was an ex-NZR DJ class.

A rearrangement of local government throughout New Zealand resulted in the functions of the Ohai Railway Board being taken over by the Southland United Council from 1 November 1989. They soon decided that they didn't want to run a railway, and NZR took over operation on 1 June 1990, although it was a few years before all the legal processes of winding up the Board's assets were completed. Now DC locomotives work right through to Ohai, with much of the coal railed to Temuka for the Clandeboyne dairy factory.

Wyndham Branch (formerly Glenham Branch)

The main line from Invercargill to Dunedin went northeast to Edendale, and then north along the west bank of the Mataura River, leaving the small town of Wyndham, on the east bank, off the main route. In response to this local agitation, a 6.5 km branch line was built from Edendale to Wyndham in 1882, and this was extended 9 km south to Glenham in 1890. There were local hopes of further extensions, but the Seaward Bush Branch was extended instead to serve the lower Mataura valley.

Traffic was always light, and the Wyndham-Glenham portion was closed in July 1930. For a few years before this, a model T bus converted for rail use had been tried on this line, but it was not successful enough to stop the closure. Passenger services to Wyndham ceased a few months later, but freight traffic was conveyed to and from Wyndham until 1962.

Browns Branch (or Hedgehope Branch)

In 1883 the Forest Hill Tramway was built in 1883, running for 8 km east from Winton, on the Kingston Branch. In 1886 it was extended another 8 km to coal mines near Hokonui. (Hokonui is some distance from the Hokonui Hills, allegedly the source of bootleg whisky.) Between 1896 and 1899 the tramway was rebuilt to railway standards, and reopened on 17 July 1899 as the Forest Hill Railway, of 21 km from Winton to Hedgehope. Passenger services ceased in 1931, and the line past Browns closed in 1953. By then, the only significant traffic on the branch was about 75,000 tonnes/

Opposite: *A southbound Dj 1206 smokes it up at Athol on the Kingston Branch on 7 January 1971.* B.J. McKENZIE

Right: An Invercargill–Lyttelton express races past a Dunedin–Invercargill railcar at Warepa north of Balclutha. Of the man-made objects in this view only the main line survives.
B.J. McKENZIE

year of lime from lime-works at Kings and Browns. Much of this lime was for farms still being developed in outlying parts of Southland, served by branches like Wyndham and Seaward Bush. As farming areas were developed and no longer needed lime, or their local branches were closed, the amount of lime railed out of this line declined, and it closed on 1 January 1968.

Mossburn Branch

This branch ran from Mararoa Junction, which was nothing but a set of points 2 km north of Lumsden, west to Mossburn. The first section to Castle Rock, crossing the Oreti River with a combined road and rail bridge, was opened in 1881. It took six more years to get the line across flat open country to Mossburn, showing the effects of the 1880s depression. Perhaps the political "pull" of this district was inadequate, because no proposal to extend the 16 km branch towards Manapouri and Te Anau ever even looked like coming to fruition. The branch was a typical branch for an area of extensive farming, with lime and fertiliser coming in, and wool and livestock out. Because the farms to the west were still being developed in the 1970s, substantial fertiliser traffic to a depot at Mossburn kept this line going after the other farm branches. Increasing road competition resulted in closure on 13 December 1982, together with the surviving Makarewa–Mararoa section of the Kingston Branch.

Waikaia Branch (or Switzers Branch)

Work on this commenced in 1884, but after about 10 km of easy formation work, and the laying of 3 km of track, work was stopped. In 1905, work started again with the laying of new track, the original track having in the intervening twenty years been taken up for use elsewhere. This time, the work was completed, with the only major work being the bridge over the Mataura River.

A photo of the official opening on 1 October 1909 shows an F class locomotive, and hardly any larger locomotives would have been needed during the life of this branch. In its early years, gold mining and dredging around the small town of Switzers (now Waikaia) contributed to the traffic, but later farm traffic was virtually all that was carried. A converted Model T bus was tried on this line without great success during the 1920s, and from 1931 on, only freight trains were run. Final closure was in 1959, after a long period of comparatively large engines, such as the A class 4-6-2's, hauling rather short trains.

Waimea Plains Railway

This connecting line from Gore on the South Island Main Trunk to the Kingston Branch from Invercargill at Lumsden was built by a private company, the Waimea Plains Railway Company, to shorten the route from Dunedin to the Lake District, and open up the Waimea plains. The 60 km over flat plains took only 16 months to build, and the line was completed by May 1878. The line was worked by the New Zealand Government Railways, who collected about 70% of the revenue. After some disputes over revenue, and over whether the Government had guaranteed a return of 7% on the railway, the Government bought out the railway company on 30 July 1886. Around the turn of the century, the passenger services on this line and the Lumsden–Kingston route became known as the "Kingston Flyer", because of the comparatively high speeds attained by K and V class locomotives with light trains.

Regular passenger services were replaced by buses in 1945, although the holiday expresses between Dunedin and Kingston continued until the late 1950s. A thrice weekly freight train mainly carried farm traffic until in 1971, with annual traffic less than 24,000 tonnes, the line was closed.

The 16 km section from Balfour to Lumsden remained open until 15 January 1978 to carry bulk wheat consignments from a silo at Balfour.

An AB double-headed goods train from Lumsden at Makarewa on 26 November 1965. NZR

Seaward Bush (Tokanui) Branch

One of the branches started in Southland soon after the completion of the Main Trunk Railway was this line, which headed south-east from Invercargill into the area known as the Seaward Bush. The first 20 km section to Mokotua was opened in January 1888. At this time, there were two alternative routes being considered for further extension into the lower Mataura area. The decision was made to extend the Seaward Bush branch across the Mataura, rather than bring the Wyndham branch south from Glenham. The section to Gorge Road opened in 1895, and with the completion of the bridge across the Mataura, the section to Waimahaka was opened in 1899.

After some years, the government bowed to local pressure, and approved a proposal to extend the line to link Waimahaka with the Catlins River branch. The section to Tokanui, 54 km from Invercargill, was opened on 20 September 1911. The rugged country ahead discouraged further construction, if indeed the link was ever more than a political ploy. The next 10 km to Marinui were surveyed, but no more construction work was done, and Tokanui became the final terminus.

Timber was a major traffic at first, and then as farms were developed, the traffic of lime and fertiliser in, and farm products out, became predominant. Mixed trains carried passengers until 1960, and the line was closed in 1966. By this time, both the farms and the roads of this district were well developed, and the railway had fulfilled its function.

Tuatapere (Orawia) Branch

This branch took nearly 50 years to grow to its greatest extent, and in the following 50 years it withered away. The first section, to the old port of Riverton, was completed in 1879. In 1885 the line reached Orepuki, which had developed as a gold mining town, but then developed an oil shale industry. This collapsed in 1902, the result of competition from imported oil, and sawmilling became the main industry. As the railway was pushed west, to reach Tuatapere in 1909, sawmills were opened to mill the beech forest. Tuatapere, 88 km from Invercargill, became the centre of this activity, and it was the timber sent from the Tuatapere mill which kept this line open until the mid 1970s. An extension to Orawia opened in 1925, and closed in 1970 soon after the closure of the cement works there.

The usual service on this line for many years was for a train to leave Tuatapere each morning for Invercargill, and return in the late afternoon, while another train did an Invercargill–Tuatapere and return trip. A carriage or car-van was attached to each train until the early 1950s. The Tuatapere locomotive shed was closed when DJ diesels replaced steam in June 1968. From then, until closure on 30 July 1976, a freight train ran three times a week to Tuatapere and back. The section to Riverton was not closed in 1976, in expectation of forest product developments, but no major development occurred, and this remaining section closed on 15 January 1978.

Waikaka Branch

This was the last branch to be authorised of the minor branches which sprouted in northern Southland around the end of the 19th century. It was authorised in 1905 after local interests had arranged to set up a company to advance half the construction cost to the Government. Once the promised money arrived progress was rapid. Formation work started in April 1907, and the 21 km line from McNab to the small settlement of Waikaka was opened in November 1908. It ran up a valley parallel to the Pomahaka valley used by the Tapanui branch; in fact it was claimed that the crew of the train on one branch could sometimes see the smoke from the locomotive in the next valley. The line was a typical farmer's branch, with no towns or industries. It would probably have closed earlier, but the lack of bridges or tunnels on the line enabled it to be used for carrying large and heavy items for the Roxburgh Dam. The line was closed in September 1962, the same year as the dam was completed.

CHAPTER EIGHTEEN

Steam lives on!

As in other parts of the world, the passing of steam on New Zealand railways was mourned by railway enthusiasts, many of whom regard the steam locomotive as man's finest creation. In a way the official steam era on NZR never really ended as soon after the Invercargill–Christchurch overnight express was hauled by steam for the last time in October 1971, NZR reinstituted the "Kingston Flyer" summer tourist train on the Kingston Branch which in 2001 was still owned by Tranz Rail. However, this was simply a heritage operation and for all intents and purposes, steam finally came to an end in 1971.

From 1872 until 1956 over 1000 steam locomotives representing 72 different classes were acquired by New Zealand Railways for use on its 3'6" gauge network. At least 200 more were acquired by private companies and bush tramways for industrial use. The substantial majority of these locomotives were cut up for scrap or dumped into river banks once they had come to the end of their useful working lives. The remains of some of these can be seen today scattered around rocky foreshores in parts of the coastline or in rivers.

Pride of the Plains Railway fleet, situated at Tinwald near Ashburton, is the restored Rogers built K 88. In a scene almost from the American "wild west", the 2-4-2 locomotive from 1877 steams through Weka Pass in September 1984 on the occasion of the filming of the TV series Hanlon. *ROY SINCLAIR*

Fortunately, however, about 100 steam locomotives have been saved from this fate and preserved. These include the first locomotive to be acquired by NZR (the 0-4-4-0 double Fairlie *Josephine*), and the last—Ja 1274. Over 30 former NZR classes and 12 private classes are represented in the locomotives now preserved, although most of these are not operational. Invariably they were acquired by preservation groups in a dilapidated and worn-out condition and many hours of painstaking and difficult work has been required to restore them with many parts having to be made from scratch. Boilers have had to be rebuilt, cylinders rebored, pistons, piston rods, running rods, valves, wheels, have all had to be remachined or remade.

The end results however, all make it worthwhile for those who have spent so many laborious hours. A working steam locomotive is now in action!

The first serious attempts to preserve items of railway equipment did not begin until the early 1960s. The preservation of some electric trams following their withdrawal from Auckland streets in 1957 was the first impetus to a wider preservation movement in the 1960s, following on from the NZR centennial celebrations in 1963. Gradually different groups were established in different centres and began acquiring various items of railway equipment with which to establish a museum railway. By 1970 nine museums were in various stages of development. With the abandonment of branch lines continuing, more groups were formed to operate tourist orientated museum railways and today there are 20 such museum railways, all except one operating on the standard New Zealand 1067 mm gauge.

For several years the attitude of New Zealand Railways towards steam excursions over main lines was not overly co-operative and apart from delivery runs, enthusiast trips were not permitted. As recently as 1985, NZR had decreed that there would be only one main line steam excursion a year. By the end of the 1980s, however, attitudes had changed and such excursions were seen as a useful contribution to revenue, as trackage rights were sold, carriages hired, and personnel are assigned to monitor the trains. The year of the 125th anniversary of NZR in 1988 saw a particularly large number of excursions, many centred around the events over Labour Weekend, when seven mainline steam engines made their way to Christchurch. The steam spectacle of the great parade on Sunday 23 October was

Right: Restored K 92, stablemate of K 88, leads the two Kingston Flyer ABs just out of Fairlight on 30 September 2000.
GRAHAM FOX

Below: The 0-6-0T Fowler from 1921 and A 67 of the Ocean Beach Railway seen in action on 17 September 1989.
LORRAINE FOX

Ferrymead Railway owned 2-6-2 type C 864 from 1931 steams up the Weka Pass Railway from Waipara on 5 June 1989 with Mt Bruce in the background.
GLEN ANTHONY

Top: The Ferrymead Railway's Baldwin built WD 357 seen at the Moorhouse Station in February 1999 MICHAEL BURT

Above: JA 1271 with a Steam Incorporated excursion on 20 May 2001 stops at the restored station of Shannon, the only surviving station built by the Wellington and Manawatu Railway (in 1893). REID McNAUGHT

Right: Pride of the Glenbrook Vintage Railway is the Alco built Mallet of 1912, ex the Taupo Totara Timber Company. DAVE SIMPSON

undoubtedly an experience that many attending would not have hitherto experienced in their lifetimes, and many will not do so again.

The running of steam excursion trips, and of the museum operations located in different parts of the country, has also brought the experience of steam to many who are too young to have any memory of it otherwise. Most no doubt view the spectacle as a curiosity, a passing novelty which they quickly forget. However, it can be said with reasonable safety that no other form of vintage transport generates quite as much admiration and enthusiasm as the steam locomotive at work. Most of the mainline steam locomotives to be restored to operationality are those from the middle decades of the 20th century, such as Ka 942, 945, J 1211, Ja 1250 and 1271. However, K 88 from the 1870s was restored in the 1980s to run steam trips on the main lines, and has recently been joined by K 92.

The most northerly museum railway in the country is the Bay of Islands Scenic Railway at Opua and the most southerly is the Ocean Beach Railway in Dunedin. The most ambitious is the Glenbrook Vintage Railway operating over most of the 7.7 km trackage between Glenbrook and Waiuku in south west Auckland, and probably the best known is the "Kingston Flyer" which has now featured for nearly three decades in television commercials for Crunchie Bars.

Other significant museum railways are located at the Museum of Transport and Technology in Auckland, at Pukemiro in the Waikato (the Bush Tramway Club), between Waihi and Waikino in the Coromandel, at the former NZR steam depot at Paekakariki 39 km north of Wellington (The Engine Shed/Steam Incorporated), at Silverstream between Upper Hutt and Lower Hutt, at Blenheim (which uses narrow gauge diesels only), at Waipara (the WekaPass Railway), Christchurch (the Ferrymead Railway), at Ashburton (the Plains Railway), and at Pleasant Point north west of Timaru (the Pleasant Point Railway).

A noted private individual preservationist is Mr Ian Welch of Wellington who has financed the restoration of several steam locomotives which are housed in depots at Parnell (Auckland) and Plimmerton in greater Wellington. His collection now includes four former South African Railways narrow gauge engines which he imported in the mid-1990s. Steam excursions using members of his fleet are operated by the Mainline Steam Trust.

Of course not only steam locomotives are included in the rosters of the railway museums—several first generation diesel and electric locomotives are also to be found. Although for enthusiasts less of a priority than the restoration of steam engines, these were also a regular part of the railway scene for many years and have now likewise disppeared from public view. Some may regard them as "boxes on wheels", but there is no doubt that a large number of people hold nostalgic memories of seeing these running regular trains too.

An ambitious project of the Pleasant Point Railway near Timaru was the recreation of RM 4, a Ford Model T railcar from 1926 of which two were built. The North Island example, RM 5, was used on the Greytown Branch, while RM 4 was used on the Switzers and Wyndham Branches because of the small amount of passenger traffic on those lines. The original was powered by a 20 hp petrol engine and weighed 2.5 tonnes. It seated 11 passengers and lasted until 1930. One notes the "toothbrushes" on the rails! BRYAN BLANCHARD

Above: Streamlined KA 942 heads an excursion train near Plimmerton on 4 October 1992. G.J. McCLARE
Below: One of the preserved JAs with an excursion train over the North Wairarapa Line on 15 August 1999. COURTESY RAILS

Top: An 0-4-2T Peckett locomotive of the Gold Fields Scenic Railway near Waihi. GOLD FIELDS STEAM TRAIN SOCIETY

Above: A Manning Wardle 0-4-0T formerly of the Imlay Freezing Works of Wanganui at one end of a train on the Tokomaru Museum track, and an ex-Napier Harbour Board 0-4-0T Fowler on the other end, photographed on 13 May 1973. MARK COLE

Left: Steam power took over from electric locomotives at Paekakariki for nearly 30 years. A scene at the depot on 25 August 1962. MARK COLE

Above: AB 663 crosses the Flat Stream Viaduct with a Mainline Steam Trust excursion to Middlemarch on 15 April 2001. REID McNAUGHT
Below: KAs 945+942 storm the Raurimu Spiral with the "Double Drivers" excursion of July 1994. TONY HURST

Index

JA 1283 on a Frankton–Te Maunga (Bay of Plenty) goods train near Athenree on 29 September 1967. J.A.T. TERRY

Bibliography

Alexander, R.B., *The Stratford–Okahukura Line*, NZ Railway & Locomotive Society, Wellington, 1983

Cassells, K.R. *The Foxton and Wanganui Railway*, NZ Railway and Locomotive Society, 1984.

Churchman, G.B., *New Zealand Locomotives and Railcars 1992*, IPL Books, 1992

Churchman, G.B., *Railway Electrification in Australia and New Zealand*, IPL Books, 1995

Churchman, G.B., *The Midland Line–New Zealand's Trans-Alpine Railway*, IPL Books 1988, 1990, 1995.

Churchman, G.B. & Tony Hurst, *South Island Main Trunk*, IPL Books, 1993

Dangerfield, J.A. & G.W. Emerson, *Over the Garden Wall: the Story of the Otago Central Railway*, NZ Railway & Locomotive Society, Dunedin Branch, 1962

Garner, John, *Guide to New Zealand Rail Heritage*, IPL Books 1996

Hoy, D.G., *Rails out of the Capital*, NZ Railway & Locomotive Society, Wellington Branch, 1970

Hurst, Tony, *Farewell to Steam: Four decades of Change on New Zealand railways*, HarperCollins Publishers, (New Zealand), 1995

Leitch, David, *Steam, Steel and Splendour*, HarperCollins Publishers (New Zealand), 1994

McClare, E.J., *Steam Locomotives of New Zealand: Part Two*, NZ Railway & Locomotive Society, 1988

McGavin, T.A., *Steam Locomotives of New Zealand: Part One*, NZ Railway & Locomotive Society, 1986

McClare, E.J., *Steam Locomotives of New Zealand: Part Three*, NZ Railway & Locomotive Society, 1991

Mahoney, J.D., *Kings of the Iron Road*, Dunmore Press, 1982

Mahoney, J.D., *Down at the Station*, Dunmore Press, 1987

Mahoney, Paul., *The Era of the Bush Tram in New Zealand*, IPL Books, 1998

Meyer, R.J., *Coaling from the Clouds*, NZ Railway & Locomotive Society, 1971, 1988

Pierre, W.A., *Canterbury Provincial Railways*, NZ Railway & Locomotive Society, 1964

Pierre, W.A., *North Island Main Trunk*, A.H. & A.W. Reed, 1981

Stott, Bob, *Kaimai: The Story of the Kaimai Tunnel and the East Coast Main Trunk*, Southern Press, 1978

Troup, G. (Ed), *Steel Roads of New Zealand*, A.H. & A.W. Reed, 1973

Turner, D.L.A., *The Last Decade*, Whitcoulls, 1977

Watt, J.O.P, *Southland's Pioneer Railways 1864–1878*, NZ Railway & Locomotive Society, 1965

Wood, Chris, *Steaming to the Sunrise: A history of railways in the Gisborne region*, IPL Books and Te Rau Herald Press, 1996

Yonge, John, *New Zealand Railway and Tramway Atlas* (3rd edition), Quail Map Company, England, 1985